# Bristol Britannia

## Other titles in the Crowood Aviation Series

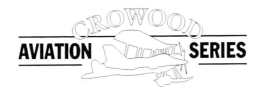

# Bristol Britannia

## Charles Woodley

The Crowood Press

First published in 2002 by
The Crowood Press Ltd
Ramsbury, Marlborough
Wiltshire SN8 2HR

**British Library Cataloguing-in-Publication Data**
A catalogue record for this book is available from
the British Library.

ISBN 1 86126 515 8

# Acknowledgements

Right from the beginning of this project I have been overwhelmed by the generosity shown by the very many people from all over the world who have contributed material in the form of photographs, access to archive material and personal reminiscences about the Britannia. During the preparation of the book I have been fortunate enough to meet some of them, but most of them I will probably never meet. Nevertheless, we are bound together by a common interest in old airliners and one in particular. To all those mentioned below, my grateful thanks, and I hope you feel I have done justice to the subject.

Mr J. A. Ligertwood and Keith Hayward at the British Airways Archives and Museum Collection and John Battersby at the Bristol Aero Collection for their kindness during my visits and afterwards. Glyn Ramsden at Air-Britain for supplying photographs from their monochrome library and granting permission to publish. Derek A. King, for loaning me the Britannia material amassed by the late Dave Williams, and for his own Britannia production history. Roger Hargreaves and Sarah Keen at the Britannia Aircraft Preservation Trust for arranging access to XM496 and permitting me to use Sarah's Cubana material. Julie McDonnell at Airbus UK for granting permission to use Bristol Aeroplane Co. Ltd copyright photos. Roger Jackson for loaning me photos from the A. J. Jackson photo collection. Tony Merton Jones for permission to use material from his *Propliner* articles. Harro Ranter for permission to use material from the Aviation Safety Network website. Adrian Bishop and John Wegg for permission to use the article on the last British Eagle Britannia flight. Kathi Austin and the *Washington Post* for permission to reproduce her Britannia arms smuggling stories. Dave Berry, for permission to use material from the Britannia Association newsletter. Linda Jones at British Airways' *Touchdown* magazine for printing my appeals for assistance. My wife Hazel, for moral support and for putting up with my reclusive behaviour during the project.

Plus the following, who all supplied photographs, printed matter or reminiscences: Mr P. Hicks, James Gay, Vic Attwood, Keith Butcher, Colin Vangen, John James, John Goring, Ian Dobinson, Peter Pavey at the Rolls-Royce Heritage Trust, Liz Bartlett at Monarch Airlines, John Kelley, Donald H. Bartlett, Mike at Air Nikon, Caz Caswell, Eduard Marmet, Lynn Wilson, P. J. S. Pearson, Captain Lincoln Lee, Manfred Borchers, Alan F. G. Hale, R. A. Backwell, Captain Brian Dawson, Mrs W. R. Waterman, Stan Verrall, Robert Wyatt, Mr D. G. Parsloe, Michael Harrison, Mrs Elizabeth Cox, Edith Mills, Mrs Julie Bowen, Dorothy A. Holman, Edward R. Belbin, Ted Ashman, Lester Stenner, Mr G. Harper, Mary Dixon, Bob Stradling, David Ayling, Mike Widdowson, Mr M. Taylor, Judith Young, Martyn Howell, Toni Marimon, Captain Raymond Dodwell, Dave Sparrow, Mr D. G. Iles, Nev Boulton, The Duxford Aviation Society, Mrs Pamela Hampson, Malcolm McCrow, Mr J. P. O'Connor, Mr A. J. L. Hickox, Steve Williams and D. G. Parsloe.

If I have forgotten anybody, please accept my apologies and thanks.

Typefaces used: Goudy (*text*),
Cheltenham (*headings*).

Typeset and designed by
D & N Publishing
Baydon, Marlborough, Wiltshire.

Printed and bound in Great Britain by Bookcraft,
Midsomer Norton.

# Contents

# Introduction

In the 1950s Great Britain's aircraft industry was still one of the foremost in the world. Indeed, only British-built aircraft and aero-engines were exhibited at the Farnborough Air Show (annual in those days), with a crop of new machines making their debuts each year. Among them were three airliners that could have dominated world markets if properly controlled and marketed. The Vickers Viscount achieved success in export markets, including the USA, and revolutionized short-haul air travel. The De Havilland Comet slashed long-haul journey times in half, but paid a tragic price for being technologically ahead of its time. By the time the revised Comet 4 appeared, American aircraft manufacturers had caught up. The third design was the Bristol Britannia.

In technical terms, the Britannia was a great British achievement. It was the world's first long-range turbine-powered airliner. It was the largest and quietest airliner in service at the time. It was the first airliner capable of reliable non-stop transatlantic service in either direction, and the first aeroplane to fly non-stop from the UK to the Pacific coast. Passengers loved its smooth, quiet ride. Many new records for long-distance flight were quickly established by this new machine, and had it enjoyed a long and substantial production run it would have gone down in history as one of the world's greatest transport aircraft. However, the aircraft suffered many teething troubles that repeatedly delayed its introduction into full airline service, and in the event only eighty-two, including the prototypes, were built, between 1952 and 1960, and the aircraft's potential was never realized.

The Bristol Type 175 Britannia was the outcome of one of the recommendations of the wartime Brabazon Committee, which had been set up to determine Britain's air transport needs once World War Two was over. The type was intended to fill the 'Medium Range, Empire' (MRE) requirement. Ordered for Britain's state airline, the British Overseas Airways Corporation (BOAC), it was originally to have been piston-engined, but in 1950 BOAC decided to order twenty-five Type 175s powered instead by the then-untried Bristol Proteus turboprop. This decision was to delay the first flight until 16 August 1952, some five years after the start of the project. Then, problems with the Proteus engines 'flaming-out' (that is, stopping) in certain icing conditions delayed the Britannia's entry into airline service until 1957, by which time the Comet 4 and Boeing 707 jet airliners were well into their test programmes, and the Britannia had effectively been left behind in the technology race.

Even then, the prospects for substantial foreign sales still seemed quite good. Following a demonstration of the aircraft in 1957, tycoon Howard Hughes was keen to purchase thirty for his airline TWA, and United Airlines were also seriously interested in buying thirty-five. Both these major US carriers were insistent on speedy deliveries, however, and Bristol could not speed up production to accommodate them and the opportunity to break open the US market was lost.

At an initial price of around £700,000 for the 90-passenger, medium-range srs 102 and around double that figure for the 114-seat long-range srs 312, the Britannia was always good value for money. After its retirement by BOAC and the other first-line operators (including the Royal Air Force) the aircraft quickly established itself as an economical and popular passenger and freight carrier with charter airlines around the world. The Proteus developed into a reliable and economical engine whose cruising fuel consumption was only around a third of that of the early jet airliners: over long distances the Britannia returned around sixty-seven seat-miles to the gallon, twice that of the contemporary jets. But above all the Britannia was quiet, emitting only 81dB when halfway into its take-off run – truly, a 'Whispering Giant'.

You'll love *The Whispering Giant*

...it's the fastest most spacious airliner in the world

**Pre-service BOAC advertisement for its newest airliner.**

# CHAPTER ONE

# A Brief History of Bristol Aircraft Ltd

## Early Years

On 19 February 1910 Sir George White formed four aeronautical companies: The Bristol Aeroplane Company Ltd, The Bristol Aviation Company Ltd, The British and Colonial Aeroplane Company Ltd and The British and Colonial Aviation Company Ltd. The only one to commence trading immediately was The British and Colonial Aeroplane Company Ltd, which began operations with operating capital of no less than £25,000, the other companies being provided with only nominal capital of £100 each. All the money was subscribed by Sir George White, his brother Samuel and his son G. Stanley White. The Bristol Tramways Company's omnibus depot and repair shop, comprising two iron sheds at their northern terminus at Filton, some 4 miles (6.5km) from Bristol city centre, were leased for use as a factory. Filton House, in private occupation until August 1911, was then bought by the Bristol Tramways Company, merged with the factory and leased to the aeroplane company as general offices. Sixty years later, the two original sheds were still in use as part of the main machine shop. Land at Larkhill on Salisbury Plain was leased from the War Office and three iron sheds were erected there. A shed on the flying ground at Brooklands was also leased, and flying schools were established at these sites, using the Bristol Boxkite.

The Boxkite, the first Bristol aircraft to fly, was an improved version of a Farman design and first flew, from Larkhill, on 30 July 1910. After demonstrations to the War Office, permission was grudgingly granted for Army officers to fly, Lieutenant H. M. Maitland and Captain H. F. Wood becoming the first pupils at the Bristol school at Brooklands. By November 1910 Boxkites were being built at Filton at the rate of two per week, and by the end of that year sixteen had been built and the sale of eight machines to the Russian government had been negotiated. In all, seventy-eight Boxkites were built.

The company experimented with licence-built monoplanes to succeed the Boxkite, but a spate of accidents led to a temporary War Office ban on monoplanes and Bristol was forced to accept a contract to build B.E.2 biplanes instead. At the same time, the company was building new biplane designs that were developed into the Bristol Scout, which was ordered by both the War Office and the Admiralty at the end of 1914. In August 1916 the first order was placed for the legendary Bristol F.2B Fighter. An initial order for fifty was followed by further contracts for batches of 550, 800, 500 and 700. However, the end of hostilities saw a rundown in military aircraft production, and on 20 September 1919 all existing contracts for the Bristol Fighter were cancelled.

Twelve months later the Bristol Fighter was adopted as the RAF's standard army co-operation aeroplane and new orders were placed. In the uncertain intervening period, however, non-aeronautical work had been sought and eventually production lines were set up to produce bus and coach bodies for the Bristol Tramways Company and saloon car bodies for Armstrong Siddeley cars. Close liaison had been maintained with Roy Fedden, chief engineer at the Cosmos Engineering Company, which had designed the promising Jupiter and Lucifer air-cooled radial engines at Fishponds in Bristol, and after that company went into liquidation in February 1920 Bristol took over the Cosmos organization as the nucleus of its new Aero-Engine Department, the deal being completed just in time for the Jupiter and Lucifer engines to be shown on the Bristol stand at the Aero Show at Olympia in August 1920. In the meantime, the business of the British and Colonial Aeroplane Company had been transferred to The Bristol Aeroplane Company Ltd, and the old company was formally wound up. During the 1930s Bristol produced nearly 450 Bulldogs for the RAF and eight other air arms. By the time Bulldog production came to an end in 1934, however, the Bristol Fighter had finally become obsolete. No

more were being returned to the works for reconditioning, so the aircraft factory was almost at a standstill, although the output of engines was higher than ever.

## The Blenheim and World War Two

On 15 June 1935 The Bristol Aeroplane Company Ltd was reorganized as a public liability company with a share capital of £1.2m. On that date there were 4,200 employees on the payroll. The same year, the Government decided at last to re-arm the RAF with modern equipment, and Bristol was ready with a twin-engined high-speed monoplane, the 'Britain First'. This had been constructed as a one-off personal transport for the newspaper magnate, Lord Rothermere. It made its maiden flight just over thirteen months from the initial go-ahead decision, and was sent to the RAF experimental station at Martlesham Heath for trials. It was found to be almost 50mph (80km/h) faster than the RAF's latest biplane fighters, and Lord Rothermere presented it to the nation. The 'Britain First' design was adapted as a bomber with 840hp Bristol Mercury engines, and renamed the Blenheim; an initial contract for 150 Blenheims was placed in September 1935. The prototype Blenheim I made its first flight from Filton on 25 June 1936 and after completing service trials was cleared for production that December. Deliveries to the RAF began in March 1937 and production at Filton rose from six per month in January 1937 to twenty-four per month in January 1938.

Production of the Blenheim required a substantial enlargement of the works at Filton, and in early 1936 a large new engine factory was built opposite the existing works to undertake production of the Mercury and Pegasus, and later the sleeve-valve Perseus, Taurus and Hercules, engines. During the war years production of Bristol designs was dispersed, and Blenheims, Beaufort torpedo bombers and Beaufighters were built elsewhere, as well as at Filton. The Beaufighter was a private-venture fighter development of the Beaufort, and went on to be developed into night-fighter and torpedo-strike versions. It came onto the scene just in time to save the Bristol company from being brought into an Air Ministry group of sub-contractors for the manufacture of Short Stirling bombers.

## Post-War Developments

The company's first post-war product was the Bristol 170, a large-capacity transport developed from the wartime Bristol Bombay. It was originally intended for use against the Japanese in Burma, but when it became clear that the war would end before it could enter service it was produced for civil use as a utility passenger and freight transport for use in underdeveloped areas. It was produced in two versions: the Freighter, with nose-doors and a strengthened floor for accepting bulky loads; and the Wayfarer, without nose doors and with seating for up to thirty-six passengers. The prototype first flew on 2 December 1945 and the following May the Bristol 170 was awarded the first post-war unrestricted

**Bristol Beaufighter TT.10 RD867.** Air-Britain

Certificate of Airworthiness. Two days later the type was in service on charter to Channel Island Airways on flights between Croydon and Jersey. In July 1948 the third prototype inaugurated a cross-Channel car ferry service, and Silver City Airways went on to develop this type of operation with

such success that a lengthened Mk 32 Superfreighter, capable of carrying three cars and thirty-two passengers, was produced to their specifications. The Bristol 170 saw service with many civil operators as well as the Royal New Zealand Air Force, the Royal Canadian Air Force and

**Bristol 170 Mk 32 Superfreighter G-AOUV in joint Air Charter/SABENA colours at Southend in September 1957.** SABENA

the Pakistan Air Force. Concurrently with the type 170, limited production was undertaken of the Brigand, a strike aircraft to replace the coastal Beaufighter. This aircraft did valuable work in the Far East, being well suited to tropical environments.

A helicopter department under Raoul Hafner was also set up, and this grew into an important activity, eventually achieving the status of a separate division at Weston-Super-Mare, occupying the Old Mixon 'shadow' factory originally built in 1940 for Beaufighter production. Among the important designs produced were the Type 171, of which 172 were produced. It was known in RAF service as the Sycamore and was also exported successfully. Also produced was the twin-rotor Type 173, which evolved into the Bristol 192 Belvedere for the RAF. The Helicopter Division was finally taken over by the Westland Aircraft group early in 1960.

## The Bristol Brabazon

Just before Christmas 1942 the Ministry of Aircraft Production called a meeting of chief designers to discuss the practicality of developing a large, long-range civil transport, as a post-war challenge to the virtual monopoly in such aircraft then held by the Americans. Bristol was not invited, but Leslie G. Frise protested against exclusion, sought BOAC opinions on large aircraft and went to the meeting in London on 14 January 1943 armed with the company's proposal for a transport derived from the '100-ton bomber' project with a range of 5,000 miles (8,000km).

The previous year the Cabinet had set up an inter-departmental committee under the chairmanship of Lord Brabazon of Tara to investigate the types of civil aircraft needed in the immediate post-war period. This committee reported to the Cabinet on 9 February 1943 with a recommendation for five basic types, ranging from a small feeder transport to a London–New York express airliner. The latter project, known as the Brabazon Type 1, was to have priority in design and prototype construction, although production models were not expected to go into service for at least five years. The project could only be undertaken by a firm with long experience of the structural problems involved, and it was assumed that the contract would go to one of the firms

already building large bombers. However, these companies were all fully committed to bomber production and had no spare capacity. Thus it was announced that, provided other work was not affected, the Bristol Aeroplane Company was to be invited to design the Brabazon Type 1 airliner.

When it was announced that Bristol were to design the Brabazon Type 1 airliner there was no consensus of opinion as to how many passengers should be carried. BOAC stated that passengers would not tolerate a flight longer than eighteen hours, and recommended an allocation of space of 200cu ft (5.7cu m) for an ordinary level of comfort and 270cu ft (7.6cu m) for luxury travel. The first layout, in April 1943, showed a body 25ft (7.6m) in diameter divided by a level floor into two decks, with sleeping berths for eighty passengers, together with a dining room, promenade and bar. Alternatively, there

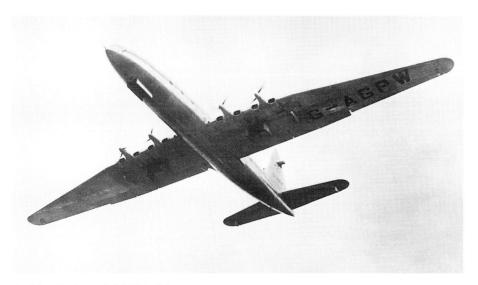

**The Bristol Brabazon G-AGPW in flight.** Air-Britain

were to be seats for 150 day passengers. However, it soon became clear that the drag from a 25ft body was too high, and on 5 August the second Brabazon Committee (including industry and BOAC members) recommended adopting the Bristol proposal for a fifty-passenger aircraft with an all-up weight of 250,000lb (113,000kg), even though BOAC would have preferred a smaller version for only twenty-five passengers.

By November 1944 the main features of the design, now known as the Bristol Type

167, had been decided: four pairs of coupled Centaurus engines mounted forward of the front spar, driving co-axial tractor propellers, a conventional tail unit, a pressurized fuselage with a maximum diameter 16ft 9in (5.1m), nosewheel landing gear with multiple wheels, and flexible fuel tanks in the outer portions of the wings. During all stages of design and construction extreme care was to be taken to reduce and control weight. At first it was proposed to build the prototypes at Weston-Super-Mare, but the subsoil there was unsuitable for a runway of the required strength, so Bristol was reluctantly obliged to extend the runway at Filton. This involved closing a new dual-carriageway bypass road and demolishing part of the village of Charlton. The local protests raised by this were only the first of the many legal, political and technical problems that delayed the first flight until September 1949.

Among the technical challenges was the construction of a new 8-acre (3.2ha) three-bay assembly hall at Filton to house the Brabazon. However, in December 1948 the completed first aircraft was rolled out for initial engine runs, and on 4 September 1949 Bristol's new Chief Test Pilot, A. J. Pegg, took the prototype up for an uneventful first flight. On 16 January 1950, during W. F. Gibb's first flight as pilot in charge, a hydraulic pipe failure caused a landing with the flaps up, but the Brabazon's reversing propellers and the long Filton runway

**Unpainted Britannia srs 317 G-APNB flying in late 1958.** Bristol

proved equal to the task. Demonstration flights at London Airport on 15 June 1950 and at the Farnborough Air Show that September earned the Brabazon critical acclaim for its smooth and easy manoeuvrability on the ground, its short take-off run and even shorter landing roll. Partial furnishing of the rear fuselage with a bar and thirty BOAC reclining seats for demonstrations to official passengers proved how quietness, comfort and freedom from fatigue and claustrophobia could be achieved in a really large aeroplane, as in no smaller type. However, due to a lack of political will to back such a colossal project, the Type 167 Brabazon never saw airline service. It had amassed fewer than 400 hours' flying time when the first prototype, G-AGPW, and the partially completed second prototype were broken up at Filton in October 1953. Soon after its demise pundits were predicting that no civil aeroplane so large would ever be built again. However, within ten years fleets of 300,000lb (136,000kg) airliners were the order of the day, and by the late 1980s weights had risen to over 850,000lb (385,500kg).

The Brabazon was a concept ahead of its time. The specially built production facilities at Filton and the experience gained in designing and building this large, pressurized airliner were, however, to prove invaluable when Bristol turned to the smaller, less ambitious, but more commercially acceptable project that was to become the Britannia.

## The Final Years

In January 1956 the manufacturing and sales activities of the Aircraft, Aero-Engine and Car divisions were further reorganized into three separate companies: Bristol Aircraft Ltd, Bristol Aero-Engines Ltd and Bristol Cars Ltd, each being wholly owned by The Bristol Aeroplane Company Ltd. The facilities belonging to Bristol Aircraft Ltd, including more recently built special laboratories and test plants, would be the main Bristol contribution to the British Aircraft Corporation, formed in June 1960 to pool the aviation interests and resources of the Company with those of Vickers Ltd and the English Electric Company. Soon afterwards the Corporation acquired Hunting Aircraft Ltd. The Bristol 221 was the last aeroplane type to be built under the Bristol name. Between February 1910 and June 1960 some 15,750 aircraft of eighty-five different designs had been built in the company's own works and in 'shadow' factories under its direct management. Only about 10 per cent of these were not of Bristol design. By contrast, some 8,320 aircraft of Bristol design had been manufactured by licencees and other contractors, giving a total world production of 22,470 Bristol aeroplanes in fifty years.

# CHAPTER TWO

# Design and Development

## Specification 2/47

The Bristol Type 175 Britannia was an ambitious, state-of-the-art design for its time, but may never have been designed at all if the Miles X.11 project of 1943 had been proceeded with. The X.11 was to have been substantially the same in size, power, weight and performance as the long-range srs 300 Britannia that eventually appeared fourteen years later: it was to have been able to carry a 24,000lb (11,000kg) payload over a still-air range of 3,450 miles (5,550km), a fuel capacity of 7,400gal (33,640ltr) and a cruising speed of 350mph (560km/h). If ordered in 1943 it would have been in service (albeit with piston engines initially) many years before the Britannia and could have given Great Britain an unassailable lead in post-war transport aircraft design and production. However, the project was rejected as inadequate by the then Ministry of Aircraft Production, the government support necessary for its development was not forthcoming, and the world's airlines looked to America for their immediate post-war needs.

The Britannia was designed under the leadership of Dr A. E. Russell (later Sir Archibald Russell) and came about in response to a 1946 BOAC requirement for a 'Medium Range, Empire' transport to service the routes to Britain's colonies in Africa and the Far East, replacing the Handley Page Hermes and Canadair Argonaut on these routes from 1954–55 onwards. The basic specification for such a transport aircraft had previously been laid down by the Brabazon Committee as its Type III, and called for an aircraft capable of operating over 1,000–2,500-mile (1,600–4,000km) stages at 300mph (500km/h) with thirty-two passengers. At that time the Lockheed Constellation was generally recognized as one of the world's most efficient, economic and versatile airliners, and Bristol pointed out that a slightly lengthened L-749 Constellation with Bristol Centaurus 660 engines would fit the bill nicely. Bristol proposed initially converting several airframes and thereafter building Constellations under licence at Filton. The Centaurus 660 conversion was designated Project 'X', and a further proposal to use Centaurus 662s was called Project 'Y'. However, Britain's foreign exchange situation at the time was so precarious that the Treasury refused to consider such a large dollar transaction.

Ten companies were officially invited to tender, and another nine later asked for copies of the invitation but took no further action. Tender applications were returned by the end of April 1946 by Armstrong Whitworth, Blackburn, Bristol, Handley Page and Avro, and initially the Avro 693 was selected, but in December 1946 BOAC requested that the specification be revised to allow their critical 1,354nm (2,509km) sector between Calcutta and Karachi to be flown at 320mph (515km/h) with thirty-two passengers plus mail. Specification 2/47 was then re-drafted around the BOAC requirements, which specified a capacity of thirty-two First Class or thirty-six Tourist Class seats on routes to South Africa, Australia and the Far East, with a maximum stage length of 1,100 miles (1,800km). The four engines must be air-cooled and the maximum operating weight was not to exceed 100,000lb (45,000kg). To prevent

**The first prototype Britannia, G-ALBO, on static display at the Farnborough Air Show.**
Air-Britain

---

### Sir Archibald E. Russell

After graduation from Bristol University, Archibald Russell started his working life in 1924 as an assistant fitter in the maintenance department of the Bristol Tramway and Carriage Company.

On his twenty-first birthday in 1925 he transferred his talents to the drawing office of The Bristol Aeroplane Company. When he retired forty-four years later it was as Managing Director, Filton, of the British Aircraft Corporation and British joint chairman of the Concorde Committee. During all this time he always had an office at Filton, and witnessed the maiden flights of thirty distinct prototypes, in all of which he had played his part. He pioneered the sophisticated theoretical system for achieving the lightest possible aircraft structures without sacrificing strength. He had a lucky escape in 1954 when he was aboard the second Britannia prototype, G-ALRX, during its emergency landing on the mud flats of the River Severn (*see* page 16).

Archibald Russell was awarded the Gold Medal of the Royal Aeronautical Society in 1951, and the CBE in 1954. He was elected a Fellow of the Royal Society in 1970, and in 1971 was awarded the Daniel Guggenheim Gold Medal for his outstanding leadership of the Bristol design team. In 1972 he was knighted for his services to aviation.

Class or forty-eight Tourist Class passengers plus their baggage and 3,370lb (1,500kg) of freight. This payload was to be carried at 310mph (500km/h) over the Johannesburg to Nairobi stage of the African trunk route, against the maximum headwind for that stage. The Britannia was originally intended to be capable of operation from grass runways, but this requirement was later dropped. Bristol Proteus turboprops and Napier Nomad compound engines were considered, but at this stage Bristol was only prepared to guarantee the performance with Centaurus engines, not with the Proteus.

## The Type 175 is Ordered

On 2 February 1948 the Ministry of Supply agreed to order several prototypes provided BOAC would agree to order at least twenty-five production aircraft. Since the new fleet was intended to be in service by 1954 it was not going to be possible for BOAC to delay a production order until after the first flight of the prototype. The technical risk involved was difficult for BOAC to accept and on 5 July 1948 the Ministry of Supply decided to order three prototypes without waiting for BOAC's production order. All three were to be Centaurus-powered, but the second and third examples were to be suitable for conversion to the Proteus, and the third was to be fully equipped for operation as part of the BOAC fleet. In October 1948, having ordered a fleet of twenty-two Canadair Argonauts as an interim fleet for the African and Far East routes, BOAC decided to take an interest in the Proteus-powered Britannia and the Bristol–BOAC working party was recalled to Filton to decide on the best parameters for a larger and more versatile Britannia, suitable for either Centaurus or Proteus power. A specification was agreed upon that included a 140ft (43m) wingspan, a wing area of 2,055sq ft (191sq m), an all-up weight of 118,000lb (53,500kg) with Centaurus engines or 119,000lb (54,000kg) with Proteus engines, and interior layouts for forty-two, fifty or sixty-four day passengers, or thirty-eight sleeping berths. In November BOAC agreed to order twenty-five aircraft of this size at a cost of £400,000 per machine, designed with eventual installation of Proteus engines in mind, but powered initially by Centaurus 663 engines developing 2,850hp and providing a cruising speed of 296mph (476km/h) at 20,000ft

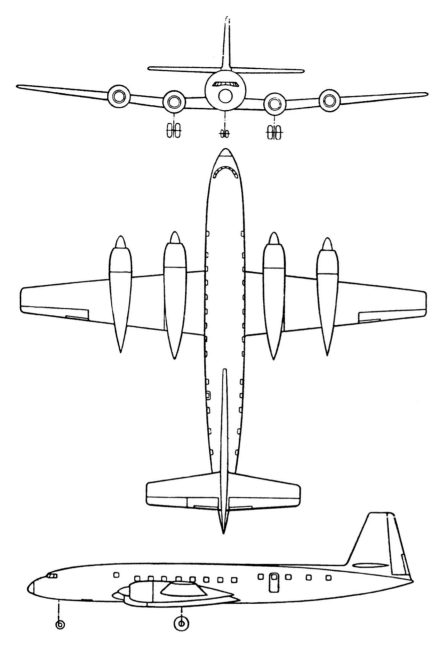

General arrangement of the Bristol Type 175, featuring Centaurus engines and with a 120ft (36.6m) wingspan, as it appeared in the first brochure submitted to BOAC. Bristol publication

the premature obsolescence of the Constellation fleet, deliveries of the new aircraft were not to commence before 1954. The maximum capacity of thirty-six passengers was chosen because this was the capacity of the standard BOAC airport bus: more passengers per flight would require a doubling of the bus fleet, which serviced nearly fifty airports along the network!

In April 1947 Bristol submitted their Type 175 project, powered by Centaurus 662 engines and with a gross weight of 94,000lb (43,000kg), a wingspan of 120ft (37m) and a payload of 11,000lb (5,000kg). This was considered the most promising design and in October 1947 a joint working party with BOAC met at Filton to decide on the optimum size for the aircraft. At this meeting the gross weight was increased to 107,000lb (49,000kg), the wingspan to 130ft (40m), and the payload to 13,300lb (6,000kg), this representing forty-two First

**General arrangement of the Centaurus-powered Britannia.**
Bristol publication via Captain Brian Dawson

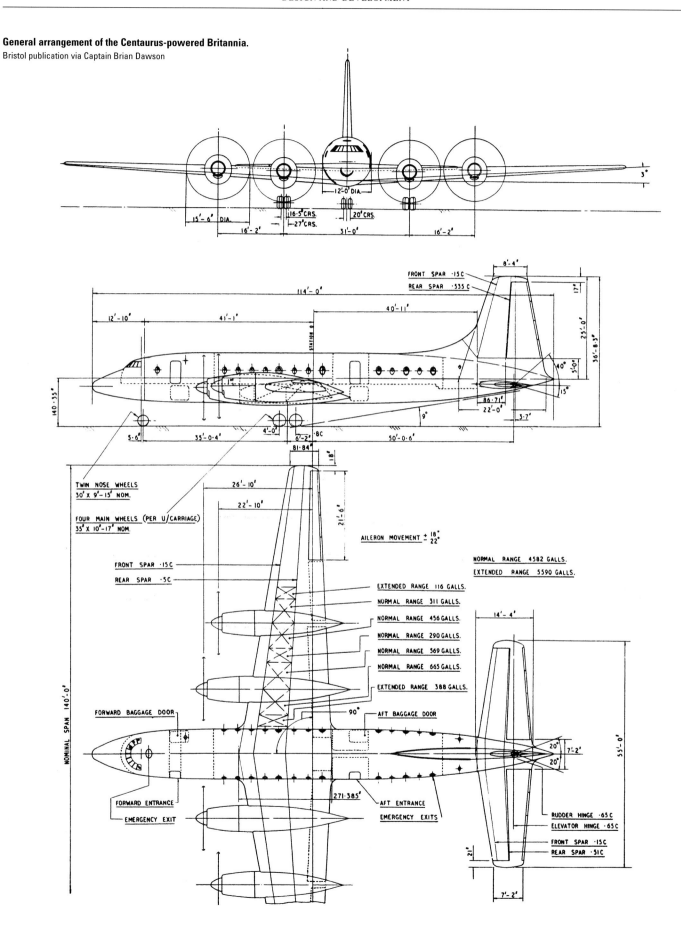

(6,000m). The payload and range, of 17,610lb (8,000kg) over a distance of 2,300nm (4,300km), was to be common to both Centaurus- and Proteus-powered variants. The Centaurus-powered Britannia was intended to fly in 1949, at which time it would rival in size the largest airliner in service, the Boeing Stratocruiser.

The formal contract was not signed until 28 July 1949, and covered the purchase of twenty-five Britannias, the first six of which were to be powered by the Centaurus 663. The price of each aircraft was £445,000, £45,000 of which represented the price of four Centaurus engines, and a further £45,000 the airframe development levy payable to the Minister of

Atlantic routes. Because the runway and terrain-clearance restrictions imposed at the secondary airports on the Empire routes did not apply to the Atlantic air terminals, an increased gross weight of 130,000lb (59,000kg) and increased fuel capacity of 5,790gal (26,320ltr) was possible. At this weight the Proteus gave an excellent take-off performance, and the payload of 23,500lb (10,600kg) would allow up to eighty-three passengers to be carried. Apart from a complete revision of the interior layout, the only major modification required was a four-wheeled bogie instead of twin wheels for each main undercarriage unit, in order to keep the runway loading down to that of the L-749 Constellation.

already made for this Centaurus prototype being used for a functional mock-up, given construction number 12825, on which a wide range of ground tests could be carried out. In order to speed up development of the Proteus, two of these engines were test-flown in the outboard engine positions of Avro Lincoln SX972 during 1950.

In January 1951 the final issue of Specification 2/47 was issued, incorporating all the features agreed to date, including a redesign of the passenger cabin floor to introduce longitudinal seat rails, at BOAC's request, and a switch from Fowler flaps to the double-slotted type. This defined the standard to which the first prototype (c/n 12873, registered G-ALBO) would be built. The structural design of the Type 175 embodied many lessons from the Brabazon project, which had provided Bristol with an unequalled store of basic design data. During 1951 a full-scale wing, with 40ft of fuselage attached, was proof-loaded and then tested to failure, which occurred at 98 per cent of the designed ultimate loading. A minor modification at the site of the primary failure then raised the ultimate strength to 104 per cent of the designed value. As a result of these tests it was possible to raise the all-up weight once more, to 140,000lb (63,000kg). The fuel capacity was correspondingly increased to 6,800gal (31,000ltr), proposed for the twenty-sixth and subsequent aircraft. However, the new fuel tankage was also incorporated into the first twenty-five production aircraft at BOAC's request, and the second prototype (G-ALRX) was also modified to this standard. Also in 1951, Bristol 170 Mk 21E G-AICT was fitted with a 0.7-scale Britannia tailplane, elevators and rudder with a representative dorsal fin to provide handling data on the aerodynamic servo-tab controls and artificial feel system adopted for the Britannia. In this configuration it was flown for some months with the experimental marks G-18-40. A further reappraisal of cabin arrangements by BOAC in November 1951 established the basic tourist-class layout as ninety seats in six-abreast configuration. By this time, the type name Britannia had been formally approved by both the Ministry of Supply and BOAC. Fuel flow tests were conducted in April 1952 using the functional mock-up in the maximum nose-up flight attitude of 15 degrees, and around the same time ditching trials were carried out with the aid of a scale model Britannia at Bristol.

**The first prototype Britannia G-ALBO at Filton.** Bristol via Ted Ashman

Supply. The payment schedule specified payment of 11 per cent of the price on signature of contract, a further 11 per cent on 1 April 1950, 1951, 1952 and 1953, and 45 per cent on acceptance of each aircraft. Under the terms of the contract Bristol agreed that it 'shall not, before one month after the first flight of the first prototype offer any Bristol Type 175 aircraft for sale to a third party civilian operator'.

In the interim period BOAC investigated the possible use of the Bristol 175 on its

At this stage provision was still made for either Centaurus 663 or Proteus 3 engines, but during 1950 such excellent progress was made with bench-running of the Proteus srs 700 (equivalent to the original Proteus 3 performance) that BOAC asked for all twenty-five of their aircraft to be delivered with the Proteus. Deletion of the provision for Centaurus power allowed the engine nacelles to be reduced in frontal area, and also meant that one prototype could be cancelled, the components

**The historic first flight of the Britannia. G-ALBO at Filton, 16 August 1952.** Bristol Aeroplane Co. Ltd, via the Bristol Aero Collection

## The Britannia Takes to the Air

G-ALBO was rolled out of the Brabazon assembly hall at Filton in July 1952. Piloted by Chief Test Pilot A. J. Pegg, it made its first flight on 16 August, powered by Proteus 625 engines with only three-quarters of the output of the developed Proteus 705. The eventful first flight revealed over-sensitivity of the elevator controls, but after a few wild manoeuvres control was regained and the crew decided to complete a circuit and land. On selection of 'undercarriage down' the starboard main bogie refused to rotate fully down. After several attempts to shake it down Pegg was resigned to making a landing with the bogie still at 90 degrees from its correct landing attitude, and with almost unusable elevators. At that moment blue smoke and a smell of burning began to waft up through the cockpit floor from an overheated electric motor. Fortunately the reluctant undercarriage bogie locked down fully just seconds before landing. The fault was later traced to the temporary seizing of a bearing, caused by overheating incurred during high-speed taxi runs and maximum breaking tests immediately before the take-off. The second flight was made on 21 August, and on this occasion the nose-wheel strut refused to lock down until after G-ALBO had touched down and about one second before the nosewheel made contact with the runway. Both the elevator and the undercarriage faults were corrected by simple modifications, and the aircraft's ninth flight was to Farnborough in September for the Britannia's appearance at the 1952 SBAC display.

Not very long after the Britannia's first flight, the type was evaluated by Royal Canadian Air Force pilots for possible use

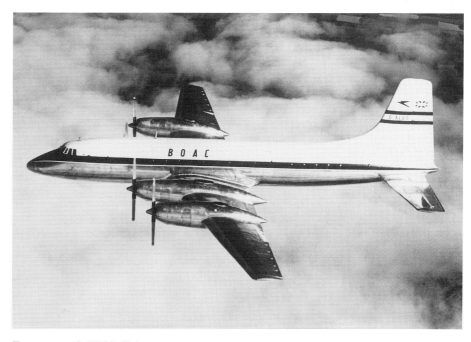

**First prototype G-ALBO in flight.** The late Dave Williams

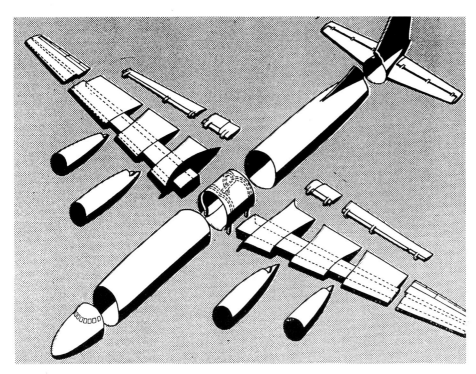

**Breakdown of the major components of the Britannia during construction.** Bristol publication

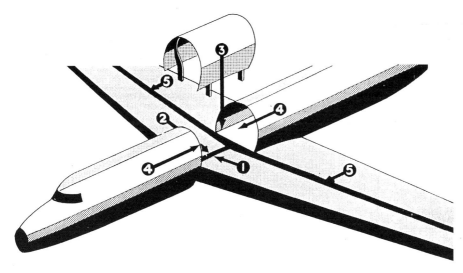

**Assembly sequence of major components of the Britannia.** Bristol publication

servo-tabs with the rudder control. In November 1952 a proposal was put forward to reduce cabin noise on the sixteenth and subsequent aircraft, by using air tapped direct from the engines for cabin pressurization and air conditioning in place of the existing Godfrey blowers. This system was finally adopted for all but the two prototypes. The more powerful Proteus 705, incorporating a prop-turbine speed limiter and increased fire protection, was installed in August 1953, in time for G-ALBO's appearance at that year's Farnborough show.

## The Crash of the Second Prototype

On 23 December 1953 the second prototype Britannia, c/n 12874, G-ALRX, was flown at the higher all-up weight of 140,000lb (63,000kg), with the fuel capacity increased to 6,750gal (30,700ltr) and with Proteus 705s from the outset, but on 4 February 1954, after only 51 hours' flying time, the No.3 engine oil temperature rose some seven minutes after take-off and the engine had to be shut down. It was relit once the oil temperature had fallen, but following the demonstration of a stall manoeuvre the oil temperature again rose. A pinion in the reduction gear at the front end of the long propeller shaft had stripped its teeth, probably as a result of resonance. Freed of its load, the big low-pressure turbine ran away, suddenly breaking from its shaft to explode with great violence into small pieces. These fortunately missed the fuselage and fuel tanks, but pierced the engine oil tank, causing an oil fire of great intensity. The fire could not be contained, so the No.4 engine was also shut down as a precautionary measure. On approach to Filton the Nos 1 and 2 engines both cut out as a result of a short circuit caused by the fire. They were quickly restarted thanks to the skill of two of the technical specialists on board, Ken Fitzgerald and Gareth Jones, but because of the intensity of the fire Bill Pegg decided on an immediate forced landing on the mud of the Severn estuary at Littleton-on Severn, in order to safeguard the passengers; these included senior Bristol executives and two representatives of KLM. The landing was made with only the two port engines running, but despite this the only injury sustained by any of the thirteen people on board was one head wound.

in the coastal reconnaissance and anti-submarine role. No order for the Britannia as such was forthcoming, but longer-term developments led to the type being developed under licence in Canada into two completely new types (*see* Chapter Six).

After the early flights, only a few substantial modifications were necessary. The nacelle shape was improved and the engine tailpipes extended aft. Lateral stability was increased by fitting up-turned wingtips of slightly greater span. (Bill Pegg had originally asked for the dihedral to be increased from 3 degrees to the 5 degrees common in contemporary four-engined airliners, but this would have been too time-consuming.) Handling during the approach was improved by introducing aileron and elevator anti-float springs, and inter-connecting the inboard aileron

**The first two Britannias, G-ALRX (nearest the camera) and G-ALBO, flying together in early 1954.** Bristol via Ted Ashman

**Mystery ship. The original caption to these photos says 'Air Transport Development Unit, Abingdon, June 1966'. Could this be c/n 12874, the second prototype Britannia?**

The second prototype Britannia, G-ALRX, on the mud-flats of the Severn Estuary after its forced landing on 4 February 1954. Bristol via Ted Ashman

The mud of the estuary doused the fire and preserved the evidence of its origins, but then the aircraft was caught by the rising tide and when RAF personnel arrived on the scene the next day, all that could be seen of it was the tail fin sticking up out of the water. The initial recovery plan was to place flotation bags under the Britannia and float her down to Avonmouth Docks, some 3 miles (5km) away. To this end, pierced steel planking was laid across the mudflats, but the aircraft was then found to have been damaged beyond repair by the salt water, and so was cut up. Components from it were subsequently used for training purposes by Bristol's Service School, and the nose section is preserved to this day at Kemble in Gloucestershire.

As a result of the crash, the reduction gear was redesigned with helical instead of straight teeth. To maintain the urgent tempo of the flight development programme G-ALBO was modified to the 140,000lb standard without the extra fuel capacity and recommenced flying in March 1954, only to be grounded in May for wing repairs after a flap torque-tube on one side

18

failed during stalling tests at 10,000ft (3,000m). A half-roll was performed before test pilot Walter Gibb could retract the extended flaps on the other side, and 7,000ft (2,000m) was lost in the rapid uncontrolled descent, and an overload of 3g was imposed on the wings. It was discovered that the inner and outer torsion tubes had been inadvertently installed in each other's positions.

## Testing Continues

It was then decided to use the first production Britannia, c/n 12902, G-ANBA, for general development flying after its first flight on 5 September 1954, and to allocate the next three examples to a 2,000-hour programme of Certificate of Airworthiness testing and 250 hours' route proving in which BOAC crews would fly with the Bristol pilots. To assist with engine development, Airspeed Ambasssador G-AKRD was equipped with Proteus 705 engines and also with a spray rig for icing trials. G-ALBO returned to service in time for preliminary tropical performance trials at Idris in October 1954, and Britannias G-ANBB and G-ANBC made their first flights on 18 January and 29 June 1955 respectively. Full tropical trials were completed by G-ANBA at Khartoum and Johannesburg in March 1955. The Britannia made the trip out to Johannesburg in a faster time than the Comet 1 had done previously, as it only needed to make one refuelling stop, at Khartoum, in either direction.

During the course of these trials it made four- and three-engined take-offs at 150,000lb (68,000kg), and this was confirmed as the take-off weight for production aircraft. It was raised to 155,000lb (70,000kg) in 1956, with an associated landing weight of 123,000lb (56,000kg) following undercarriage modifications. After completing 652 hours and 277 hours, respectively, on this intensive development programme G-ANBA and G-ANBB were flown to Belfast for completion and furnishing to BOAC standard by Short Bros and Harland.

A 1955 Bristol publication details the total hours flown by each of the first five Britannias up to August 1955, as shown in the table. These hours were used for general development, tests to establish compliance with British Civil Airworthiness Requirements and endurance flying.

The same document goes on to give a brief history of flight tests. From August

An early shot of srs 102 G-ANBA being used for development flying before delivery to **BOAC.** Bristol via Ted Ashman

**Britannia Development Programme Flying to August 1955**

| Aircraft | Total Hours | | | |
|---|---|---|---|---|
| G-ALBO | 1,028 | | | |
| G-ALRX | 51 | | | |
| G-ANBA | 652 | | | |
| G-ANBB | 277 | | | |
| G-ANBC | 19 | | | |

| Aircraft | Development | Compliance with BCAR | Endurance | Miscellaneous |
|---|---|---|---|---|
| G-ALBO | 424 | 184 | 393 | 27 |
| G-ALRX | 30 | 21 | – | – |
| G-ANBA | 208 | 421 | – | 23 |
| G-ANBB | 61 | 174 | – | 42 |

1952 to August 1954 flying covered general development of all systems including flying controls, handling characteristics and preliminary performance data for the airframe and engines. During September 1954 preliminary tropical trials were undertaken with G-ALBO, at Idris in North Africa. Some thirty hours were spent obtaining performance data for airframe and engines, and the results showed close agreement with calculations.

Until October 1954 it had been planned that BOAC should take delivery of early aircraft with a Special Category Certificate of Airworthiness and undertake crew familiarization and training while full certification tests were carried out by the Bristol Aeroplane Company at Filton. It was now decided that Bristol should carry out all the flight work necessary to obtain a full Certificate of Airworthiness before delivery. This change

**The first four Britannias together at Filton. G-ALBO nearest camera, then G-ANBA, G-ANBB and G-ALRX.**
Bristol via Ted Ashman

## Flight Tests From October 1954

| Aircraft | Flight Tests |
|---|---|
| G-ALBO | Engine and power plant endurance flying |
| | Propeller endurance flying |
| | Structure strain gauge |
| | Radio (VHF, ILS, ADF, HF, search radar) |
| G-ANBA | De-icing |
| | General performance (aircraft and engines) |
| | Pressurization and air conditioning |
| | Hydraulic system |
| | Preliminary auto-pilot |
| | Preliminary handling tests (Bristol Aeroplane Co., Air Registration Board, Royal Aircraft Establishment) |
| | Tropical tests |
| | Fuel System |
| | Electrical system load measurement |
| G-ANBB | Handling tests (for Royal Canadian Air Force) |
| | Final handling |
| | Final auto-pilot |
| | Final radio |
| | Fuel system |
| G-ANBC | Certificate of Airworthiness route tests |
| | Production fuel system |
| | Production electrical system |
| | Production jet pipe |
| | Pilot emergency procedure |
| | Certificate of Airworthiness acceptance (series flight tests) |
| | ARB acceptance of prototype |

## Certificate of Airworthiness Tests

| Test | Hours Flown |
|---|---|
| Performance | 130 (UK) |
| | 30 (Tropics) |
| Handling | 60 (UK/Bristol) |
| | 69 (UK/ARB) |
| | 5 (Tropics/Bristol) |
| Structure strain gauging | 150 |
| Air conditioning and pressurization | 25 (UK) |
| | 5 (Tropics) |
| De-icing | 40 |
| Fuel system | 30 |
| Auto-pilot | 30 |
| Electrics | 20 (Load measurement) |
| | 50 (Load endurance) |
| Radio | 75 |
| Power plant | 50 (UK) |
| | 10 (Tropics) |

*Major Items Requiring Intensive Flight Development*

Development of tab-operated flying control system

Vibratory torque in flap system and high-operating motor currents

Miscellaneous troubles with undercarriage, covering hydraulic and mechanical failures forcing use of emergency system in flight

Rates of roll

Aileron control system torques

Excessive wheel-brake torques

Wing and tail anti-icing system

Propeller development, including difficulties with unfeathering, failure to reverse pitch and failure to cancel reverse pitch

Position of jet pipe efflux and shape of jet pipe

Pressurization and air conditioning, including the change from engine-driven cabin blowers to tapping the engine compressor

Development of radio equipment as installed in Britannia 100, including positioning of aerials and establishment of satisfactory performance had a profound effect on the flight testing programme: all available aircraft were now to be used for test work and endurance flying, with the object of achieving some 2,000 hours' flying by the time the Britannia srs 100 qualified for a normal full Certificate of Airworthiness. This figure was to include at least 250 hours of route proving with an aircraft of full production standard. To achieve the 2,000-hour total and to obtain the maximum number of flying hours for Proteus engines it was decided to allocate the work to the four aircraft available as shown in the table on the opposite page (left).

This intensive flight programme, particularly that covering endurance flying, was carried out with the help of BOAC pilots, and by November 1954 G-ALBO was being flown on test work and endurance flying by these pilots without the assistance of Bristol staff, following a period of crew training. To establish data for the pressure-tank fatigue tests at the Royal Aircraft Establishment, Farnborough, some 150 hours' flying was carried out, during which strain gauge measurements were taken at various parts of the airframe structure. This work was done in G-ALBO.

During March 1955 G-ANBA went to Johannesburg and Khartoum for full tropical trials. A total of 90 hours was flown, including the transit flights, during which full tropical performance and handling was established. By June 1955 the majority of development flying had been completed, apart from that required to establish satisfactory wing and tail anti-icing. The period of development was now complete, and the Certificate of Airworthiness tests were nearly so. These tests included the establishment of correct heat distribution over the wing and tail surfaces, and proof that the aircraft handled satisfactorily when flown in light ice without the anti-icing system functioning. During the period of flying, the ARB pilots had flown the various aircraft for some 100 hours and carried out detailed checks of their handling characteristics. Following general development flying, the full series of tests to obtain all the data were carried out, the hours flown being broken down as shown in the table on the opposite page (right).

By August 1955 the immediate flight tests outstanding in relation to the srs 100 were the completion of the wing and tail anti-icing tests, and the 250 hours' route proving, which were about to commence using G-ANBC.

G-ANBC was already furnished to BOAC standards for the programme of 250 hours of route-proving flights under normal traffic conditions to Nairobi, Entebbe, Johannesburg, Karachi, Khartoum, Lod, Cairo, Idris and Rome. On the flights to the last two destinations a full complement of ninety-eight crew and passengers (Bristol and BOAC employees) was carried. The flights took place from 9 September to 19 November, representing an annual utilization of 2,150 hours. The fourth production Britannia, c/n 12905 G-ANBD, was furnished with First Class seating and a lounge bar and did not fly until November 1955, so was too late to participate in the main development programme, but along with G-ANBC was formally handed over to BOAC at London Airport on 30 December 1955, immediately after the full Certificate of Airworthiness had been granted.

After 20 hours of performance flying between 1–4 January 1956 to establish cruising control techniques, these aircraft were then based at Hurn Airport, Bournemouth, where BOAC crews were mustered for training by senior pilots, who had themselves completed some 600 hours conversion flying on G-ALBO at Filton under Bristol supervision. During this intensive crew-training programme it was sometimes known for up to sixty landings to be made in a single day.

## Icing Problems

Six more Britannias were delivered to BOAC during 1956, and a programme of South African route familiarization flights from Hurn started in March, but that same month the airline experienced its first case of engine 'flame-out', whilst an aircraft was flying in icing cloud conditions in the intertropical front over Uganda. This was followed on 4 April by G-ANBD suffering flame-outs on all four engines within five minutes over the Rift Valley, about 200 miles (320km) south of Nairobi. The pilot, Captain Rendall, BOAC's Britannia Flight Manager, managed to restore full power, however, without the loss of too much altitude. A similar occurrence happened to Captain Lincoln Lee, when all four engines failed due to ice forming in the intakes on 27 April. Captain Lee was later to be second-in-command on the inaugural Britannia passenger service, before eventually converting onto Comet

4s. On another occasion a Britannia flying between Singapore and Calcutta suffered a total of seven flame-outs and completed the leg with the No.2 engine shut down and its propeller feathered.

The icing problem seemed to occur only in tropical zones and its cause was initially obscure: it was in fact a type of icing only found in certain cloud conditions found in tropical areas. It had in fact first been encountered during a flight to Bombay by G-ANBC in 1955, but the cause had been wrongly diagnosed at that time as compressor stalling in turbulence. Small modifications were made and as the trouble did not reoccur in test flights over Britain, it was thought to have been cured. It was eventually found to be caused by the design of the engine air intake, which curved through 180 degrees. In certain conditions this resulted in 'dry' ice crystals forming on the inner walls of the engine cowlings. When the ice reached a sufficient thickness it would break away and enter the engine compressor in quantities large enough to produce either a 'bump stall' or a flame-out. 'Bump stalls' were caused by the interruption of the airflow through the compressor and could be both felt and heard in the passenger cabin. The icing problem in tropical climes had been initially camouflaged by the fact that the Proteus had been subjected to and had passed rigorous icing trials in Canada.

At first, various modifications to cure the problems were only partially successful, but by the end of the year the 'slush-icing' phenomenon was fully understood, thanks partly to the ingenious use of industrial television cameras inside the engine cowlings, and had been remedied by a combination of hot-air jets to remove ice precipitation in the air intake and platinum glow plugs in four of the eight combustion chambers to ensure automatic relighting immediately a flame-out occurred. During flight tests to prove the various engine de-icing modifications G-ALBO was fitted with a water-spray rig ahead of the starboard inner nacelle, which at one stage contained an engine fitted with eight separate NACA ramp-type flush intakes. This was reasonably ice-free, but extracted too high a performance penalty, as the intakes scooped away the boundary layer air so that vortices were induced on the wing behind the nacelle and the increase in drag led to a range penalty of some 4 per cent.

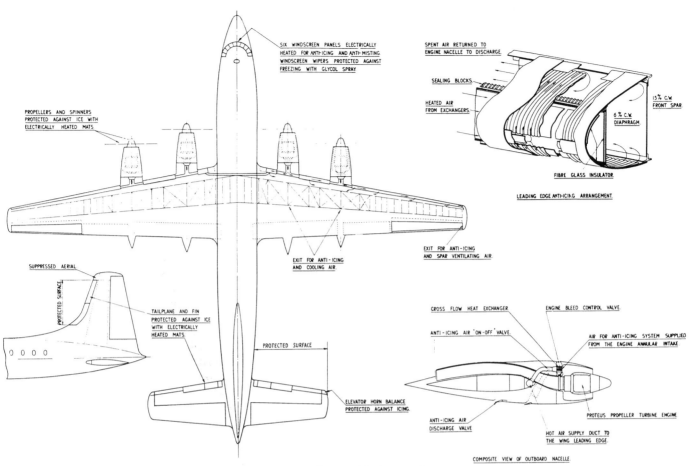

SIX WINDSCREEN PANELS ELECTRICALLY
HEATED FOR ANTI-ICING AND ANTI-MISTING
WINDSCREEN WIPERS PROTECTED AGAINST
FREEZING WITH GLYCOL SPRAY

PROPELLERS AND SPINNERS
PROTECTED AGAINST ICE WITH
ELECTRICALLY HEATED MATS

SUPPRESSED AERIAL

PROTECTED SURFACE

TAILPLANE AND FIN
PROTECTED AGAINST ICE
WITH ELECTRICALLY
HEATED MATS.

PROTECTED SURFACE

EXIT FOR ANTI-ICING
AND COOLING AIR.

ELEVATOR HORN BALANCE
PROTECTED AGAINST ICING.

EXIT FOR ANTI-ICING
AND SPAR VENTILATING AIR.

SPENT AIR RETURNED TO
ENGINE NACELLE TO DISCHARGE.

SEALING BLOCKS

HEATED AIR
FROM EXCHANGERS.

15% C.W.
FRONT SPAR.

6% C.W.
DIAPHRAGM.

FIBRE GLASS INSULATOR.

LEADING EDGE ANTI-ICING ARRANGEMENT.

CROSS FLOW HEAT EXCHANGER.

ENGINE BLEED CONTROL VALVE.

ANTI-ICING AIR 'ON-OFF' VALVE.

AIR FOR ANTI-ICING SYSTEM SUPPLIED
FROM THE ENGINE ANNULAR INTAKE

PROTEUS PROPELLER TURBINE ENGINE

ANTI-ICING AIR
DISCHARGE VALVE

HOT AIR SUPPLY DUCT TO
THE WING LEADING EDGE.

COMPOSITE VIEW OF OUTBOARD NACELLE.

SECONDARY SURFACE

PRIMARY SURFACE

CONTINUOUSLY HEATED
LEADING EDGE STRIP

TYPICAL SECTION OF TAIL UNIT L.E.

**Ice protection systems on the Britannia srs 310. From** *Britannia Descriptive Notes and Performance Data,*
**published April 1956.** Bristol Aircraft via Mr D. H. Bartlett

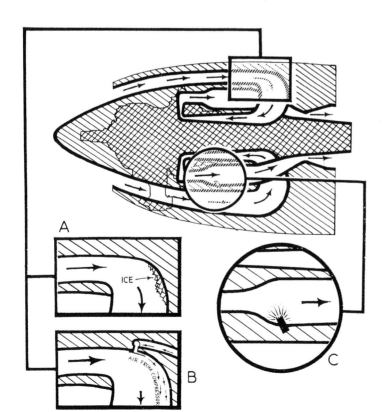

A

ICE

AIR FROM COMPRESSOR

B

C

**Diagram of measures to cure Proteus icing
problems.** Bristol publication via Bristol Aero Collection

**Surface controls systems on the Britannia srs 310. From *Britannia Descriptive Notes and Performance Data*, published April 1956.** Bristol Aircraft via Mr D. H. Bartlett

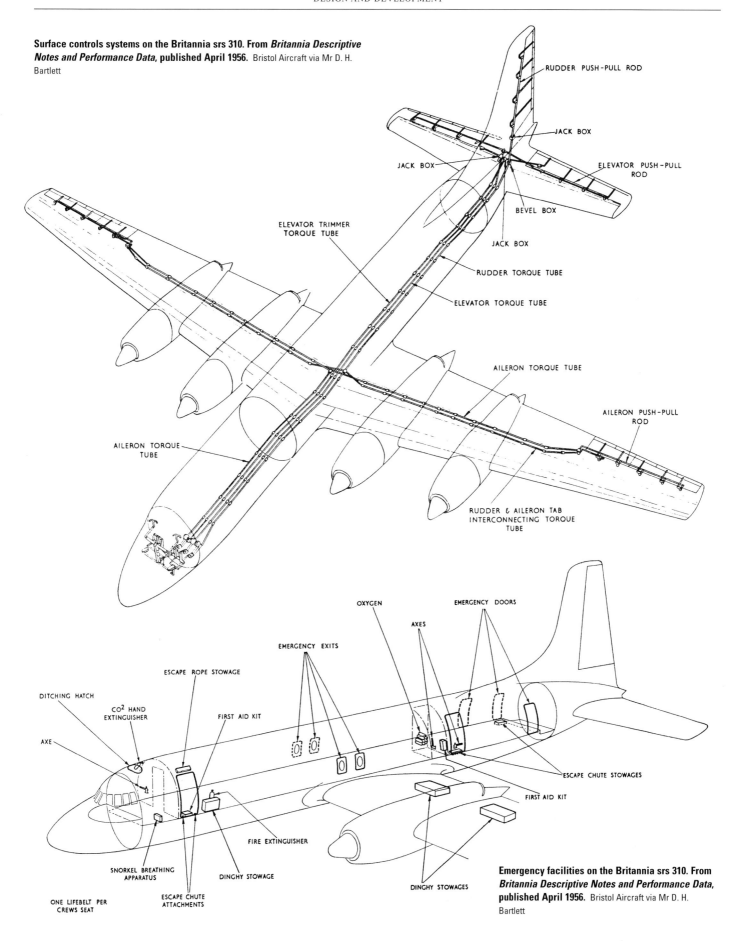

RUDDER PUSH-PULL ROD

JACK BOX

ELEVATOR PUSH-PULL ROD

JACK BOX

BEVEL BOX

JACK BOX

ELEVATOR TRIMMER TORQUE TUBE

RUDDER TORQUE TUBE

ELEVATOR TORQUE TUBE

AILERON TORQUE TUBE

AILERON PUSH-PULL ROD

AILERON TORQUE TUBE

RUDDER & AILERON TAB INTERCONNECTING TORQUE TUBE

OXYGEN

EMERGENCY DOORS

AXES

EMERGENCY EXITS

ESCAPE ROPE STOWAGE

DITCHING HATCH

$CO_2$ HAND EXTINGUISHER

FIRST AID KIT

AXE

ESCAPE CHUTE STOWAGES

FIRST AID KIT

FIRE EXTINGUISHER

SNORKEL BREATHING APPARATUS

DINGHY STOWAGE

ONE LIFEBELT PER CREWS SEAT

ESCAPE CHUTE ATTACHMENTS

DINGHY STOWAGES

**Emergency facilities on the Britannia srs 310. From *Britannia Descriptive Notes and Performance Data*, published April 1956.** Bristol Aircraft via Mr D. H. Bartlett

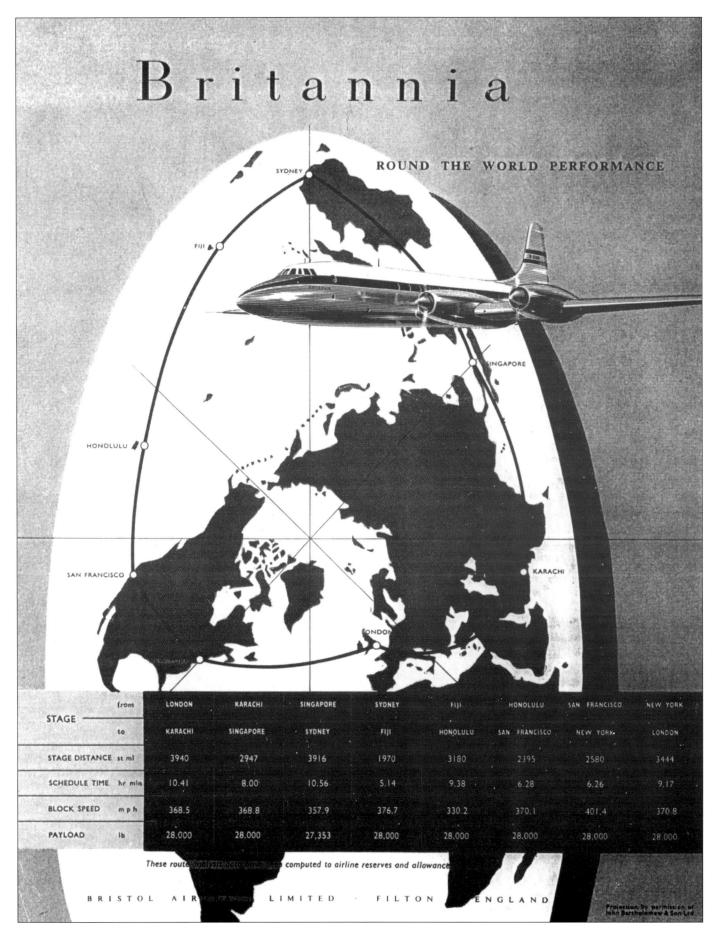

# Britannia

## ROUND THE WORLD PERFORMANCE

| STAGE | from | LONDON | KARACHI | SINGAPORE | SYDNEY | FIJI | HONOLULU | SAN FRANCISCO | NEW YORK |
|---|---|---|---|---|---|---|---|---|---|
| | to | KARACHI | SINGAPORE | SYDNEY | FIJI | HONOLULU | SAN FRANCISCO | NEW YORK | LONDON |
| STAGE DISTANCE | st ml | 3940 | 2947 | 3916 | 1970 | 3180 | 2395 | 2580 | 3444 |
| SCHEDULE TIME | hr min | 10.41 | 8.00 | 10.56 | 5.14 | 9.38 | 6.28 | 6.26 | 9.17 |
| BLOCK SPEED | m p h | 368.5 | 368.8 | 357.9 | 376.7 | 330.2 | 370.1 | 401.4 | 370.8 |
| PAYLOAD | lb | 28,000 | 28,000 | 27,353 | 28,000 | 28,000 | 28,000 | 28,000 | 28,000 |

These route _____ computed to airline reserves and allowance

BRISTOL AIR____ LIMITED · FILTON · ENGLAND

Projection by permission of
John Bartholomew & Son Ltd

**Bristol advertisement for the Britannia, from the February 1956 edition of *BOAC Review*.** British Airways Archives

## The Sales Effort

In the spring of 1956 G-ANBE undertook a European sales tour, with visits to Lufthansa at Hamburg and Cologne and SAS at Stockholm (Bromma) and Copenhagen. A BOAC crew flew the transit flights between the various cities, but the demonstration flights given at each were carried out by a Bristol crew under the command of Bill Pegg. Travelling as passengers on the aircraft were the Britannia's design team leader, Dr A. E. Russell, and the Managing Director of Bristol Aircraft, Peter Masefield.

The European tour was followed in the summer by another, more ambitious, sales tour, this time of North America. On 12 August, only seven days after its first flight, G-ANBJ was flown by a crew under the command of Bill Pegg from London to Montreal non-stop in 10 hours 52 minutes on what was the first transatlantic crossing by a Britannia. After a 75-minute stopover the aircraft was on its way again, to New York in 1 hour 34 minutes. At New York the new airliner was demonstrated to representatives of Pan-American, Eastern Airlines, American Airlines, TWA and Northeast Airlines. Then it was on to San Diego, the 2,180 miles (3,500km) being covered in 8½ hours, the first US transcontinental flight by a turboprop airliner. After three days at San Diego, G-ANBJ flew to Burbank and Los Angeles, then onwards to Vancouver and to San Francisco, where it was demonstrated to United, Pan-American and Western Airlines. The next stops on the itinerary were Denver, to be shown to Continental and United, and Chicago. Next came New York again and Miami, followed by Washington and Ottawa, where the Britannia was demonstrated to officials of the Royal Canadian Air Force and the Canadian government. Finally, G-ANBJ was shown to Trans-Canada Air Lines at Montreal before flying back non-stop to London Airport. The tour took in fourteen cities in the USA and Canada and included thirty-two demonstration flights, and no major snags were encountered during the 24,000-mile (40,000km) trip. The transatlantic legs were flown by BOAC flight crews, with Bristol pilots carrying out the demonstration flights. Over 4,000 people walked through the aircraft whilst it was on the ground during the tour and the only major item requiring replacement at the end of it was the carpet in the passenger cabin!

**Srs 301 G-ANCA, the srs 300 prototype, in partial Capital Airlines colour scheme after its US sales tour in 1956.** Air-Britain

Sales efforts continued and an August 1956 brochure offered potential Britannia operators a choice of several different cabin configurations, including a First Class sleeper version with seventeen single-width upper berths and fifteen double-width lower berths, plus four fully-reclining First Class seats. For daytime services, sixty-six First Class passengers could be accommodated in fully-reclining seats in four-abreast configuration, with a cocktail bar and aft lounge. There was also the option of a 93-seat, six-abreast Tourist Class layout.

A brochure was also produced for the Britannia srs 323, intended expressly for use by the other state airline corporation, British European Airways (BEA). This was to have been powered by Proteus 755 engines, giving a cruising speed of 400mph (640km/h) at 23,000ft (7,000m). It was claimed that the exterior noise level on take-off would be less than that of the DC-3s still widely used by BEA at that time. Delivery was promised for September 1958, or possibly from July 1957 if existing Britannnia options were not taken up. A range of seating arrangements was offered, including a five-abreast 87-seat Tourist layout, a four-abreast 73-seat First Class layout, and a mixed-class layout of eighteen First Class seats in a section aft of the rear galley and eighty-four Tourist Class seats in six-abreast configuration. All these versions would also have a six-seat rear lounge compartment. Also on offer was a 107-seat, six-abreast Night Tourist layout, and a high-density version with 133 seats at 34in (86cm) pitch. Bristol figures claimed a

break-even load factor on the London–Paris route of 63 per cent in First Class and 70 per cent in Tourist Class, and on the London–Rome route 34 per cent in First Class and 39 per cent in Tourist Class. The Britannia 323 was also claimed to be highly suitable for domestic routes such as London–Manchester and London–Belfast, and was offered to BEA at a purchase price of £1,613,600 per aircraft, including spares. However, no sale was forthcoming, and BEA eventually purchased a fleet of Vickers Vanguard turboprops instead. This was not the end of BEA's association with the Britannia, though, as a shortage of Vanguard capacity in the summer of 1961 led to the airline chartering BOAC Britannias for use on its European routes.

At the 1956 Farnborough Air Show G-ALBO was demonstrated with Proteus 705s in the inner nacelles, a Proteus 755 in the port outer position and a Bristol Orion in the starboard outer. During the demonstration it made a flypast with the inner Proteus 705s shut down. Also at the show was the Britannia 301 demonstrator, G-ANCA, and both these aircraft appeared again at the 1957 show, accompanied by Britannia srs 313 4X-AGB, ordered by El Al. By 17 January 1957 total Britannia flying hours, logged on fifteen different aircraft, totalled 8,194. Of these, 3,726 had been amassed by Bristol and 4,468 by BOAC. The aircraft with the most hours (the first prototype G-ALBO) had logged 1,471 hours and 993 landings. BOAC's hours included 3,257 landings, most of these on training sorties.

**First prototype Britannia G-ALBO flying in 1956 with a Bristol Orion in the port outer position, a Proteus 755 in the starboard outer, and Proteus 705s in the inner nacelles.**
Bristol via Ted Ashman

## Into Service

The Britannia entered public service on 1 February 1957, when G-ANBI operated the inaugural BOAC service from London to Johannesburg. During 1957 several BOAC srs 102s were flown into Weston-Super-Mare (Locking) Airport for modifications by Western Airways Ltd before delivery and that same year a pair of srs 302s for Aeronaves de Mexico were also flown in for fitting out, becoming the largest aircraft ever to land on Weston-Super-Mare's 4,200ft (1,280m) runway. Delivery of the first fifteen aircraft for BOAC was completed in August when G-ANBA re-emerged, fully furnished, from Belfast. The aircraft, allocated the registration G-ANBG, was later re-registered as G-APLL, after BOAC Chairman Sir Basil Smallpiece had decided after an annual inspection of the fleet that NBG might be construed as meaning 'no bloody good'. By August 1958 the annual utilization of the fleet had reached the unprecedented figure for this type of trunk route of 3,750 hours per aircraft, and the Proteus 705 engines had been approved to run 1,600 hours between overhauls. By 1962 this figure was to be increased to 2,400 hours.

## The Stretched Versions

The remaining ten aircraft of the original BOAC contract were not built, as a result of discussions that had begun in August 1952 regarding a possible srs 200 freighter version of the Britannia. Apart from increasing internal space for this role it was necessary to lengthen the fuselage forward of the wing to obtain clearance between the proposed large cargo door and the port inboard propeller. The fuselage was therefore lengthened by 82in (208cm) forward of the wing and 41in (104cm) aft to maintain the best centre of gravity position for the payload; this was also found to improve the aircraft's all-round performance and handling. BOAC took an option on five of the freighter version, but support could not be obtained from the International Air Transport Association for BOAC all-cargo operations on profitable routes, and so the airline then examined the economics of a long-bodied Britannia in either an all-passenger configuration or a mixed traffic layout with a strengthened cargo floor forward of the wing. To distinguish between these variants, the original Britannia was designated the srs 100, the all-cargo version the srs 200, the mixed-traffic version the srs 250 and the long-bodied passenger version the srs 300.

The all-up weight for all three of the longer variants was to be 155,000lb (70,000kg). In 1953 QANTAS of Australia wrote a letter of intent for six of the srs 250 variant, but this was not proceeded with.

BOAC considered the srs 300 for possible operation on the Atlantic routes, as it initially seemed to be more suitable than the Comet 2 for these duties on account of its greater volumetric payload. This was only achieved at the expense of fuel capacity, however, which left the srs 300 initially slightly worse off than the srs 100. Nevertheless, BOAC agreed to take ten srs 300s in place of the last ten of its original order of srs 100s, in addition to the option on five srs 200s, which had not been cancelled. Design studies then revealed that the extra fuel that was needed could be carried in the outer wing without exceeding existing wing strength limits, and the basic design for what was initially called the srs 300LR, incorporating these changes, was completed in May 1955. The landing gear and fuselage skin were strengthened and up-rated Proteus 755 engines allowed the maximum take-off weight to be increased to 175,000lb (80,000kg). Three months previously, manufacture of the first Britannia 300 had begun at Filton, along with seven more at a second production line that had been set up by Short Bros and Harland at Belfast. (Bristol had negotiated an agreement with Shorts in 1953 and had acquired a 13.5 per cent holding in the company in July 1954.) BOAC asked for long-range tanks to be incorporated into their srs 300s during manufacture and agreed to order ten srs 300LR aircraft if this could be done, at the same time cancelling two of the original srs 300s order, as well as the option on the five srs 200s. In fact, the new fuel system could only be installed in the last five srs 300s, since the earlier two were already too far advanced in manufacture to be modified at that stage.

As soon as news of the Britannia srs 300 and 300LR was announced interest was shown by long-haul operators worldwide, and negotiations began with El Al Israel Airlines and Canadian Pacific Air Lines that led to orders for three and four srs 300LRs, respectively, for use on the Atlantic routes. As each customer specified a different interior layout and instrumentation and equipment, the designation 300LR was changed to 310 and the sub-variants were numbered 311 for the prototype, 312 for BOAC, 313 for El Al and 314 for Canadian Pacific.

**(*Above*) Artist's impression of a srs 300 Britannia in the colours of Hunting-Clan Air Transport.** Bristol via Lester Stenner

**(*Below*) Artist's impression of a srs 300 Britannia in the colours of L.A.V. of Venezuala, who never actually placed an order.** Bristol via Lester Stenner

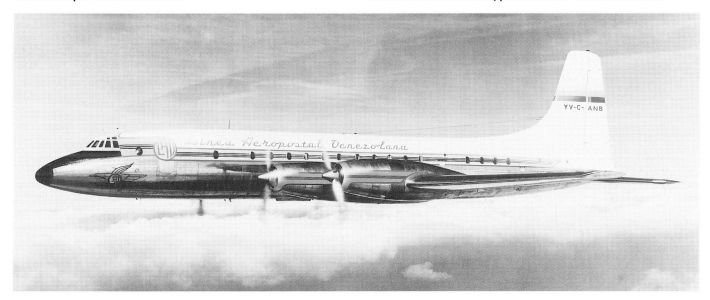

**(*Right*) Srs 305 G-ANCA in Northeast Airlines colours in early 1958.** Air-Britain

The five srs 300s converted to long range at Belfast still retained their original thinner fuselage skin and lighter landing-gear, which limited their take-off weight to 165,000lb (75,000kg), and these were designated srs 305s. By this time BOAC would have preferred not to take delivery of these interim aircraft, and when the Ministry of Supply agreed to buy the Filton-built srs 300 as a prototype (designated srs 301) and Bristol received a firm enquiry from Capital Airlines for the five srs 305s, a new contract was signed on 10 August 1955 that released BOAC from its obligation to take them. In return, BOAC placed a firm order for eighteen srs 312s which, with the fifteen srs 100s, brought the total BOAC fleet up to thirty-three Britannias.

The Capital Airlines sale was eventually frustrated by financial difficulties, but another US carrier, Northeast Airlines, placed a $17m bid for the five srs 305s in December 1956. With delivery planned

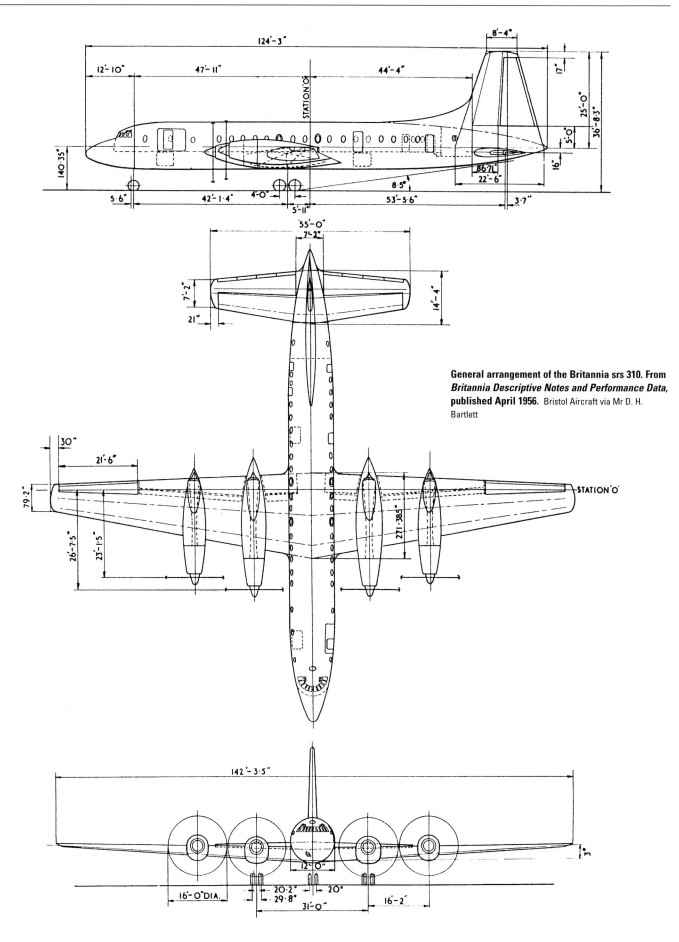

General arrangement of the Britannia srs 310. From *Britannia Descriptive Notes and Performance Data*, **published April 1956.** Bristol Aircraft via Mr D. H. Bartlett

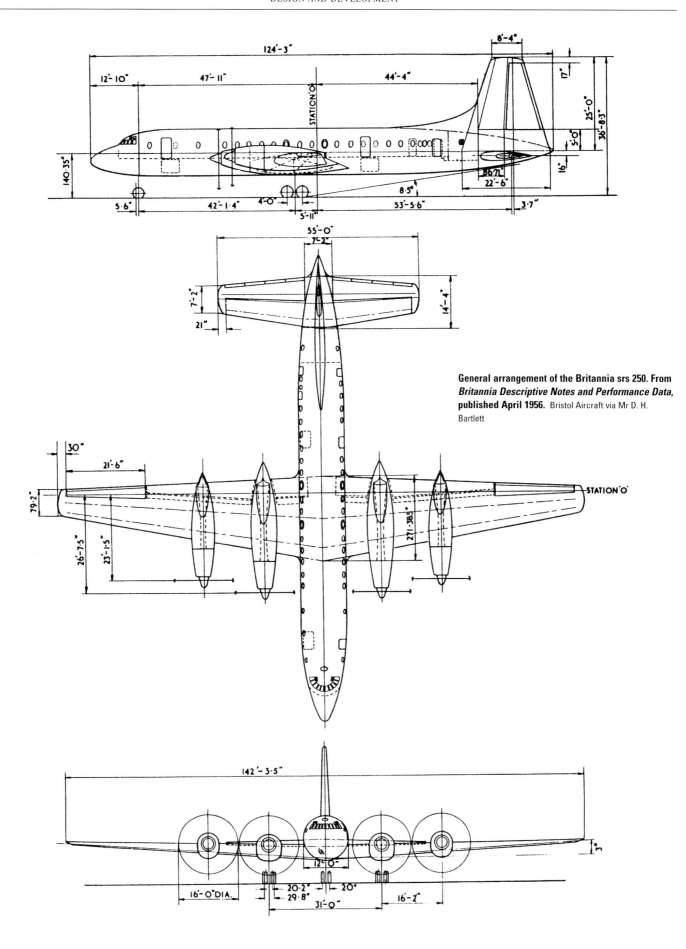

**General arrangement of the Britannia srs 250. From** *Britannia Descriptive Notes and Performance Data*, **published April 1956.** Bristol Aircraft via Mr D. H. Bartlett

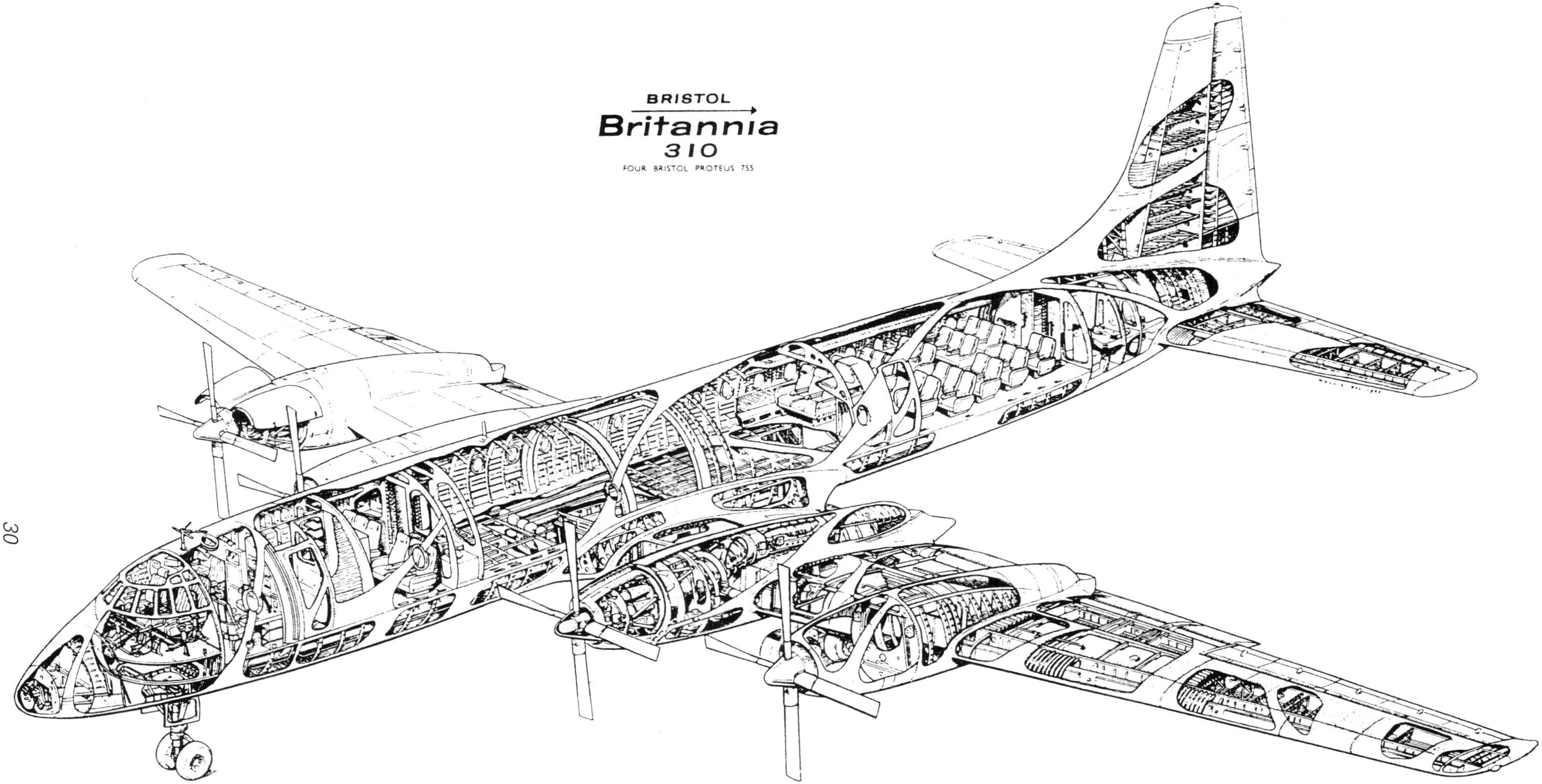

BRISTOL
**Britannia**
310
FOUR BRISTOL PROTEUS 755

30

**Cutaway diagram of the Britannia srs 310.** Bristol publication via Bristol Aero Collection

for October 1957, they were intended for use that winter on the airline's lucrative routes from New York and Washington to Miami. However, in order to meet American airworthiness requirements over 114 modifications had to be made first, and the first example, G-ANCE, the first Belfast-built Britannia, was delivered to Filton immediately after its first flight for American certification flying. By November, Northeast had realized that the aircraft were not going to be ready for service that winter and postponed the order until the spring of 1958. FAA approval was granted in April 1958, but in June of that year Northeast cancelled the contract as they had been unable to arrange suitable long-term credit facilities. The five srs 305s did, however, eventually prove attractive to independent operators tendering for Air Ministry trooping charters and, under revised designations, became the last Britannias to be sold. As for the two srs 300s that had been completed at Belfast without the long-range tanks, following earlier enquiries by Mexican carrier Aerovias Guest, they were bought by Aerovias de Mexico, designated srs 302.

The Britannia 301 G-ANCA first flew on 31 July 1956 and was earmarked for Certificate of Airworthiness testing and engine development at Filton. Prior to this, however, it was painted in Capital Airlines livery and sent to the USA on a sales tour. On its return a modified version of the Capital colour scheme was retained, but with Bristol Britannia titles instead.

The first Britannia srs 310, G-AOVA, made its maiden flight on 31 December 1956. With a fuel capacity of 8,580gal (39,000ltr), it was earmarked for Certificate of Airworthiness tests to supplement G-ANCA's programme. Designated as a Britannia 311 for development flying, although actually earmarked as the first production srs 312 for BOAC, it was based in Canada for cold weather trials between 30 January and 23 February 1957. The aircraft was based at Stevenson Field, Winnipeg, for the trials, and also made flights from Fort Churchill and Vancouver, with transit stops at Edmonton, Regina and Calgary. The lowest ground temperature was recorded at Winnipeg, where it dropped to −28°C. During the outward flight from Prestwick to Winnipeg the rudder control jammed for some two hours, and was still jammed on landing. The trouble was traced to a build-up of ice on the stringer immediately below the starboard rudder/aileron

**Srs 302 G-18-1, the first Belfast-built Britannia, later delivered to Aeronaves de Mexico as XA-MEC.** Air-Britain

**Landing shot of srs 300 prototype G-ANCA in partial Capital Airlines colour scheme.** Bristol via S. Verrall

interconnection torque tube, which had frozen the tube to the aircraft skin at the point where it passed through the fuselage.

G-AOVA also undertook a number of long-distance proving flights, including one from New York to Rome, a distance of 4,750 miles (7,640km). It later took part in a long series of Proteus 765 engine development tests culminating in flights to Singapore in December 1957 under monsoon conditions, during which the engines remained unaffected by the severe icing encountered. On 29 June 1957, in the course of a proving flight, it made the first ever non-stop airliner flight from London to the Pacific coast of Canada, covering the 5,100 miles (8,200km) to Vancouver in 14 hours 40 minutes. However, during a subsequent flight from Vancouver to Honolulu with the President of Canadian Pacific Airlines, Mr Grant McConochie, aboard, it suffered a runaway propeller on the No.4 engine whilst at 30,000ft (9,000m) over the middle of the Pacific. The propeller refused to feather and set up a vibration that led to compressor failure on the No.3 engine. Eventually, nine hours out from Vancouver, G-AOVA was safely landed in the dark at San Francisco on just the two port engines by Walter Gibb, a tribute to his skill and to the docile handling of the Britannia.

It was also around this time that millionaire Howard Hughes expressed an interest in acquiring thirty Britannia 320s for his airline, TWA. The srs 320 was a specialized short- and medium-haul development of the srs 310 aimed specifically at the North American market. It would have been capable of carrying up to 133 passengers in 'Coach' configuration at 400mph (640km/h) over stage lengths of 200–2,600 miles (320–4,200km). Features introduced for American users included hydraulically operated airstairs and a 'carry-on' luggage compartment. As related by Sir Archibald Russell in his autobiography *A Span of Wings* (Airlife, 1992), the negotiations with Howard Hughes were in keeping with the eccentric nature of the man. Hughes would talk to no-one but the boss, so Sir Reginald Verdon-Smith had to meet a barefoot Hughes alone at a certain street corner in Montreal at midnight. The two of them took a walk around the block, during which Hughes expressed his desire to fly the Britannia himself. He refused contact with any Bristol pilot and instead demanded the keys to the aircraft and the pilot's

manuals. He sat alone in the aircraft for the best part of a day, familiarizing himself with the controls and systems, before starting the aircraft up, taxiing out and taking off for his personal check flight. The TWA order was valued at around $100 million, but one of the terms of the proposed purchase was that seventeen examples must be delivered to TWA within six months, so that the airline could begin US transcontinental services with them in 1958. Unfortunately, Bristol could not promise to achieve this, as the production rate of twenty-eight aircraft per year could not be increased and they were already committed to existing customers for the next twelve months, and so no TWA order was forthcoming.

The first srs 312, G-AOVB, first flew on 5 July 1957 and was delivered from Filton to BOAC at London Airport on 10 September by Chief Test Pilot Walter Gibb. On 28 September it set off from London on a series of proving flights in the USA and the Caribbean in a 99-seat configuration, making the crossing from London to Idlewild Airport, New York, non-stop in 11 hours 39 minutes. Unfortunately, the aircraft was forced to make an unscheduled landing at Miami on 30 September after sustaining damage to two engines in storm clouds near Jacksonville. The incident received much publicity in the American press; the cause was traced to a change in stator material, which led to rubbing and seizure of the compressor blades when suddenly doused by heavy concentrations of slush-ice. This further complication to the Proteus icing problems was finally cured and the inaugural BOAC Britannia 312 service to New York took place on 19 December 1957.

Meanwhile, El Al had taken delivery of their three Britannia 313s, and on 19 December 1957 4X-AGA made a spectacular non-stop proving flight from Idlewild to Tel Aviv, a distance record for civil aircraft of 6,100 miles (9,800km) covered at an average speed of 401mph (645km/h). Aeronaves de Mexico began operating an arduous six days a week schedule between Mexico City and New York on 18 December 1957 and maintained this frequency with just a single aircraft for a whole month until their second example was delivered. Canadian Pacific's four Belfast-built srs 314s were delivered between April and June 1958 and entered service on the Polar route from Vancouver to Amsterdam on 1st June.

## Losses

In the first two years of commercial service, two Britannias were lost. Ministry of Supply-owned srs 317 G-ANCA, under the command of Bristol test pilot Hugh Slatham, took off from Filton on 6 November 1957 for a 1 hour 40 minute sortie including strain-gauge measurements on the non-standard propeller of the No.2 engine, and high-speed upset manoeuvre recovery tests in connection with the US certification of the type. On completion of the tests the Britannia returned to Filton and entered the circuit. At this point partial landing-gear extensions occurred for unknown reasons. They may have been part of attempts to complete undercarriage free-fall tests, which had been started on the previous day, but such tests were not scheduled for the programme for 6 November. At 1,500ft (460m) a left turn onto base leg was initiated, but the right wing suddenly dropped and the aircraft went into a very steeply banked right-hand turn. The Britannia recovered briefly, but then banked steeply again and struck the ground in a wood near the residential area of Downend. All fifteen on board were killed. The reason for the steeply banked turn prior to the impact could not be determined, but the possibility of an autopilot malfunction was not ruled out. Some two months later an incident occurred during the first flight of G-AOVG, a production srs 312 for BOAC. Shortly after disengagement of the autopilot, dangerous aileron control difficulties were encountered. The emergency lasted several minutes, and was only ended when the power supply to the autopilot was cut off. As a result of this incident a modification was introduced to prevent a repeat of the problem.

BOAC suffered its first Britannia 312 loss on 24 December 1958 when G-AOVD crashed near Hurn during a Certificate of Airworthiness renewal check. This was only the second Britannia fatal accident and they were to fly half a million more hours before the third fatal accident, the first involving fare-paying passengers. On the night of 22 July 1962, Canadian Pacific's CF-CZB crashed at Honolulu, killing twenty-seven of the forty persons on board. Despite this tragedy, the Britannia had established an exceptional safety record when compared to the established average of 300,000 hours between fatal accidents of the large piston-engined airliners of the day.

## The Orion Engine

It had been intended to use G-ANCA for the development of the high-powered Bristol Orion turboprop, with which BOAC planned to re-engine their Britannia fleet at a later date. One was installed in the port outer nacelle of G-ALBO in August 1956, the aircraft being fitted with a Proteus 755 in the starboard outer and Proteus 705s in the inner positions. Promising results were obtained by the Orion, whose development contract had been awarded in 1954 on the basis of £6.5m being spent over six years up to type test. By March 1957, however, the estimated cost up to type test in 1959 had risen to £12.9m. Of this increase, £3.65m was the result of underestimating the cost of the work to be done and overlooking the need for an additional six engines for the test programme. At this time, the sales prospects for the Orion were good. BOAC, for example, had undertaken to buy sixty, and the recovery of the development expenditure seemed likely. However, late in 1957 a government report explained that the Ministry of Supply and Bristol Aero-Engines had found that 'for technical reasons' advantage could not be taken of the increased power of the Orion as a Proteus-replacement in Britannias without modifying the wing – with subsequent expense and delay – and that even then there would not be much improvement in speed and range. In January 1958, when the RAF decided to keep to Proteus engines for its second squadron of Britannias, and BOAC asked to be relieved of its obligation to buy Orions, the Ministry of Supply decided to withdraw financial support, and Orion development was abandoned.

## Britannias for the Ministry of Supply and Royal Air Force

In February 1955 Bristol had received an order from the Ministry of Supply for three mixed-traffic Britannias, which it at first hoped to lease to charter operators for use on trooping work. The Ministry owned about two-thirds of Short Bros and Harland (the balance being held by Bristol and by Harland and Wolff) and, being anxious to find employment for its Belfast plant, hoped that Bristol would consider laying down a second Britannia production line in Northern Ireland. Bristol agreed to build a minimum of eight Britannia srs 250s at Belfast, these aircraft

Srs 252 G-APPE, later delivered to the RAF as srs 252, C.2 XN392. Air-Britain

having a mixed cargo/passenger configuration, the fuselage forward of the wing being specially adapted for the carriage of heavy freight. The specifications for the three Ministry of Supply srs 252s referred to a maximum payload of 31,000lb (14,000kg), a strengthened freight floor, installation of a hydraulic jack (for shifting heavy equipment such as aircraft engines), provision for stretcher points, a large (6ft × 8ft, 1.8 × 2.4m) freight door forward, and accommodation for eighty-seven passengers. When the Ministry came to issue tenders for the Britannia contract, two alternative proposals were invited from each interested airline. The first involved the purchase of the three aircraft a cost of around £4m, including spares and ground equipment. A five-year contract would then be awarded, which would cover the purchase price of the aircraft. The second option proposed that the three Britannias be lent gratis to the airline for a three-year period and operated on the Ministry's behalf. The three srs 252 aircraft were duly constructed and initially placed onto the civil register as G-APPE, G-APPF and G-APPG. However, a year passed and there were no takers among the charter airlines, probably because they considered that the special cargo-passenger configuration of the aircraft did not offer the optimum economy for the predominantly passenger-carrying work involved. The three srs 252s were then assimilated into the fleet of twenty Britannia srs 253s that had been ordered for RAF Transport Command.

The first flight of the srs 253, renamed Britannia C.1 by the Air Ministry, took place at Belfast on 29 December 1958. The RAF aircraft had improved Proteus 765 engines of higher output, fittings for aft-facing seats, stretchers or cargo and RAF-standard instruments and radio facilities. Five were built at Filton and fifteen at Belfast, and the last two Belfast-built examples (c/n 13508 and c/n 13509) were also the last two Britannias to be completed, being delivered on 17 September and 2 December 1960, respectively. (The full story of the Britannia C.1 and C.2 is recounted in Chapter Five.)

## Production Comes to an End

On 7 June 1958, inspired by an order for two srs 318s from Cubana, G-ANCD, painted in Cubana livery, was despatched from Filton on a 23-day sales tour of Spain, Portugal, Cuba and Latin America. Fourteen cities in ten countries were visited and over 1,200 passengers were carried on twenty-one demonstration flights. These included a Havana–Washington–New York–Havana flight with eight ambassadors among the passengers, and a flight between Rio de Janeiro and Caracas at a record block speed of 338mph (544km/h). The tour also included a take-off from the 5,000ft (1,500m) runway at Aeroparque Airport in Buenos Aires, and the final 3,350-mile (5,390km) leg from Bermuda direct to Filton was completed in just 8 hours 50 minutes. After the demonstration Cubana ordered two examples of yet another version, the Britannia 318, with an option on two more, and Bristol decided to risk building two aircraft to srs 320 standard, for stock.

After this, the market for new Britannias became quiet. In spite of its reputation for reliability and economy, the Britannia was beginning to encounter competition from the turboprop Lockheed Electra and

Srs 305 G-ANCD in Northeast Airlines colours at Filton in early 1958. Bristol via Michael Harrison

jet transports such as the Comet 4 and Boeing 707/720 family. By end of 1960, Boeing had delivered 173 of the latter, and indeed by now the twelve Britannia 102s had each flown 30,000 hours. It was therefore decided not to continue production unless an order for a really substantial number of one variant was received.

The two srs 320s, the last Britannias to be laid down, were furnished to Canadian Pacific requirements and leased to them for eighteen months under the designation Britannia 324. When the hire terminated they returned to Filton and were sold to Cunard Eagle Airways. Apart from those for RAF Transport Command, only three more Britannia deliveries were to be made in 1960, one from Belfast and two from Filton. The first was the ex-srs 305 c/n 12924, which became a srs 309 for Ghana Airways and was delivered as 9G-AAG on 17 July. The second was the veteran G-AOVA, rebuilt to a similar srs 319 standard and delivered to Ghana Airways as 9G-AAH on 8 November. The last Britannia to leave Filton was the very first of all the eighty-five aircraft to be built, G-ALBO. Still fitted with Proteus 705 engines inboard, a

Proteus 755 in the starboard outer position and an Orion in the port outer, the aircraft was ferried to RAF St Athan on 30 November 1960 to become an instructional airframe with the new identity 7708M. It was finally scrapped in June 1968, having flown nearly 1,800 hours.

In the annual report and accounts of The Bristol Aeroplane Co. Ltd for 1960, the Chairman, Sir Reginald Verdon Smith, made the claim that 'the aircraft will not itself have involved any significant cost to the taxpayer'. The basis of this claim was that 'contributions towards aircraft development received from the Ministry of Supply have been substantially balanced by repayments to the Ministry by way of royalties on sales and licence receipts and an appropriate allowance for the proportion of development expenditure attributable to the aircraft purchased by the Ministry for the Royal Air Force'. The Ministry of Aviation told the press at the time that the Government had contributed about £6.5m towards

(*Top*) **Britannias in production at Filton.** Bristol via Lester Stenner

(*Above*) **Srs 317 G-APNA unpainted at Filton in late 1958.** Bristol

(*Left*) **The first prototype Britannia, G-ALBO, seen carrying its maintenance serial 7708M, was broken up at St Athan in 1968.** Air-Britain

Britannia airframe development, including the purchase of three prototypes. RAF orders for the Britannia represented some 37 per cent of the total built. If the development costs were assumed to have been distributed in the same proportion, Bristol's claim seemed to be that some £4m had been repaid in levies on the fifty-nine Britannias sold at that time to civil operators, and on the licence fees from production of the CL-28 and CL-44 by Canadair (*see* Chapter Six). This arithmetic, however, took no account of the Government spending on the Proteus engine, which had no other production application than the Britannia. Total Ministry expenditure on the Proteus at that time was in the order of £13m.

Sir Reginald recorded in his statement that the total sales value of the eighty-three Britannias sold up to the end of 1959, and their spares, amounted to about £100m. Sir Reginald went on 'We can now look forward to a modest profit on the sale of spare parts and to income from licences. I doubt whether any other recent civil aircraft project, whether undertaken in this country or in the USA, would present a better picture.'

## The Bristol Britannia – a Brief Technical Summary

The Britannia was a conventional low-wing monoplane whose primary structural material was high-strength aluminium alloy. Although nothing revolutionary was introduced, the design team under Dr Russell devoted a great deal of care and

| Britannia Production and Models |
|---|
| *Series 100* |
| Basic series designation of initial version, with 114ft (35m) fuselage length, medium-range fuel capacity and four Proteus 705 engines. |
| Srs 101 – Two prototypes with Proteus 600 series engines. |
| Srs 102 – Production series 100 for BOAC. Initial order for twenty-five, but ten cancelled. |
| *Series 200* |
| All-cargo version with 124ft 3in (38m) fuselage length. Option on five aircraft for BOAC later cancelled. |
| *Series 250* |
| Basic series designation for long-fuselage Britannia cargo/passenger version of the srs 200, with longer range and four Proteus 755 engines. |
| Srs 252 – Ministry of Supply order for three aircraft intended for leasing to military charter operators. Scheme abandoned and aircraft transferred to RAF Transport Command. Fitted with heavy-duty flooring and freight doors. Later designated Britannia C.2. |
| Srs 253 – RAF Transport Command order for twenty aircraft designated Britannia C.1, with metal flooring, capacity for 115 troops, 53 stretcher cases or equivalent cargo. Civilianized designation srs 253F. |
| *Series 300* |
| Passenger-only version of srs 200, with medium-range fuel capacity. |
| Srs 301 – Filton-built prototype srs 300. |
| Srs 302 – Belfast-built production, initially for BOAC but order later cancelled. Seven aircraft laid down but only first two completed to this standard. Initial interest by Aerovias Guest, but actually delivered to Aeronaves de Mexico. *See* srs 305 (*below*) for remaining five. |
| Srs 305 – Five built at Belfast modified to longer-range specification but limited to 165,000lb (75,000kg) take-off weight due to thinner fuselage skin and lighter landing gear. BOAC released from contract and aircraft transferred to Capital Airlines order. Capital suffered financial setbacks and Northeast Airlines took over order, but Northeast order also collapsed in June 1958. One example became a srs 306 and then a srs 307, one a srs 307, two srs 308s and one a srs 309 (*see* separate entries). |
| Srs 306 – Former srs 305 for El Al pending delivery of final srs 313. |
| Srs 307 – Srs 305 in trooping charter configuration. Strengthened wings, long-range fuel tanks. Two built. |
| Srs 308 – Srs 305 built for Transcontinental SA in 104-passenger configuration. Two built, which were later converted to same specification as srs 252 by British Eagle and redesignated as srs 308F. |
| Srs 309 – Srs 305 built for Ghana Airways. One built. |
| *Series 310* |
| Basic designation for civil variant with long-range fuel capacity, thicker fuselage skin and strengthened landing gear for all-up weight of 175,000lb (80,000kg). Initially designated as srs 300LR. |
| Srs 311 – Prototype srs 300LR |
| Srs 312 – BOAC production. Eighteen built. |
| Srs 313 – El Al production. Four built. |
| Srs 314 – Canadian Pacific Air Lines production. Six built. |
| Srs 317 – Hunting-Clan Air Transport production, in 124-passenger configuration for trooping flights. Two built. |
| Srs 318 – Cubana production. Four built. |
| Srs 319 – Ghana Airways production. One built. |
| Srs 320 – Canadian Pacific Air Lines production. Later converted to srs 324. Two built. |
| Srs 324 – Two examples converted from srs 320. |

thought to achieving their object of weight control, which resulted in the bare structure weight being only 23.5 per cent of the laden weight, giving the maximum lifting ability for fuel or payload. It was actually as a result of the work done on the earlier Brabazon that the Bristol idea of the 'optimum structure formula' came into being. For the Brabazon a close theoretical study was made into structural forms, and arising from this came the thought that there must be one best arrangement of structural members for any given kind of material and any given kind of loading. Such a thought brought with it the implication that there would then be an almost standard structural form

very high-strength materials. It also contributed to another of the aims of the Britannia design, namely, good fatigue characteristics. A conscious effort was made to avoid stress concentrations, with the box-spar structure of the wings being a good example of 'spreading the load', so as not to have any single part bearing too large a responsibility for the safety of the whole.

All three major variants of the Britannia had a virtually identical external appearance, with a 12ft (3.7m) diameter fuselage, giving a centre gangway headroom of 80in (2m). There were no bulkheads or other structural intrusions anywhere in the usable part of the fuselage, permitting the utmost versatility in cabin layouts. A com-

original srs 100 into the later versions was done by lengthening the component panels, adding two bays of 41in (104cm) each to those ahead of the central fuselage section, and a single bay of the same length to each of those behind. The fact that the stretch was embodied in the part of the fuselage where there were in any case joints, and where the form was parallel, made the process a comparatively simple matter.

The cabin was equipped with up to three galleys and had toilet facilities at the front and rear. All models had windows of vertical ellipse shape at 41in (104cm) pitch, affording excellent views to the passengers. Underneath the cabin floor were

**This view of a srs 312 illustrates well the size and power of the Britannia.** Air-Britain

for any given set of circumstances. A comprehensive analysis of structures was therefore put in train, and it became apparent before this had progressed very far that unique curves of structural efficiency could in fact be plotted, and that the choice of material was also dictated by the predicated circumstances.

In the Britannia the principle of optimum design was widely used in evolving the stiffened skin-and-frame combinations of which the structure largely consisted. The wing structure, for example, was so designed that both the flexural strength and torsional stiffness requirements were satisfied. The use of structural curves also ensured that the stress was not higher than it needed to be, avoiding the use of

plete cylindrical section of the fuselage was made up of ten panels with a ring frame at each end, which provided the attachment to the next section. The two main sections of the fuselage, the front and rear portions, were connected by a much shorter central section, which carried the heavier wing attachment frames. The fuselage panels were manufactured by Blackburn and General Aircraft at Dunbarton, and other parts were made by Douglas Motors and by Bristol's own satellite at Weston-Super-Mare. And of course there was also the second assembly line at Short Bros and Harland at Belfast. The srs 200 and 300 were 124ft 3in (37.9m) in length, compared to the 114ft (34.8m) of the original srs 100. The lengthening process necessary to 'stretch' the

two large freight holds. The srs 200 was fitted with an integral freight door on the forward port side. Some srs 300s were also fitted with these doors, usually at a later stage in their careers. Two main passenger cabin doors were fitted on the port side, one just forward and one just to the rear of the wing, the forward one being incorporated into the freight door in aircraft so equipped. The srs 200 and 300 also had an additional door at the extreme rear of the port side of the fuselage, principally for use in emergencies. Two starboard side doors, one at the front and one at the rear, were used for loading catering supplies and as emergency exits. Overwing emergency exits were fitted as standard on all variants, usually two on each side of the cabin.

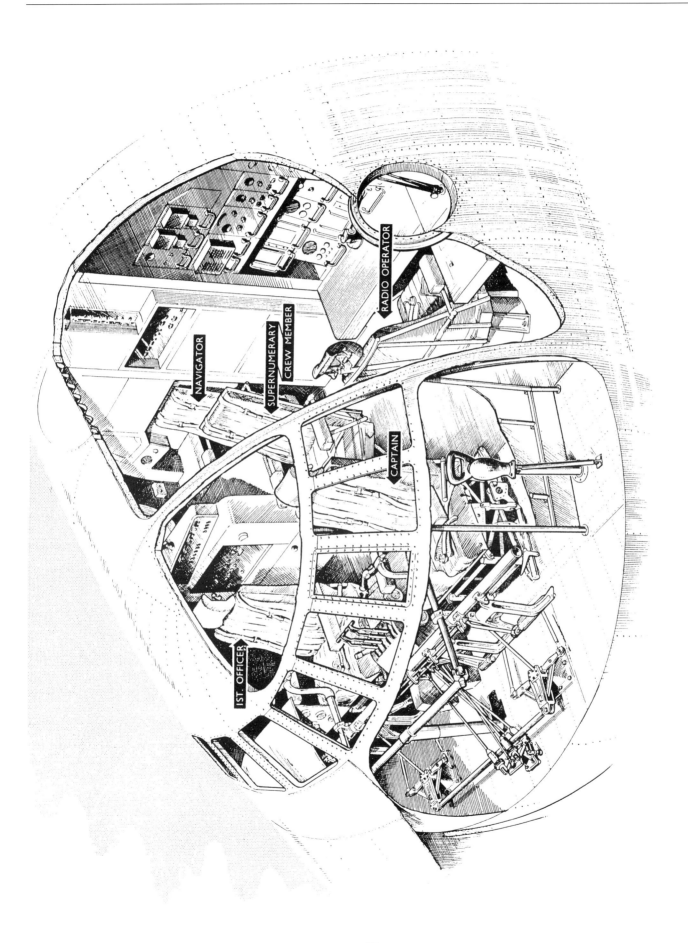

**Crew stations. From *Britannia Descriptive Notes and Performance Data*, published April 1956.** Bristol Aircraft via Mr D. H. Bartlett

| Britannia srs 102 Specifications | |
| --- | --- |
| Powerplant: | 4 × Bristol Proteus 705 turboprops of 3,900hp each, driving DH 4-bladed 16ft propellers. |
| Dimensions: | Length 114ft; height 36ft 8in; wingspan 142ft 3½in; cabin volume 5,150cu ft. |
| Weights: | Max takeoff 155,000lb; max landing 125,000lb. |
| Fuel capacity: | 6,690 imp gal. |
| Performance: | Continuous cruising speed 362mph at 20,250ft. Landing distance from 50ft = 5,200ft. |
| Range: | With max payload 2,945 miles; with max fuel, optimum cruise 3,690 miles. |

| Britannia srs 253 (RAF C Mk 1) Specifications | |
| --- | --- |
| Powerplant: | 4 × Bristol Proteus 255 turboprops of 4,445hp each, driving DH 4-bladed propellers. |
| Dimensions: | Length 124ft; height 36ft 8in; wingspan 142ft 3½in. |
| Weights: | Max takeoff 180,000lb; max landing 135,000lb. |
| Fuel capacity: | 8,580 imp gal. |
| Performance: | Continuous cruising speed 345mph at 20,000–36,000ft. Landing distance from 50ft = 3,700ft. |
| Range: | With 35,000lb payload 2,500 miles. With 20,000lb payload 3,450 miles. |

All models were fitted with a pressurization system with associated air conditioning and cabin heating systems. The pressurization system was designed to maintain a cabin altitude of about 6,000ft (1,800m) while flying at altitudes of up to 35,000ft (11,000m). A cabin de-humidifier was also provided, which would be useful for operation in hot and humid areas. The pressurization and associated systems also served the two underfloor holds, allowing the carriage of livestock below the main

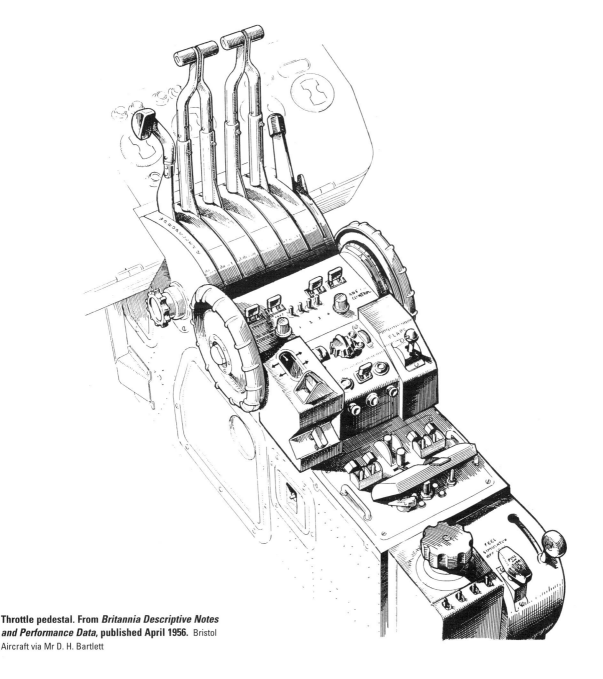

**Throttle pedestal. From** *Britannia Descriptive Notes and Performance Data*, **published April 1956.** Bristol Aircraft via Mr D. H. Bartlett

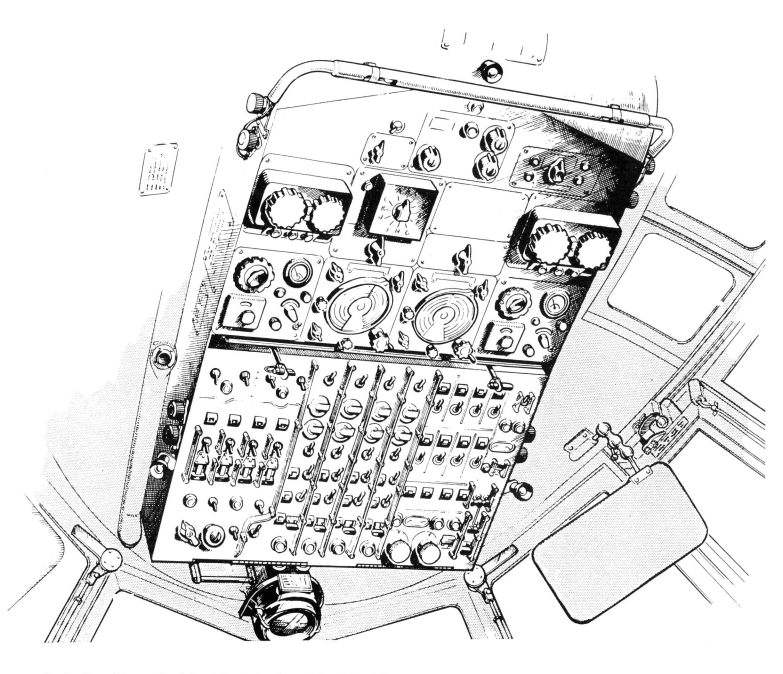

**Starting, fire and king panel, and above it the pilot's radio panel. From *Britannia Descriptive Notes and Performance Data*, published April 1956.**
Bristol Aircraft via Mr D. H. Bartlett

### Britannia srs 312 Specifications

| | |
|---|---|
| Powerplant: | 4 × Bristol Proteus 755 turboprops of 4,120hp each, driving DH 4-bladed propellers. |
| Dimensions: | Length 124ft 3in; height 37ft 6in; wingspan 142ft 3½in. |
| Weights: | Max takeoff 185,000lb. |
| Fuel capacity: | 8,486 imp gal. |
| Performance: | Continuous cruising speed 357mph at 2,600ft. Max speed 420mph. |
| Range: | Max payload 4,268 miles. |

### Britannia srs 324 Specifications

| | |
|---|---|
| Powerplant: | 4 × Bristol Proteus 765 turboprops of 4,445hp each, driving DH 4-bladed propellers. |
| Dimensions: | Length 124ft 3in; height 37ft 6in; wingspan 142ft 3½in. |
| Weights: | Max takeoff 180,000lb; max landing 135,000lb. |
| Fuel capacity: | 8,580 imp gal. |
| Performance: | Continuous cruising speed 397mph at 22,000ft. Landing distance from 50ft = 3,050ft. |
| Range: | Max payload 3,620 miles; max fuel 4,530 miles. |

**Navigating station. From *Britannia Descriptive Notes and Performance Data*, published April 1956.** Bristol Aircraft via Mr D. H. Bartlett

deck. Former BOAC Captain Lincoln Lee recalls that the Britannia's air conditioning system was notorious for generating what on the ground looked suspiciously like smoke. 'More like smoke than smoke' was the phrase often used to describe the billowing clouds of steam that sometimes filled the passenger cabin, frightening passengers and crew alike. Of course, the crews soon got used to the sight of this condensation, and could calm those passengers who needed it.

The stubs for the tail assembly were an integral part of the fuselage construction, and the fin and tailplane simply bolted on to these stubs. This allowed for easy replacement of these parts and gave the whole tail assembly greater strength.

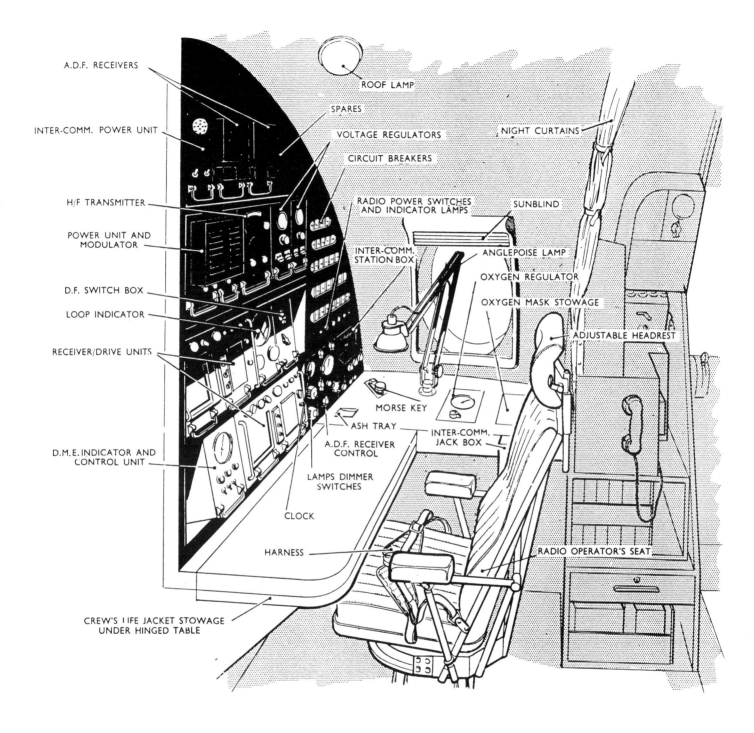

A.D.F. RECEIVERS

INTER-COMM. POWER UNIT

H/F TRANSMITTER

POWER UNIT AND MODULATOR

D.F. SWITCH BOX

LOOP INDICATOR

RECEIVER/DRIVE UNITS

D.M.E. INDICATOR AND CONTROL UNIT

CREW'S LIFE JACKET STOWAGE UNDER HINGED TABLE

ROOF LAMP

SPARES

VOLTAGE REGULATORS

CIRCUIT BREAKERS

RADIO POWER SWITCHES AND INDICATOR LAMPS

INTER-COMM. STATION BOX

MORSE KEY

ASH TRAY

A.D.F. RECEIVER CONTROL

LAMPS DIMMER SWITCHES

CLOCK

HARNESS

INTER-COMM. JACK BOX

NIGHT CURTAINS

SUNBLIND

ANGLEPOISE LAMP

OXYGEN REGULATOR

OXYGEN MASK STOWAGE

ADJUSTABLE HEADREST

RADIO OPERATOR'S SEAT

**Radio station. From *Britannia Descriptive Notes and Performance Data*, published April 1956.** Bristol Aircraft via Mr D. H. Bartlett

The wing tapered uniformly from centreline to tip and the span of 142ft 3½in (43.4m) was the same on all the various versions. Each wing had an inner and an outer spar, both in the form of a large box occupying some 35 per cent of the wing chord. The inner and outer sections of wings were manufactured as separate parts, which were then bolted together onto the box spar. The wings were equipped with double slotted flaps, split into two sections on both sides of the wing. These amounted to about 20 per cent of the gross wing area. No power-operated controls were provided, the main flying control systems on both the wing and the tail being operated by aerodynamic servo-tabs which were mechanically connected to the control column. Each

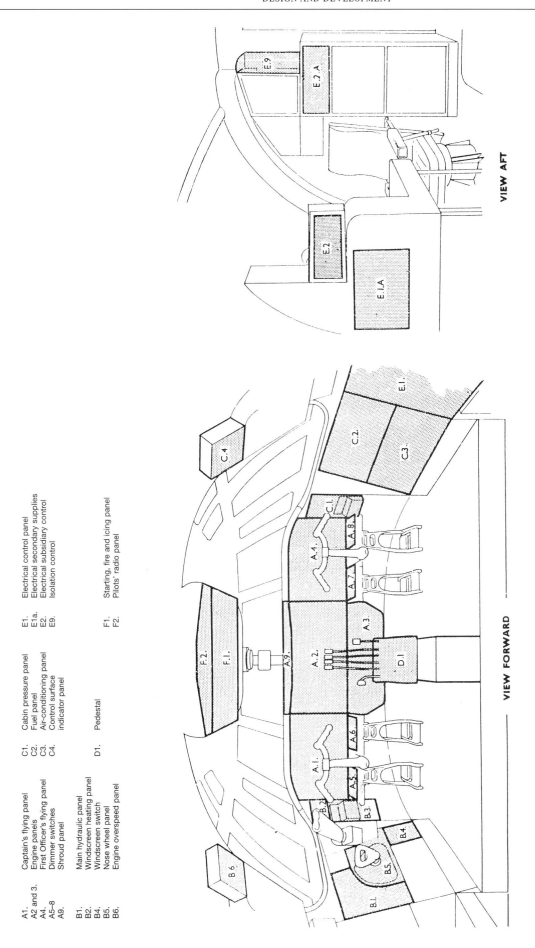

A1. Captain's flying panel
A2 and 3. Engine panels
A4. First Officer's flying panel
A5–8 Dimmer switches
A9. Shroud panel

B1. Main hydraulic panel
B2. Windscreen heating panel
B4. Windscreen switch
B5. Nose wheel panel
B6. Engine overspeed panel

C1. Cabin pressure panel
C2. Fuel panel
C3. Air-conditioning panel
C4. Control surface
indicator panel

D1. Pedestal

E1. Electrical control panel
E1a. Electrical secondary supplies
E2. Electrical subsidiary control
E9. Isolation control

F1. Starting, fire and icing panel
F2. Pilots' radio panel

**VIEW FORWARD**

**VIEW AFT**

**Panel identifications. From _Britannia Descriptive Notes and Performance Data_, published April 1956.** Bristol Aircraft via Mr D. H. Bartlett

43

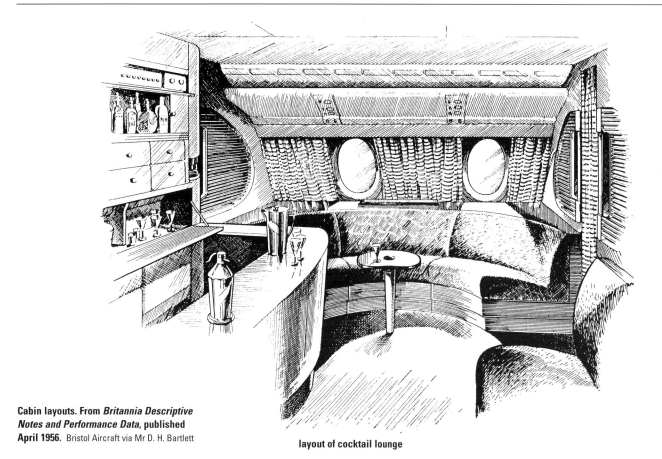

**Cabin layouts. From *Britannia Descriptive Notes and Performance Data*, published April 1956.** Bristol Aircraft via Mr D. H. Bartlett

**layout of cocktail lounge**

**layout of rear cabin tourist version**

aileron had five servo-tabs, of which four were used to drive the surface under the command of the control column. The fifth was connected to the rudder controls, and ensured that when a turn was initiated by the use of the rudder, the aircraft was banked in the proper direction. Each elevator had four tabs, three used for flying control and one for trimming.

The Britannia's fuel was stored in flexible fuel bags within the box spar of the mainplane. There were four main tanks and three smaller ones, and fuel could be transferred between all these tanks. The ribs between the tanks took the form of webs, and were of sandwich construction with a corrugated inner sheet, Reduxed between the two flat outer sheets. The initial srs 100 had a fuel capacity of about 6,690gal (30,400ltr). On the longer range srs 200s and 300s the capacity was increased to 8,580gal (39,000ltr), and on the srs 300s the outer wing section was built as an integral fuel tank to accommodate the extra fuel.

Wing de-icing was achieved by taking heat from the engine compressors and channelling it via heat exchangers along the leading edge; the leading edge consisted of a double skin of light alloy, the inner skin being corrugated and Reduxed to the outer skin so as to provide a large number of chordwise ducts, from the extreme leading edge to about 14 per cent of the chord. De-icing for the tail fin and tailplane leading edges was provided by electric heater mats. The six forward windscreen panels were also electrically heated, as were the propeller blades and spinners.

The nose undercarriage (of British Messier design) consisted of a steerable, forward-retracting two-wheel unit without brakes. Each of the two main units carried a four-wheel bogie, the rear wheels of which had a rather greater track than the front pair. The wheels, tyres, brakes and anti-skid units were manufactured by Dunlop. The bogie retracted into a bay in the nacelle of the inner engine and was covered by three pairs of doors; the position of the Proteus' exhaust pipe meant that rearwards retraction was necessary. Upon retraction the bogie-beam pivoted about a lateral axis until it was in line with the leg, whereupon the entire unit retracted backwards, the bogie being finally stowed in an inverted position. The undercarriage system was operated hydraulically, with pressure for the emergency back-up system supplied by an independent pump. The Britannia's four hydraulic pumps were electrically driven,

and the hydraulics system powered the undercarriage retraction system, control-surface locking and nosewheel steering.

The flight-deck layout on the later srs 250/310 models provided for a maximum of five crew members, although the aircraft could be operated by a minimum of two if necessary. The full complement was two pilots, a flight engineer, a radio operator, and a navigator. The navigator was provided with a large chart table and access to the roof sextant. No separate flight engineer's panel was provided, but this function could be performed from a detachable seat at the supernumerary crew station. Technical log stowage was provided, and all the engine and propeller controls were within reach from here. On the srs 312 the Smiths flight director system was fitted as standard. Two crew bunks could be fitted if required, on the starboard side immediately aft of the flight deck.

The aircraft's electrical supply came primarily from four engine-driven generators producing a three-phase output. The highest output was 208V, chiefly used for powering the hydraulic pumps. Other outputs were 104V and 65V, rectified to give a 112V and 28V DC supply for electrical services requiring less power. A second electrical system of 115V was provided for the aircraft instruments and there was also an emergency battery back-up supply. The aircraft was an absolute maze of complicated electrics. There were over 100 relays with thirty-two electrical contacts each (reputedly of the same design as those used by the Post Office), and there were always a few unreliable contacts. From experience, these could be overcome by using slightly unconventional methods. For example, in the case of the BOAC srs 312s, on start-up, if the Jet Pipe Temperature gauge failed to give an indication the engineer officer (as BOAC called their flight engineers) would fix it by giving a few hard thumps on the floor of the ladies' toilet. A similar remedy could be applied to the flap relays. However, as these were situated near the rear main passenger door the engineer officer was in full view of the rather nervous passengers while this was going on.

The engines on all production models of the Britannia were four Bristol Proteus turboprops, each driving a De Havilland constant-speed four-bladed hollow steel propeller. The initial srs 100s were fitted with the Proteus 705, giving an output of 3,900hp per engine. The srs 200s had the

4,400hp Proteus 765, fitted with a water–methanol injection system to boost performance out of hot and high airfields with shorter runways. In the srs 300s three different variants of Proteus engines were used. Virtually all of the srs 300 to srs 305 aircraft, and the srs 318, were fitted with Proteus 755 engines with an output of 4,120hp. The srs 317 used Proteus 765s, similar to those fitted to the srs 200s. All the remaining srs 300 variants were equipped with Proteus 761s with an output of 4,175hp. All Britannia variants were constructed in such a way that engine changes could be undertaken quickly and without the need for a large amount of ground support equipment. For ease of maintenance, the engine cowlings were of a petal design, opening upwards and outwards. The top cowling panel could be lifted off after releasing its fasteners. The remainder of the cowling was formed by two large panels, which hinged upwards to provide access to the engine and oil cooler. The engine positions were interchangeable for maximum flexibility.

## The Bristol Proteus

The Bristol Proteus was designed by Frank Owner, Chief Stress Calculator at Bristol's Engine Division, in response to an instruction from Roy Fedden to design and develop a gas turbine engine capable of driving a propeller. The Proteus was a high-compression turboprop engine designed expressly for civil aircraft, where reliability and economy are paramount, and was originally intended as the engine for the second prototype Bristol Brabazon. It was a high-compression descendant of the Bristol Theseus, which first bench-ran in July 1945 and became the first turboprop engine in the world to pass a type test.

The first version to enter service was the Mk 705, the powerplant of BOAC's Britannia 102s. These engines were rated at 3,900hp, and during their first two years of service their time between overhaul rose from 500 hours to 2,000 hours. This rate of progress was unequalled by any other aero engine, civil or military, piston or turbine.

From the Mk 705 was evolved the Proteus 755, used in the srs 300 and srs 310, and rated at 4,120hp. This differed from the 705 chiefly in having improved material specifications (including Nimonic 100 blades in the first turbine assembly) and a redesigned power-turbine assembly. Later

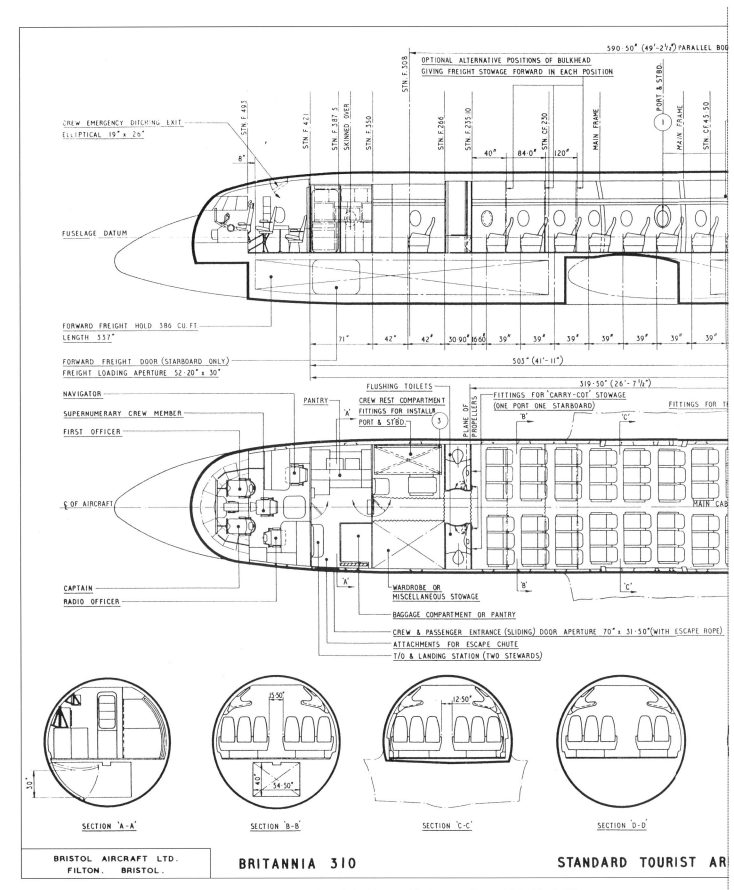

**Layout of the Britannia 310 in 93-seat Tourist arrangement. From *Britannia Descriptive Notes and Performance Data*, published April 1956.**
Bristol Aircraft via Mr D. H. Bartlett

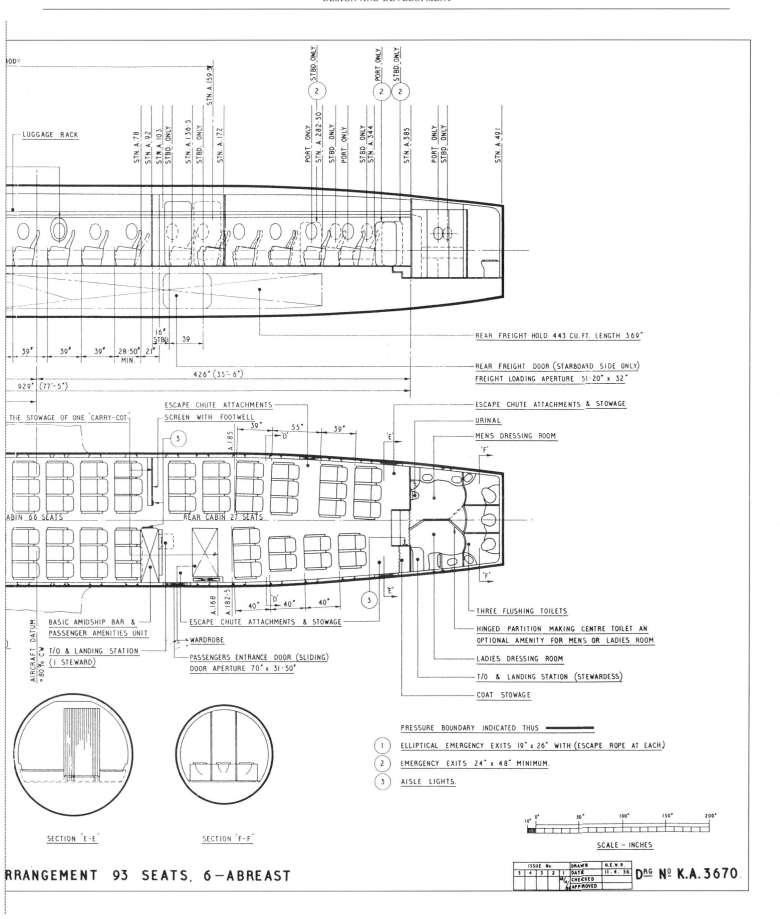

LUGGAGE RACK

STN.A.78
STN.A.92
STN.A.103 STBD. ONLY
STN.A.136.5 STBD. ONLY
STN.A.172
STN.A.159.5

PORT ONLY
STN.A.282.50
STBD. ONLY
PORT ONLY
STBD. ONLY
STN.A.344
STN.A.385
PORT ONLY
STBD. ONLY
STN.A.491

REAR FREIGHT HOLD 443 CU.FT. LENGTH 369"

16"
STBD
39

REAR FREIGHT DOOR (STARBOARD SIDE ONLY)
FREIGHT LOADING APERTURE 51.20" x 32"

39"    39"    39"    28.50"  21"
MIN.

39

426" (35'-6")

929" (77'-5")

THE STOWAGE OF ONE 'CARRY-COT'

ESCAPE CHUTE ATTACHMENTS
SCREEN WITH FOOTWELL

39"     55"     39"

ESCAPE CHUTE ATTACHMENTS & STOWAGE
URINAL
MENS DRESSING ROOM

A.185

'D'    'E'    'F'

ABIN 66 SEATS          REAR CABIN 27 SEATS

A.168  A.182.5

40"   40"   40"

'D'        'E'

BASIC AMIDSHIP BAR &
PASSENGER AMENITIES UNIT

T/O & LANDING STATION
(1 STEWARD)

ESCAPE CHUTE ATTACHMENTS & STOWAGE

WARDROBE

PASSENGERS ENTRANCE DOOR (SLIDING)
DOOR APERTURE 70" x 31.50"

AIRCRAFT DATUM
= 80% CW

THREE FLUSHING TOILETS

HINGED PARTITION MAKING CENTRE TOILET AN
OPTIONAL AMENITY FOR MENS OR LADIES ROOM

LADIES DRESSING ROOM

T/O & LANDING STATION (STEWARDESS)

COAT STOWAGE

PRESSURE BOUNDARY INDICATED THUS ━━━━

(1) ELLIPTICAL EMERGENCY EXITS 19" x 26" WITH (ESCAPE ROPE AT EACH)

(2) EMERGENCY EXITS 24" x 48" MINIMUM.

(3) AISLE LIGHTS.

SECTION 'E-E'          SECTION 'F-F'

10"  0"      50"      100"      150"      200"

SCALE - INCHES

RRANGEMENT  93  SEATS,  6—ABREAST

| ISSUE No. | | | | DRAWN | H.E.W.R. | |
|---|---|---|---|---|---|---|
| 5 | 4 | 3 | 2 | 1 | DATE | 11.4.36. |
| | | | | N/4 | CHECKED | |
| | | | | | APPROVED | |

Dʀɢ Nº K.A.3670.

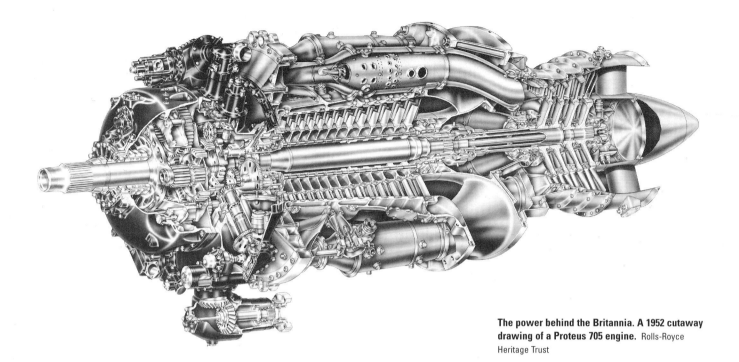

The power behind the Britannia. A 1952 cutaway drawing of a Proteus 705 engine. Rolls-Royce Heritage Trust

improved models included the Mks 761, 762 and 765, and the 4,400hp Proteus 255 for the RAF Britannia 253s, which was fitted with water injection to give maximum power in adverse altitude/temperature conditions. In early 1960, after three years as the Britannia's engine, the Proteus had logged over a million flying hours.

The Proteus featured the Bristol free turbine principle, in which the compressor and the propeller turbine systems were mechanically independent of each other. This arrangement allowed both systems to operate at optimum efficiency. Furthermore, in the event of engine failure in flight, the propeller windmilling drag was extremely low.

The air intake was situated towards the rear of the engine. Air entered the intake casings all around the compressor and travelled forward through twelve axial stages to the single centrifugal stage. Here the air flowed tangentially outwards and was then caused to flow rearwards to the combustion chambers through elbows fitted with cascade vanes to ensure losses were small. The axial compressor had a low hub-tip ratio, which allowed for a small overall diameter. This made it possible to arrange the centrifugal stage immediately next to the last axial stage to eliminate transfer losses and improve entry conditions. Tappings from the compressor provided air for engine cooling and pressurizing, and for aircraft pressurization.

The eight combustion chambers were of conventional design with centrally placed burners at the upstream end. Two were equipped with igniter plugs, and the flame spread to the other six chambers through pipes interconnecting them all. There were four turbine stages, coupled in pairs. The first pair drove the compressor, the second pair the reduction gear and propeller. They were housed in a common casing of heat-resisting steel, which was supported at eight points from the compressor air intake casing in such a manner as to preserve concentricity whilst allowing for expansion. A bleed of exhaust gas was available if required for anti-icing, via a heat exchanger on the aircraft.

The reduction gear contained a torquemeter, consisting of eight piston and cylinder assemblies, supplied with oil by a simple high pressure pump. The pressure in the cylinders was measured and was in direct proportion to the torque on the reduction gear stationary wheel. The system allowed complete freedom for self-alignment and gave uniform distribution of load on the planet gears, an important consideration in the gear design. Initially the reduction gear consisted of straight spur gears, but it was subsequently proved that straight spurs caused a vibration at certain critical speeds, which subsequently caused engine failures. A hasty changeover to double helical gearing, introduced on the Proteus 705 along with a propeller turbine speed limiter and

increased fire protection, at a weight penalty of 200lb (90kg), solved the problem. An electrically operated brake prevented windmilling of the propeller when the aircraft was parked.

## Flying the Britannia

The following notes are reproduced from *Britannia Crew Training Notes*, issued by Bristol Aircraft Ltd on 7 May 1958.

ENGINE FAILURE ON TAKE-OFF BELOW V1
If an engine fails below V1, the following are the immediate actions to be taken:-

1. Close Throttles.
2. Apply wheel brakes.
3. Brake Dwell on all four engines and apply Full Reverse Power on the good engines.

Keep the aircraft straight by use of the nose-wheel steering and by coarse use of the rudder. Normally there is no difficulty in keeping straight with asymmetric reverse, but if there is a strong cross-wind blowing from the opposite side to that of the dead engine it may be necessary, after reversing has begun, to come out of reverse on the outboard engine for a short time to straighten the run.

The recommended drill when necessary to abandon take-off is as follows:

1. Engine failure reported.

2. Captain orders take-off to be abandoned, throttles back on all four engines and applies full wheel brakes.

3. Engineer moves reversing lever to reverse position and all throttle levers to brake dwell.

4. Engineer applies Full Reverse Power on good engines.

## ENGINE FAILURE ABOVE V1

In the event of engine failure above V1 the take-off should be continued. The Captain will order simulated feathering/ fire drill as required, and hold the nosewheel firmly onto the ground, keeping the aircraft straight by coarse use of rudder and nosewheel steering.

At V2 minus 5 knots, or at 115 knots, whichever is the higher speed, the nosewheel should be raised, the aircraft flown off and then kept straight by use of rudder and not more than 5 degrees against the live engines. The brakes should be applied, undercarriage retracted and the aircraft should be climbed away at the Free Air Safety Speed up to 400ft. Speed should then be increased to the Flaps Up Safety Speed, the flaps retracted and the climb continued to the 5 Minute Point, where climb power should be selected.

From this point the climb should be continued at the En-Route climbing speed up to 1500ft, where the aircraft may be levelled and the Captain's decision regarding further action may be made.

The above speeds are given appropriate to the weight, and the aircraft should be climbed at these speeds when obstacle clearance is limiting. If clearance is not critical, and the maximum performance is not required, speeds may be increased and take-off power reduced at an earlier point.

After confirmation of engine failure, and when ordered by the Captain, the Co-Pilot will throttle back the appropriate engine and carry out the simulated feathering/fire drill and complete the After Take-Off Check. The Flight Engineer will monitor the drill and then ensure that the subsequent Emergency Actions are carried out.

## 4-ENGINE TAKE-OFF

The following drill is recommended for take-off after completion of the pre take-off checks:-

## CAPTAIN

1. Calls for full power and places right hand on top of the throttle lever.

2. Releases brakes after overspeed limiters have been checked to 'ARM'.

If the take-off is weight-limited, brakes should not be released until full power has been attained.

3. Keeping steering limiting button depressed, steers aircraft with left hand on the nosewheel steering handle up to the steering abandon speed of 106 knots.

4. At 106 knots, transfers his left hand to the control column.

5. At V1 transfers his right hand from the throttles to the control column.

6. Raises the nosewheel about 5 knots below the unstick speed so that take-off occurs smoothly at the correct speed.

7. As soon as comfortably airborne applies wheel brakes and calls for undercarrriage up. Climbs aircraft at the free air safety speed.

8. At 400ft allows speed to increase to flaps up safety speed and calls for flaps up and maximum continuous power.

## SECOND PILOT

1. Checks and reports overspeed limiters to 'ARM' above 10,500 C.R.P.M., during application of power.

2. During take-off run holds control column slightly forward of neutral to keep the nosewheel firmly on the ground, up to V1.

3. Calls out 'V1' at appropriate speed.

4. Monitors flight and engine instruments.

5. Raises undercarriage on Captain's order.

6. Raises flaps on Captain's order.

## FLIGHT ENGINEER

1. Opens throttles up to full power.

2. Keeps hands on throttles below the Captain's hand to make adjustments to maintain full power without exceeding limitations.

3. Monitors all engine instruments.

4. Reduces power to maximum continuous on Captain's order.

## TRAINING NOTES ON 3-ENGINE LANDINGS

The normal landing procedure applies with the following exceptions:-

DOWNWIND

1. Torque settings for circuit flying should be increased by one-third.

2. 920 P.R.P.M. should be selected.

ON FINAL

1. Target threshold speed should be constant at 110 knots, at all weights below 116,000lb.

AFTER LANDING

1. Reverse power should be used on the symmetrical pair of power units, and if necessary on all three live ones.

2. In emergency (i.e. slippery runway with adverse crosswind) an outer power unit may, if

the opposite one has failed, be kept in flight fine pitch for a short period while the inboards are reversed.

## TRAINING NOTES ON LANDINGS WITH TWO ENGINES INOPERATIVE ON ONE SIDE

Before joining circuit, throttle back two engines on same side, then:-

1. Set rudder trim one division against live engines.

2. Select 920 P.R.P.M.

3. Select 1/3rd flap and landing gear down at end of downwind leg, and 2/3rds flap when in line with runway, maintaining speed above 130 knots.

4. Full flap should be selected only when it is certain a landing can be achieved.

5. After flaps are fully down speed can be reduced to 125 knots, in order to achieve a target threshold speed of 120 knots. These speeds do not vary with weight, being dictated solely by considerations of controllability.

6. Reverse power should be used on the inboard engine only, keeping the outer power unit in flight fine, until speed has reduced to about 70 knots, when any swing produced by selecting superfine is easily controllable. If possible, cancel reverse pitch on inner power unit at the same time as the outer engine goes into superfine.

## BAULKED LANDING

The decision to discontinue the approach should be made above 500ft before full flap is selected, take-off power selected, undercarriage retracted, and the speed maintained at 130 knots. 1/3rd flap should then be selected and the aircraft climbed away at 130 knots. Flaps fully up should be selected at not less than 400ft.

## FLAPLESS LANDING

The flapless landing procedure does not present any undue difficulties, apart from the fact that it is difficult to reduce airspeed, due to the clean aerodynamic lines of the Britannia.

A normal circuit should be made and the the checks completed in the usual manner. The outboard throttles should be retarded to 'FLIGHT IDLE' on the downwind leg, and height and speed maintained on inboard engine power only. The turn onto the final approach should be made after a slightly longer downwind leg, to allow a longer and flatter approach, taking care not to allow the speed to increase during the turn.

Once on the final approach, speed should be gradually reduced to 130 knots to allow the aircraft to assume a tail-down attitude, which increases drag and allows a better control over

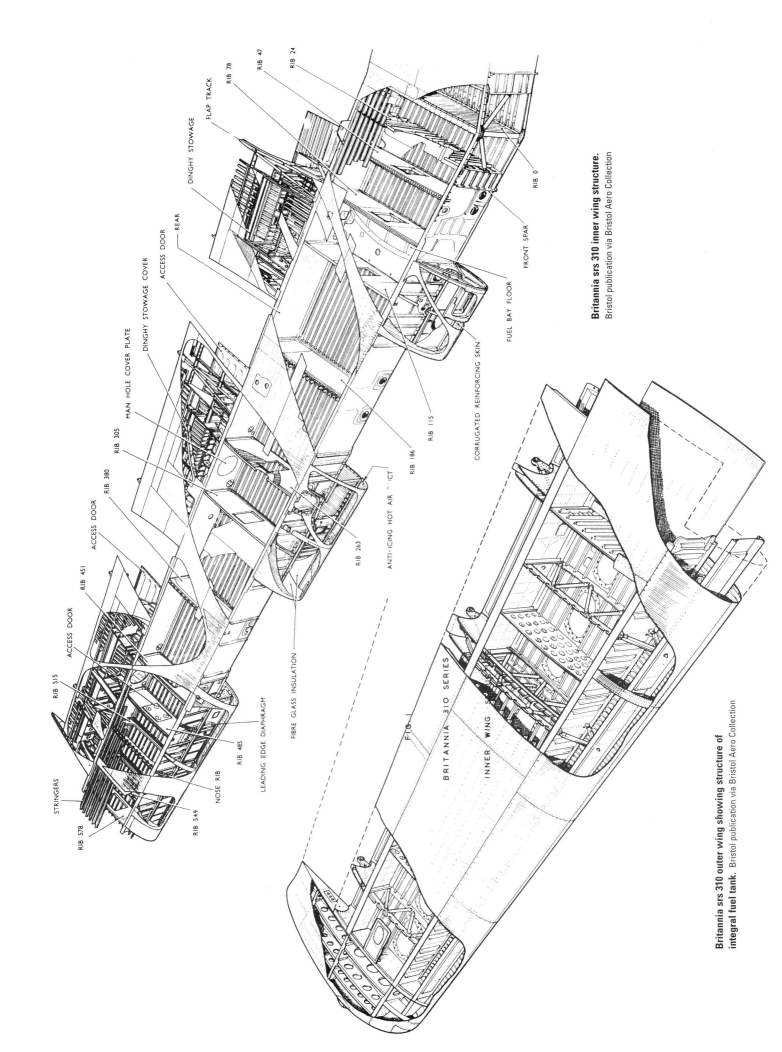

RIB 24

RIB 47

RIB 78

FLAP TRACK

DINGHY STOWAGE

REAR

ACCESS DOOR

DINGHY STOWAGE COVER

MAN HOLE COVER PLATE

RIB 305

RIB 380

ACCESS DOOR

RIB 451

ACCESS DOOR

RIB 515

ACCESS DOOR

RIB 578

STRINGERS

RIB 549

NOSE RIB

RIB 485

LEADING EDGE DIAPHRAGM

FIBRE GLASS INSULATION

RIB 263

ANTI-ICING HOT AIR DUCT

RIB 186

RIB 115

CORRUGATED REINFORCING SKIN

FUEL BAY FLOOR

FRONT SPAR

RIB 0

**Britannia srs 310 inner wing structure.**
Bristol publication via Bristol Aero Collection

BRITANNIA 310 SERIES

INNER WING

FIG.

**Britannia srs 310 outer wing showing structure of
integral fuel tank.** Bristol publication via Bristol Aero Collection

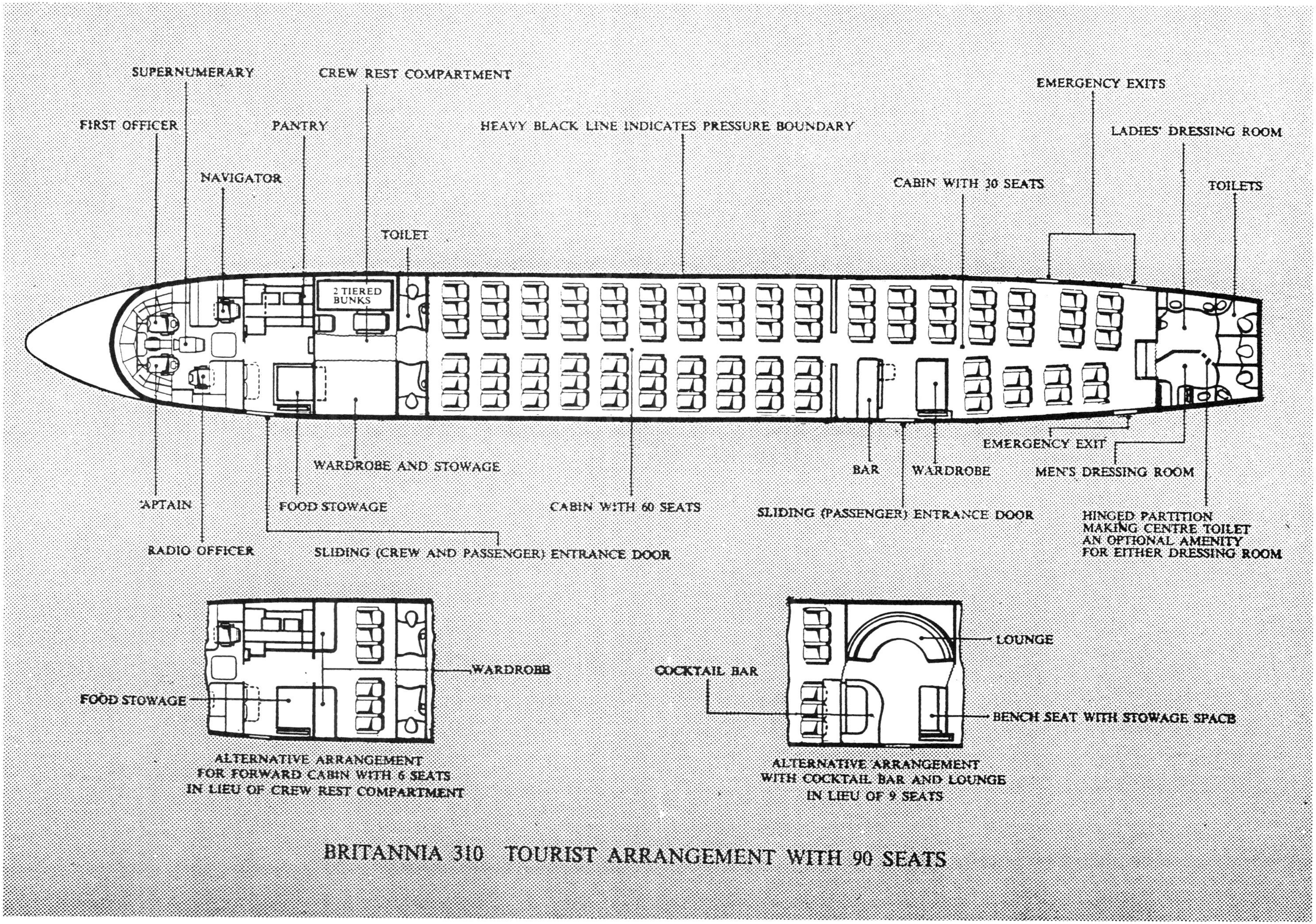
SUPERNUMERARY
CREW REST COMPARTMENT
EMERGENCY EXITS
FIRST OFFICER
PANTRY
HEAVY BLACK LINE INDICATES PRESSURE BOUNDARY
LADIES' DRESSING ROOM
NAVIGATOR
CABIN WITH 30 SEATS
TOILETS
TOILET
2 TIERED BUNKS
EMERGENCY EXIT
WARDROBE AND STOWAGE
BAR
WARDROBE
MEN'S DRESSING ROOM
'APTAIN
FOOD STOWAGE
CABIN WITH 60 SEATS
SLIDING (PASSENGER) ENTRANCE DOOR
HINGED PARTITION
MAKING CENTRE TOILET
AN OPTIONAL AMENITY
FOR EITHER DRESSING ROOM
RADIO OFFICER
SLIDING (CREW AND PASSENGER) ENTRANCE DOOR
WARDROBE
FOOD STOWAGE
ALTERNATIVE ARRANGEMENT
FOR FORWARD CABIN WITH 6 SEATS
IN LIEU OF CREW REST COMPARTMENT
LOUNGE
COCKTAIL BAR
BENCH SEAT WITH STOWAGE SPACE
ALTERNATIVE ARRANGEMENT
WITH COCKTAIL BAR AND LOUNGE
IN LIEU OF 9 SEATS
BRITANNIA 310 TOURIST ARRANGEMENT WITH 90 SEATS

**Proposed Britannia srs 310 90-seat Tourist Class cabin layout from September 1956.** Bristol publication via Bob Stradling

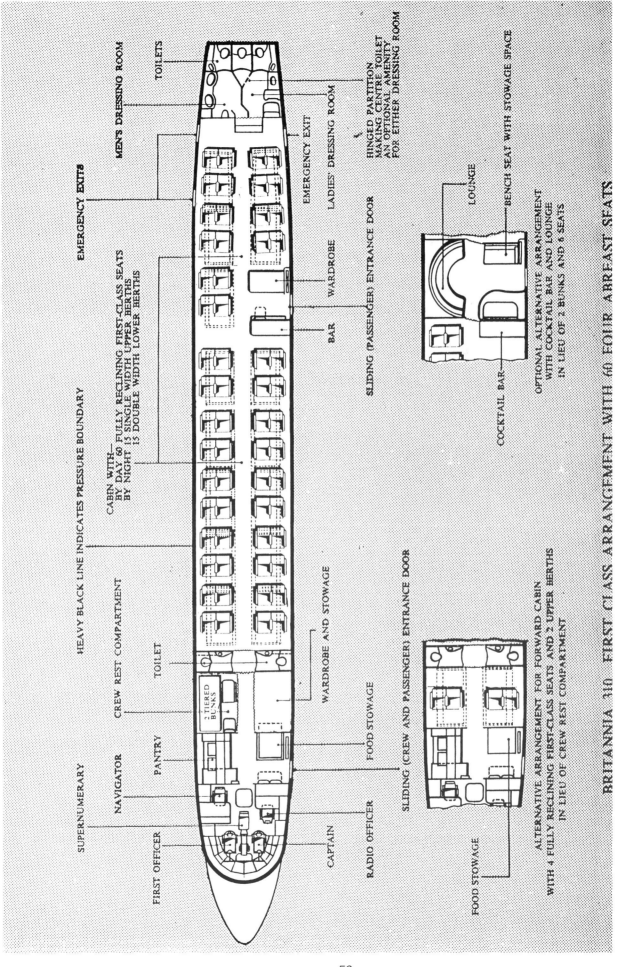

SUPERNUMERARY

NAVIGATOR

FIRST OFFICER

PANTRY

CAPTAIN

RADIO OFFICER

SLIDING (CREW AND PASSENGER) ENTRANCE DOOR

FOOD STOWAGE

ALTERNATIVE ARRANGEMENT FOR FORWARD CABIN
WITH 4 FULLY RECLINING FIRST-CLASS SEATS AND 2 UPPER BERTHS
IN LIEU OF CREW REST COMPARTMENT

HEAVY BLACK LINE INDICATES PRESSURE BOUNDARY

CREW REST COMPARTMENT

TOILET

WARDROBE AND STOWAGE

2 TIERED BUNKS

FOOD STOWAGE

CABIN WITH—
BY DAY 60 FULLY RECLINING FIRST-CLASS SEATS
BY NIGHT 15 SINGLE WIDTH UPPER BERTHS
15 DOUBLE WIDTH LOWER BERTHS

EMERGENCY EXITS

MEN'S DRESSING ROOM

TOILETS

EMERGENCY EXIT

LADIES' DRESSING ROOM

WARDROBE

BAR

SLIDING (PASSENGER) ENTRANCE DOOR

HINGED PARTITION
MAKING CENTRE TOILET
AN OPTIONAL AMENITY
FOR EITHER DRESSING ROOM

LOUNGE

BENCH SEAT WITH STOWAGE SPACE

COCKTAIL BAR

OPTIONAL ALTERNATIVE ARRANGEMENT
WITH COCKTAIL BAR AND LOUNGE
IN LIEU OF 2 BUNKS AND 6 SEATS

**BRITANNIA 310   FIRST CLASS ARRANGEMENT WITH 60 FOUR ABREAST SEATS**

**Proposed Britannia srs 310 sixty-seat First Class cabin layout from September 1956.** Bristol publication via Bob Stradling

52

the rate of descent by providing a greater range of engine acceleration.

The runway threshold should be crossed at 125 knots, at the maximum landing weight of 135,000lb, with a reduction of 3 knots per 7,000lb, down to 110 knots at 100,000lb.

When over the runway do not allow the aircraft to float excessively, but fly the aircraft down until the main wheels are on the ground, taking care during the flare-out to avoid touching the tail on the ground. Lower the nosewheel as soon as possible and keep it on the ground by holding the control column forward of neutral. Superfine and reverse thrust should then be used, and wheel braking as required.

The following notes are reproduced from *Hints and Tips on Britannia Handling*, produced by Kenneth M. Ashley, Test Pilot, Bristol Aircraft Ltd, on 17 September 1958.

### MANOUEVRING ON THE GROUND
1. Toe and Parking Brakes. ... The parking brake is an 'all or nothing' device. Thus, when bringing the aircraft to a halt, do so by gentle application of the toe brakes. When halted, hold the aircraft on the toe brakes, apply the parking brake and release the toe brakes. When starting from rest (at idling power), the parking brake may be released without use of the toe brakes. On take-off, however, apply the toe brakes, release the parking brake and, whilst opening the throttles, gently release the toe brakes.
2. Turning on the ground. ... The nosewheel steering should not be hard to apply. If it seems to be stiff the reason is either (a) that the aircraft is moving too slowly, or (b) you are trying to turn too sharply. Either fault will produce excessive tyre wear and will tend to strain the steering selector mechanism. The only exception to the above is that when full lock has been applied, considerable pressure may be needed to start the steering on its return to neutral. Once away from the full lock position, however, very little pressure should be needed. On lining up for take-off, or when making sharp turns at awkward taxiway intersections, take a wide sweep and start turning as early as possible without running the inside bogie off the track. In this way the least steering application is necessary and the turn is more comfortable. When a sharp turn is necessary, for example when turning 180 degrees to backtrack, slow the aircraft to the speed at which you feel you can comfortably make the turn, then gently apply full steering lock and free-wheel round the turn. It should seldom be necessary to to use any brake at all. Never apply brake to the inside wheels. If you find the speed too high during the turn, apply very gentle braking to the outside wheels only.

3. Use of brake dwell for taxying. ... Reverse dwell is best used as follows. Start rolling and allow speed to build up to a fairly slow taxying speed. If, due to low all-up weight and/or tailwind, you feel that the power at idling is accelerating you too much, select brake dwell on the inboards. Don't wait until the speed is already excessive before applying it. If this is still insufficient, keep the speed low by very smooth and gentle applications of toe brakes at intervals. Never taxy for long periods with even pressure applied all the time. This will cause overheating and steady deterioration of the brakes which will not be apparent at all until they finally fail, maybe several flights later, and they usually all have to be replaced at once. Remember–there's a lot of aeroplane–give the brakes a fair deal and they will never let you down.

### NOSEWHEEL STEERING ON TAKE-OFF
Points to watch. ... Up to a speed of about 40 knots the rudder is not fully effective. However, above this speed full rudder control is available and should be used for directional control on take-off. Thus, from the point of initial roll, use nosewheel steering plus coarse rudder. As speed increases use rudder only, leaving the left hand on the steering handle in case of engine cut. Above 106 knots the nosewheel steering can be abandoned entirely, as, even in the event of a failure of no.4 engine (the worst case), rudder control alone will provide full compensation. Use of coarse rudder is stressed because, if nosewheel steering alone is used, engine torque, offset propeller thrust, crosswind effects and the effect of slipstream on the fin are all being taken by the nosewheel tyres. This causes excessive wear and is particularly expensive in time and money during training. Use of rudder above 40 knots relieves the strain on the nosewheel and tyre wear is almost halved.

### CONTROLS
The servo-tab controls are very light and sensitive. There is practically no lost motion in any control run, so that any movement of a control, however small, will affect the aircraft's flight path. Thus you will find an initial tendency to over-control the aircraft, and the old adage about allowing the machine to fly itself holds very true with the Britannia. The best method is to apply pressure to the controls rather than movement. A few words on each control and its characteristics may be of value.

### The Elevators
Due to the lightness and effectiveness of the servo-tab elevators, a feel system must be used to prevent over-stressing of the airframe – particularly in turbulent conditions. However, the

feel system reacts to two effects:- (a) Dynamic pressure (I.A.S.); (b) Stick displacement. Thus, as airspeed increases the pressure required on the control column is increased. Also, the greater the movement of the control either fore or aft, the harder it becomes to move it. In normal routine flying, therefore, when comparatively small control movements are required, you will find the elevators light and very effective. But in any manouvre calling for large elevator movements the control becomes much heavier. This will be noticed particularly in steep turns (45 degrees of bank or more) and on round out over the threshold when landing. The only method of relieving the load is by means of the trimmer, and one of the answers to good landings in the Britannia is use of the elevator trimmer to relieve stick loads prior to the round out. This will be discussed later.

### Ailerons
There is only a straight spring feel in the aileron circuit in addition to the normal feed back through the control run. They are therefore pleasantly light and very effective. The smallest movement of the yoke control will produce an immediate and proportionate rate of roll. Thus, hold the spectacles lightly and merely press in the required direction. If you hold it tightly and move it you will almost certainly overdo it.

### Rudder
Except on take-off and landing, or when under asymmetric power, the rudder is almost superfluous. No rudder is required for balanced turns, even in turbulence. In fact, most pilots experienced on the type hardly put their feet on the rudder pedals at all during normal flying. Of course, when initiating a rapid 'S' turn on the approach at low speed, or when making a rapid reversal from one direction of turn to another, moderate rudder will be very helpful. But in general it is better left alone.

As most troubles with a new type are experienced during take-off and landing, perhaps a few words on each may be of help...

### TAKE-OFF
When starting the take-off, the First Officer should hold the nosewheel in contact with the ground by keeping the control column just forward of the neutral position. Except on a very slippery runway with a crosswind and an aft C.G. it is not necessary to push it fully forward. Open the throttles smoothly and, when at about half power, slowly release the brakes using the toe-brakes. Control the direction by coarse use of rudder, assisted (only for as long as necessary) by nosewheel steering. When the Second Officer confirms full power transfer the right hand from

throttles to control column and allow the stick to move back to neutral. At 106 knots abandon the nosewheel steering grip and use both hands on the stick. At about 10 knots below V2 apply firm back pressure to the control column and watch the nose of the aircraft. As soon as the nose begins to rise, gently release the pressure and the aircraft will fly off smoothly. Although this sounds very elementary, most pilots at first try to haul the stick back, with the result that instead of smoothly flying off the ground the aircraft rears up like a startled deer and leaps off the ground. Inevitably the pilot then slams the stick forward, setting up a pitching oscillation and frightening himself (not to mention his long-suffering instructor) silly. During training the aircraft will be very light, and, with highly effective controls, smoothness and relaxed handling cannot be over-emphasized.

Once off the ground, due to the large amount of engine power and, therefore, torque effect, there is a tendency for the nose to move slightly to the right. A little left rudder will correct this tendency. Otherwise, you will tend to drop the left wing instinctively. As the speed increases to about 135 knots the torque effect disappears, and

it is therefore less noticeable during take-offs at maximum all-up weight when V2 is 137 knots.

### APPROACH AND LANDING

The most comfortable type of approach for the Britannia is at about 4 degrees, i.e. rather steeper than a normal ILS glide path. The approach should be initially at about 135 knots, using 2/3 flap and approximately 200–250lb torque on all engines. Final approach speed should be about 5 knots above threshold speed. Threshold speed is scheduled on elevator control, not stalling speed. At the schedule threshold speed for landing weight you have an ample margin of safety, so don't add anything for your wife and children, except in very gusty wind gradients, and then never more than 15 knots. More bad landings have been made in Britannias through excessive speed at the round-out than through any other cause.

Due to the fact that, when windmilling, the propeller is not driving anything (free turbine principle!), there is no propeller drag when the throttles are closed. Again, even at idling power, quite a lot of thrust is still being produced. Therefore, the throttles should be closed

much earlier than on a piston-engined aircraft. Close off all power at about 100ft and make the final 100ft a glide approach. It won't fall out of the sky, in fact it will float for at least 300ft after the threshold if your threshold speed is correct.

At about 100–150ft make an initial check on rate of descent, raising the nose a little, and re-trim the elevators until you are just pushing on the stick. Then, on the round-out the stick loads will be pleasantly light and you will not over-control. If you try to make the round-out all in one pull the stick movement is large and the pressure demanded by the feel simulator will be very high, so that you will lose the sensitive control you need for a really smooth touchdown. In all probability you will eventually heave a little too hard and the aircraft will balloon. We all know how difficult it is to correct that error!

There are two good reasons for the technique recommended above. The initial check at 100–150ft reduces the amount of pitch change necessary at the flare-out and therefore the stick loads. The retrimming helps the stick loads and also counteracts the loss of slipstream over the elevators once the throttles are closed. On closing the throttles the propellers move onto the fine-pitch stop and become virtually four flat plates, cutting down the airflow over the elevators. This means that a greater elevator movement is required to achieve the change in flight path at the round-out. Retrimming at 100ft until a slight push force is felt just counteracts this and makes the round-out smooth and comfortable. Unlike most aircraft, there is no danger in trimming back on final, and even with full power on the aircraft is easily controllable until retrimmed. No difficulty will be experienced therefore, even if an overshoot from ground level becomes necessary.

### Britannia Service Time Savings from Sept 1958 Bristol Publication

| Stage | Britannia Time | Fastest Other Service | Percentage Improvement |
|---|---|---|---|
| London–Tokyo | 37hr 30min | 45hr 30min | 17.6 |
| London–Sidney | 47hr 35min | 56hr -min | 15.0 |
| London–Colombo | 21hr 35min | 29hr 20min | 27.0 |
| London–Singapore | 29hr 45min | 37hr 30min | 20.7 |
| New York–Tel Aviv | 16hr 20min | 21hr 45min | 24.9 |
| London–Chicago | 15hr 20min | 18hr 20min | 16.4 |
| London–New York | 10hr 50min | 13hr 35min | 20.2 |
| New York–London | 8hr 50min | 10hr 45min | 17.8 |
| New York–Mexico | 6hr 30min | 7hr 45min | 16.1 |
| Vancouver–Amsterdam | 13hr 40min | 19hr 30min | 30.0 |
| Tokyo–Vancouver | 14hr 00min | 19hr 25min | 27.9 |

### Britannia Record-Breaking Flights from September 1958 Bristol Publication

| Date | Sector | Time | Sector Distance (miles) | Average Blockspeed (mph) |
|---|---|---|---|---|
| 08 Jan 58 | New York–London | 7hr 44min | 3,443 | 445 |
| 10 Mar 58 | London–New York | 9hr 22min | 3,443 | 368 |
| 31 Jan 58 | New York–Paris | 8hr 47min | 3,621 | 401 |
| 19 Dec 57 | New York–Tel Aviv | 14hr 56min | 6,100* | 401 |
| 01 Jan 58 | Mexico City–New York | 5hr 8min | 2,093 | 401 |
| 21 Jul 58 | London–Montreal | 8hr 57min | 3,241 | 362 |
| 24 Feb 58 | Vancouver–London | 13hr 57min | 5,102 | 366 |
| 29 Jun 57 | London-Vancouver | 14hr 40min | 5,102 | 350 |
| 09 May 58 | San Franciso–London | 17hr 6min⁺ | 6,020 | 352 |
| 16 Jul 58 | Amsterdam–Vancouver | 13hr 53min | 4,800 | 346 |
| 20 Sept 58 | Tokyo–Vancouver | 11hr 44min | 4,700 | 400 |

* claimed as a long-distance record for a commercial aircraft
⁺ includes stop at New York

### Britannia Logbook (at Nov 1962)

Built: 85
In service: 79
Mileage flown: 222 million plus
Hours flown: 717,000 plus
Revenue hours flown: 671,000 plus
Landings: 200,000 plus
Passengers carried: over 3 million

Hours flown (by operator):
BOAC (srs 102s); 220,000
BOAC (srs 312s); 189,000
CPAL; 83,900
RAF Transport Command; 57,100
BUA; 56,100
El Al; 45,000
Aeronaves de Mexico; 20,200
Cubana/CSA; 17,400
Cunard-Eagle; 11,700
Transcontinental SA; 9,900

# CHAPTER THREE

# The Britannia in BOAC Service

The first two BOAC Britannia 102s, G-ANBC and G-ANBD, were delivered from Filton to BOAC's base at London Airport on 30 December 1955, following the issue of the Britannia's Certificate of Airworthiness by the Air Registration Board a few hours earlier. The aircraft were flown into London Airport by Captains A. S. M. Rendall and F. W. Walton, respectively Flight Superintendent and Training Captain of the BOAC Britannia fleet, and the log books were ceremonially handed over to Sir Miles Thomas, Chairman of BOAC, by Sir Reginald Verdon Smith, Chairman of the Bristol Aeroplane Company. G-ANBC was equipped as a 94-seat Tourist Class aircraft and G-ANBD was furnished in a 54-seat First Class layout, complete with a horseshoe-shaped lounge bar amidships. Crew training began at 0800hr the following morning, initially from London Airport. A week later, after some minor modifications had been carried out, the training base was transferred to Hurn Airport, near Bournemouth. At that time no Britannia had ever spent a night in the open in frosty conditions, and when the crews arrived to start training flights they found that the elevator controls had frozen solid. It was not a difficult problem to resolve, but it did cast some doubts on the thoroughness of the ARB's certification testing.

Srs 102 G-ANBD was later to serve with BKS Air Transport when the BOAC fleet was disposed of. The late Dave Williams

## Crisis Duties

Six more Britannias were delivered during 1956, and it was while they were being used for crew training from Hurn that they carried out their first revenue-earning operations, well before they entered scheduled service. In August 1956 Egypt's claim to the Suez Canal led to fighting in the Middle East, and Prime Minister Anthony Eden decided to send troops to reinforce the British bases in Cyprus. The BOAC Britannias were judged to be ideal for this as they could each carry 116 troops non-stop to Nicosia. The first BOAC trooping flight left Hurn at 0700hr on 5 August 1956 and the flights continued, without incident, for the next two or three weeks; in all sixty-eight trooping flights were made, by G-ANBE and G-ANBJ. Mike Widdowson, a BOAC Senior Engineer Officer at the time, recalls that on the arrival of one of these flights the Regimental Sergeant Major in charge fell his troops in and yelled at them 'Right you bastards, BOAC has been taking good care of you, now its my turn … Double march!' Five minutes later, a pale-faced 18-year-old soldier approached Mr Widdowson.

'Please Sir, may I go back on the aircraft?'

'Of course', he said, 'but why?'

'I've left my bayonet behind', the soldier replied.

Srs 102 G-ANBD in the early white-tail colour scheme. Air-Britain

## History of BOAC

The British Overseas Airways Corporation (BOAC) was formed on 24 November 1939 by the merger of Britain's major international airline, Imperial Airways, and the original British Airways, an independent operator of domestic and European services. The new state-owned airline began life with quite a sizeable fleet, much of which was impressed into military service, but despite wartime restrictions it still offered limited services throughout the war years with such types as the Mosquito and the ubiquitous DC-3. The resumption of civil flying on 1 January 1946 saw BOAC operating a very mixed bag of aircraft types, including converted bombers such as Avro Lancastrians and Consolidated Liberators, Boeing and Shorts flying boats, Armstrong Whitworth Ensigns and, of course, DC-3s. These were to be taken over by British European Airways (BEA) when that new state airline was established on 1 August 1946 to operate domestic and European routes.

BOAC (and BEA) had a major say in the specifications for any new British airliner project, including the new Avro Tudor, which was intended for use on BOAC's transatlantic routes. When it became obvious that the Tudor was going to be hopelessly uneconomical for this purpose BOAC caused a controversy by ordering US-built Constellations and later Boeing Stratocruisers instead of British aircraft, but there was no real home-grown alternative at the time. During 1948 a coherent aircraft procurement policy for BOAC emerged. Wherever possible British designs were to be ordered, and even the farthest-flung parts of the British Empire were to be served by medium-range aircraft

making frequent stops en route. Thus it was that the Britannia and also the Comet began life as medium-haul designs, and had to be developed into long-range versions before they could compete with the new types coming out of America.

Over the next few years many new types joined the BOAC fleet, including the Canadair Argonaut, the Handley Page Hermes, Constellations and Stratocruisers. Then, on 2 May 1952, BOAC inaugurated the world's first scheduled passenger service by a jet airliner when Comet 1 G-ALYP left London for Johannesburg. The Comets slashed flying times on BOAC's routes to Africa and the Far East, and established the airline as the world leader. Sadly though, a number of Comet 1 crashes led to the grounding of the type and the airline had to struggle on with piston-engined types once more.

The Britannia and the re-designed Comet 4 were to spearhead BOAC's re-equipment with modern British types, but delays with delivery of the Britannia fleet led to BOAC buying a small fleet of Douglas DC-7Cs to retain its competitive position on the Atlantic in the interim. Boeing 707s were later ordered for the North Atlantic routes, followed in 1965 by the highly popular Super VC-10; the standard version of the VC-10 was operated on the African and Far East network. BOAC inaugurated Boeing 747 services on 14 April 1971, after a delay of almost a year caused by a pilots' pay dispute.

In the meantime, political pressures had been mounting for a merger of Britain's two state airline corporations, and on 1 April 1974 BOAC and BEA were officially merged to form British Airways.

(*Top*) A BOAC Canadair Argonaut in flight. This type was replaced by Britannia 102s on the Far Eastern route network. BOAC

BOAC Stratocruiser G-AKGH 'Caledonia'. The Stratocruiser was replaced on the North Atlantic routes by the much faster Britannia 312. BOAC

Riots in Lebanon in the autumn of 1956 led to the evacuation of British civilians, and the Britannia proved its usefulness as a long-range load-carrier by carrying 200 British wives and children direct from Bahrain to Aden on a single flight. Another crisis in 1956 saw the BOAC Britannias in action again, this time carrying refugees from Vienna to London during the Hungarian uprising against the Soviet occupation. A total of twenty-four sorties were flown during November and December, carrying 2,699 refugees in 1,307 flying hours.

**Srs 102 G-ANBA was eventually delivered to BOAC on 22 August 1957, after use on tropical development trials work.** Air-Britain

**A Britannia in the BOAC blue-tail colour-scheme runs up its engines.**
Bristol via Michael Harrison

---

### Something Nasty in the Toilet?

Former BOAC Britannia Captain Lincoln recalls one frightening (at the time) and later amusing incident that happened in December 1957, soon after the srs 102s entered service on the Tokyo run. A Captain M. was detailed to fly to Tokyo and, although he had been there before, those visits had been in other types of aircraft, so he had to be cleared to fly into Tokyo by a Captain N., who had been there several times in the Britannia. There was no problem going into Tokyo and about an hour after the aircraft had taken off again for Hong Kong, Captain N. handed over the controls to Captain M. and disappeared into the passenger cabin. In fact, he headed for the First Class toilet, which was at the very rear of the aircraft, and settled himself down comfortably. Moments later he heard a terrifying noise, which had him leaping to his feet and dashing forward to the cockpit with his trousers still around his ankles. Captain M. and the rest of the crew greeted his arrival with amazement – nothing untoward had been noticed on the flight deck. It was at Hong Kong that the mystery was solved. In order for the toilets to be cleaned and drained there was an access pipe fitted, covered by a metal flap. While Captain N. had been enjoying the relative silence of the rear toilet this metal flap had come unfastened and, after creating a hideous vibrating sound, had broken away altogether, landing somewhere over the China Sea. Little wonder that Captain N. (who was nominally in command of the aircraft) had dashed frantically forward. Little wonder also that Captain M. and the rest of the crew were mildly amused.

---

## Scheduled Services Begin

The Britannia commenced scheduled airline services on 1 February 1957 when G-ANBI operated BOAC's inaugural turboprop service from London to Johannesburg. The thrice-weekly service included stops at Rome, Khartoum and Nairobi or Salisbury in each direction, and the scheduled journey time was 22 hours 50 minutes. By this time eight Britannias had been delivered to BOAC. The last srs 102 to be delivered was in fact G-ANBA, which had been used for development work and was delivered on 12 August 1957. For the next five years the srs 102s served BOAC's African and Eastern route networks, replacing Canadair Argonauts and Lockheed Constellations. When the Britannia entered scheduled service it was the largest airliner in service, exceeding by some 3,000lb (1,400kg) the weight of its nearest rival. It was also the fastest and the quietest, fully justifying its advertising slogan 'The Whispering Giant'.

A month after the first London–Johannesburg service, Britannias were introduced on the Sydney route, reducing the overall journey time by nearly thirty hours and offering both 'Majestic' First Class and 'Coronet' Tourist Class accommodation. The thrice-weekly service operated via Zurich, Istanbul, Karachi, Calcutta, Singapore, Jakarta and Darwin. On 16 July the Tokyo route became Britannia-operated, and on 22 August Britannias replaced Constellations on the London–Aden route, cutting the scheduled time to fifteen hours. Similar time savings were seen on the Colombo service when Britannias entered service on 17 September, slashing the journey time to 22½ hours.

By December 1957 annual utilization of the Britannia 102 fleet had reached an average of 3,000 hours per aircraft. However, during the first eight months of service there had been no fewer than forty-nine unplanned engine changes and sixteen engine failures due to icing problems. In the later months of 1957 modifications to all the Proteus engines had finally overcome the icing troubles, but BOAC's schedules had been thrown into confusion for several weeks. It was also during the second half of 1957 that the Britannia fleet started to receive BOAC's new colour scheme, with the dark blue cheat line being extended to cover most of the nose area, and a dark blue tail fin in place of the previous white one.

Srs 102 G-ANBB in the later BOAC blue-tail colour scheme at the airline's Heathrow maintenance base. Air-Britain

## Transatlantic Services Begin

On 19 December 1957 BOAC introduced the long-range Britannia srs 312 into service on the prestigious London–New York route. The inaugural service was operated by G-AOVC, with Captain A. Meagher in command. The aircraft took off from London Airport at 1035hr, and its track took it via Prestwick, the southern tip of Greenland, Gander and Boston. During the flight G-AOVC was diverted some 350 miles (560km) from its intended course in order to avoid headwinds of 146mph (235km/h), but as it was it still encountered headwinds of around 100mph (160km/h) at times. The average true airspeed was 350mph (560km/h), an average groundspeed of 305mph (490km/h) for the total distance of 3,750 miles (6,000km), and the Britannia

landed at Idlewild Airport at 2310hr. The return flight left Idlewild at 2312hr on 21 December and went via Gander, the south of Ireland, and Bristol, landing at London at 0800hr on 22 December. On this leg, tailwinds averaging 55mph (88km/h) allowed the distance of 3,515 miles (5,656km) to be covered at an average groundspeed of 405mph (652km/h). Initially, just one service a week was operated by Britannias, with the westbound flight being flown wholly in daylight on Fridays and the eastbound flight overnight on Sundays. These were the first transatlantic services by turboprop airliners and the first North Atlantic scheduled services by a British-built aircraft.

By 31 December six srs 312s had been delivered from Filton and Belfast, via Cambridge where Marshalls of Cambridge

installed the BOAC furnishings. However, because of delivery delays the srs 312s entered service just ten months ahead of the first jet services (by Comet 4 and Boeing 707) on the same route, where BOAC had once anticipated a three-year lead with the Britannia. The last srs 312 to be delivered was G-AOVT, which arrived at London Airport on 1 January 1959.

In BOAC transatlantic service the Britannias were operated in an all-First Class configuration. The airline's luxury 'Majestic' Class cabin was furnished for only fifty-two passengers, with twenty-six 'Slumberette' fully reclining sleeper seats and twenty-six conventional First Class reclining seats. At the rear of the cabin were two spacious dressing rooms, with specially toned lighting, opening into three separate toilets. According to the load carried, two toilets could be made available for ladies and one for men, or vice versa, by means of an adjustable partition between the dressing rooms. The dressing rooms featured a ladies' powder room with cushioned seating, a dressing table and plenty of well-lit mirrors. Yardley toilet requisites were provided for the gentlemen, and Elizabeth Arden cosmetics for the ladies. Because of the low passenger load even when full, BOAC were able to make most crossings non-stop, although strong headwinds sometimes obliged the Britannias to land and refuel at Goose Bay or Gander. The eastbound scheduled flight time was set at 12 hours, although it was frequently operated in less: in 1958 one flight took just 9½ hours. The westbound service was scheduled to take 11 hours, due to the usually favourable westerly winds.

The normal crew was two pilots, a flight engineer and a navigator. Two crew bunks were provided, one above the other just aft of the flight deck. The air conditioning and heating systems kept the passenger cabin at an acceptable temperature in winter, but not so the flight deck. Crews would often wear their uniform overcoats over their jackets when the outside air temperature was exceptionally low. Navigation over the ocean depended primarily on the LORAN system, whereby master and slave systems on land transmitted pulses that the navigator translated from his cathode ray tube. He then referred to a chart overprinted with the LORAN chain lines. There was also the periscopic sextant for astro-navigation. Assistance was also obtained from radar-equipped weather ships, whose position was marked on the aircraft's charts.

BOAC Britannias had only a short life on the Atlantic run, due to the introduction of Boeing 707-121s such as N707PA by Pan American. Air-Britain

## Operations Expand

At the end of its first year of service BOAC's fifteen Britannias were flying an average eight hours daily, equivalent to 3,000 hours per year, a figure that until then was not expected until a new type had been in service for 2–3 years. During 1958 both the srs 102s and the srs 312s continued to take over from piston-engined types throughout the BOAC network. On 17 April 1958 G-AOVH inaugurated Britannia 312 services on the London–Chicago route, with stops en route at Prestwick, Shannon or Gander, Montreal and Detroit. Two days later G-AOVF was used by Princess Margaret for her West Indies Royal Tour. Britannia 102s re-opened the London–Teheran service, which had been closed down since October 1952, and in May this mark also began operating between London and Melbourne, while srs 312s replaced Douglas DC-7Cs on London–New York–San Francisco services.

On 27 July srs 312s replaced the earlier 102s on the London–Johannesburg route, operating to a 23 hours 15 minutes schedule. Former BOAC Britannia 312 Engineer Officer Nev Boulton remembers a trip from Nairobi to Johannesburg via Salisbury when a compressor turbine suffered some damage. In order to maintain the compressor RPM more fuel had to be fed to the engine, resulting in a higher jet pipe temperature. The turbines that drove the propeller were separate from the compressor turbines, so as a result of this increased fuel supply (which was now maintaining the compressor turbine at the correct RPM) more power was felt on the propeller turbines. This increased power resulted in an increased propeller torque indication. A 20°C rise in jet pipe temperature required a mandatory engine shutdown. The Captain took the view that they had a more efficient engine (with more torque/power) even though it was 'a bit hotter'(!), and refused to let him shut it down. As a result, by the time they reached Johannesburg there was significant vibration damage at the rear end.

On 8 September 1958 srs 102 G-ANBC ran off the end of the wet runway at Rangoon whilst landing in drizzle. None of the forty-two persons on board were injured, but the aircraft was seriously damaged in the incident. The nose-gear radius rod was broken, and the leg folded too far back, forcing the nosewheel up into the front freight hold. The forward fuselage was severely buckled and damage was sustained to both the inner engine nacelles and all four propellers. Temporary repairs were carried out at Rangoon with the aid of air bags and a high-capacity crane, and after a satisfactory test flight on 27 March the Britannia left Rangoon on the following day piloted by Walter Gibb, Bristol's Chief Test Pilot, on an unpressurized ferry flight, cruising at 8,500ft (2,600m) and 205kt (380km/h), with the main undercarriage doors removed, and the nose wheel fixed down and its well faired over. A faulty engine had the accessory drive blanked off, eliminating that engine's alternator and the auto-pilot. The flight home was made in easy stages, and from Rome Gibb cabled Bristol 'Golf Alfa November Broken Carcass arrived Rome by hand with four burning three generating two up and one dangling.' In this condition G-ANBC eventually arrived at Filton on 1 April. Here a new front fuselage section was fitted and various modifications were carried out while the repairs were being made. The aircraft was test-flown on 15 August, re-delivered to BOAC on 20 August, and re-entered revenue service two days later. At the time this was the most extensive repair operation yet undertaken on a commercial aircraft by a British company. However, all this work was later to be undone in 1960, when G-ANBC was written off in another accident!

In October 1958 BOAC resumed its services to South America, which had been suspended for four years. On 28 October Britannia srs 312 G-AOVL inaugurated a twice-weekly run from London to Bermuda, Port of Spain and Caracas, with an optional stop at Barbados. This was the first ever turboprop service between Europe and South America, and the journey time was scheduled at 21 hours 25 minutes with the stop at Barbados omitted. On 6 October, G-AOVJ had inaugurated Britannia srs 312 services to East Africa.

1958 ended with the loss of a BOAC Britannia srs 312. At 1010hr on 24 December G-AOVD took off from London Airport for a test flight in connection with the renewal of its Certificate of Airworthiness. After completion of the tests the crew requested a descent from 12,000ft to 3,000ft. Some three minutes after starting the descent the aircraft struck the ground, which was obscured by fog, at Winkton. Of

**Srs 312 G-AOVR.** Air-Britain

the twelve people on board, nine lost their lives. The subsequent enquiry blamed the Captain and First Officer for failing to establish the altitude of the aircraft before and during the descent, but also cited the possibly confusing layout of the three-pointer altimeter as a contributory cause.

At the end of BOAC's first year of transatlantic Britannia srs 312 operations (19 December 1958), figures were published showing that 645 transatlantic crossings had been made, 40,550 passengers had been carried, at a 62.5 per cent load factor, compared to the required break-even load factor of 71 per cent (calculated up to 11 October 1958). Of the crosssings, 522 had been non-stop, 81 per cent of the total. Only 50 per cent of the crossings arrived within one hour of their scheduled timing. A loss of some £500,000 was incurred on the srs 312 services, mainly attributed to the

still-developing San Francisco and midwest routes, as the New York services actually produced a profit.

1959 began with a new Britannia 102 service to the Middle East, with G-ANBA inaugurating a London–Rome–Beirut–Kuwait–Bahrain–Doha route on 6 January. By March 1959 all thirty-three of the srs 102s and 312s ordered were in BOAC service, and on 31 March a srs 312 set off from London on BOAC's inaugural round-the-world service. The aircraft flew westbound across the Atlantic and Pacific to Tokyo via New York, San Francisco, Honolulu and Hong Kong. Meanwhile, a Comet 4 departed London for Tokyo on 1 April, travelling eastbound and arriving there on the 3rd and departing again on the 4th to complete the circuit originated by the Britannia. However, delays in obtaining full traffic rights across the Pacific meant that

the start of regular services on this route had to be postponed until 22 August 1959.

In April 1959 the Britannia started West African routes, with G-ANBK inaugurating London–Lagos services on the 13th and London–Accra three days later. On 9 August the Lagos route was upgraded to an eight-times weekly express service, with a daylight crossing of the Sahara for the first time. The 11 hours 30 minutes schedule included only one stop en route, at Barcelona.

The Britannia's engine problems were still not over, and the following incident was related by former BOAC Captain Raymond Dodwell, who was co-pilot on a London–Montreal flight in srs 312 G-AOVK under the command of Captain Harrison on the night of 16–17 July 1959. The first leg, from London to Shannon, passed without incident, but somewhere in the cruise between Shannon and Montreal one of the right-hand engines had to be shut down. The flight continued towards Montreal, descending as normal, with the power on the remaining three engines reduced to idle. On increasing power at a lower level the other right-hand engine seized and would not respond to throttle movements or de-icing procedures. This

(*Left*) Srs 312 G-AOVJ. Air-Britain

(*Below*) A night-time shot of srs 312 G-AOVD at Idlewild Airport, New York, in February 1958. Bristol via Michael Harrison

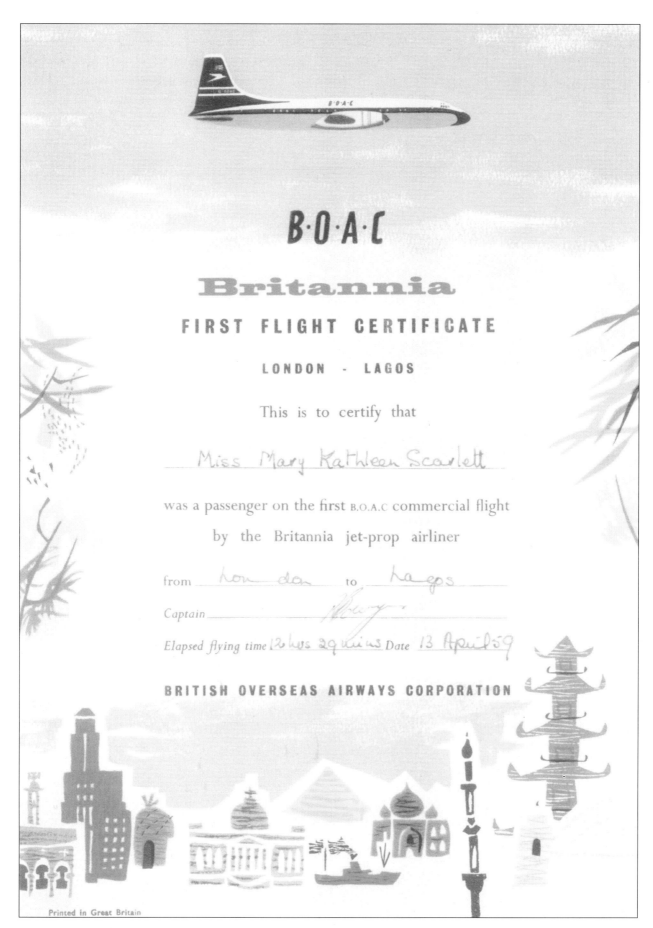

# B·O·A·C

## Britannia

### FIRST FLIGHT CERTIFICATE

#### LONDON - LAGOS

This is to certify that

*Miss Mary Kathleen Scarlett*

was a passenger on the first B.O.A.C commercial flight

by the Britannia jet-prop airliner

from *London* to *Lagos*

Captain _____

Elapsed flying time *12 hrs 29 mins* Date *13 April 59*

**BRITISH OVERSEAS AIRWAYS CORPORATION**

Printed in Great Britain

**A First Flight Certificate presented to Mary Dixon (neé Scarlett) from the inaugural BOAC Britannia service to Lagos, flown by G-ANBK on 13 April 1959.** Mary Dixon

61

engine was then shut down, and the aircraft was safely landed without further incident with just the two port engines running. Captain Dodwell was not impressed with the reliability of the Britannia, and grabbed the opportunity to join one of the first BOAC Boeing 707 training courses. He eventually progressed onto the 747, but the incident described above was the only example of double engine failure he experienced in 40 years of flying.

In November 1959 srs 312s were used to re-open BOAC services to Tel Aviv, operating alongside those of BEA, and on 7 January 1960 srs 312s inaugurated a new 23-hour service from London to Bogota via Trinidad, Bermuda and Caracas. Thirty-four First Class and thirty-nine Tourist Class seats were provided on the Britannias. During the financial year ending March 1960 the Britannia 102 and 312 fleets contributed 58 per cent of BOAC's total capacity.

On 13 April 1960 Britannia 102s took over from Canadair Argonauts on a 13 hours 25 minutes service to Abadan via Beirut and Damascus, and on 25–26 September srs 312 G-AOVN carried HRH Princess Alexandra to Lagos for the Nigerian independence celebrations. The 3,180-mile (5,120km) flight was accomplished non-stop in 10 hours 30 minutes, and is believed to have been the first non-stop flight over that route by a commercial aircraft.

After much argument between member airlines during 1959, from 1 May 1960 the International Air Transport Association introduced a 7 per cent propeller fare differential on the North Atlantic routes, helping operators of propeller airlines to remain competitive by letting them charge lower fares than jet operators. However, this meant in practice a fare reduction on Britannia services of only £7 or so each way, compared with travel on the much faster Boeing 707 and DC-8 jets being introduced by BOAC's competitors. October 1960 saw the introduction of low-cost 'Skycoach' services by BOAC in conjunction with UK independent airlines. On 15 October a monthly Britannia 312 service to Montego Bay and Kingston was inaugurated, followed a

week later by a similar service to Barbados and Port of Spain, and on 5 November by a two-monthly schedule to Bermuda and Nassau. On 1 December a twice-weekly, conventional fare, service to Tripoli and Benghazi was inaugurated.

On 11 November srs 102 G-ANBC, back in service after its mishap in 1958 and subsequent lengthy repairs, was en route to Khartoum with eighteen passengers and nine crew aboard. At 20,500ft (6,250m) a loss of hydraulic fluid occurred, accompanied by a reduction in airspeed from 210kt (390km/h) to 180kt (334km/h). During the descent into Khartoum it was discovered that the landing gear could not be lowered and locked down by using either

**Srs 312 G-AOVP on final approach.** Air-Britain

the normal or emergency systems. The Britannia was landed on a strip alongside the runway with the nosewheel up and the main landing gear trailing. None of those on board were injured, thanks to the skill of Captain Alfred S. Powell and his crew, but the aircraft was written off. It was later found that a failure of the support member for the starboard maingear uplock had permitted the gear to fall during flight, damaging the hydraulic system lines. Captain Powell was later awarded a BOAC certificate of commendation for 'his outstanding qualities of leadership and airmanship'.

1961 was to be the last complete year of operations by the full BOAC Britannia fleet. During the spring, sister airline BEA experienced a shortage of Vanguard

capacity and leased three BOAC srs 312s (G-AOVG, G-AOVP and G-AOVT) for use on European routes, chiefly to Copenhagen, Frankfurt and Nice. After America's 'Bay of Pigs' incident in Cuba, BOAC Britannias were given permission to fly into Havana to fly out the remaining American nationals. One such mission was undertaken by srs 312 G-AOVL on 17 September 1961.

## The End of BOAC Britannia Operations

In late 1961 BOAC began advertising Britannia 102s for sale for delivery during 1962, although the type was still used to inaugurate a new through-plane service to Mauritius, via Rome, Khartoum, Nairobi and Tananarive, on 6 January 1962. The Economy Class return fare to Mauritius was £309.12.0; the comparable return fare in First Class was £489.12.0, and for their money First Class passengers received a seven-course meal and travelled in a cabin equipped with five toilets and two dressing rooms, complete with cosmetic accessories.

In November 1962 BOAC withdrew all fourteen srs 102s from service, although a few remained on lease to Malayan Airways until the spring of 1963. The final BOAC srs 102 service was operated from Hong Kong to London on 22 November by G-ANBH and all the 102s were then stored at Cambridge and London Airport pending disposal, eventually being sold to Britannia Airways, BKS and Laker Airways. One of these aircraft, G-ANBO, had by then carried the fuselage titles of five different airlines: as well as its original BOAC titling it had carried the names of Nigeria Airways, Ghana Airways, Cathay Pacific and Malayan Airways as the result of various leases over the years.

The srs 102 had never been certificated by the American Federal Aviation Authority for passenger use in the USA, and so prospects for resale in America were practically non-existent, but there was much speculation at the time that the fleet could be sold to China for operation by CAAC.

A delegation from China visited Britain for talks with BOAC, and even took a short demonstration flight in a srs 102 from London Airport, but in the end the negotiations fell through, as did those with Brazilian airline Paraense Transportes Aereos for the sale of three srs 102s. It was understood at the time that a reserve price of £150,000 per aircraft had been set, and this deterred many potential buyers. In September 1962 British United Airways had made an offer to BOAC for the entire Britannia fleet, but the price offered was considered unacceptable. In 1964 a new Peruvian airline, Compania Peruana de Aviacion, was formed with the intended aim of purchasing a Britannia (presumably from BOAC) for use

Blue-tailed srs 312 G-AOVG. Air-Britain

(*Below*) Srs 102 G-ANBO at Filton in the early white-tail BOAC colour scheme. Air-Britain

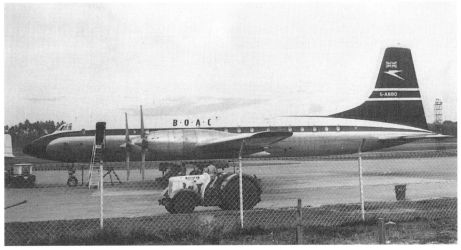

The later blue-tail colour scheme applied to srs 102 G-ANBO. Air-Britain

on domestic and international routes, but no such purchase was forthcoming.

Withdrawal of the srs 312s began in September 1963 when G-AOVT was sold to British Eagle. The final official BOAC transatlantic Britannia schedule was operated by G-AOVH on 1 March 1964 and the remainder of the fleet was progressively withdrawn as VC-10s entered service. However, several scheduled services continued to be operated from Manchester and Prestwick by srs 312s for a while, as well as transatlantic charter flights. The final BOAC Britannia 312 service was operated from Bermuda to New York by G-AOVL on 26 April 1965. This aircraft was then flown back to the UK for eventual

**BOAC VC-10 G-ARVA on lease to Nigeria Airways. The VC-10 replaced BOAC Britannias on the West African route network.** Air-Britain

**Srs 102 G-ANBF, seen here at Heathrow in the late-1950s, later served with Britannia airways.** Malcolm D. Stride

service with British Eagle, who took on the majority of the srs 312 fleet.

BOAC's total investment in the Britannia was £42m including spares, and the airline was believed to have lost in the region of £12m as a result of the fleet's premature retirement. At the time there were two reasons put forward for this large loss: the aircraft's service life had been truncated, due to delivery delays and technical problems (it was originally planned to introduce the two versions in 1955 and 1956); and BOAC had not sufficiently allowed for depreciation in their accounting.

Many BOAC pilots, although initially suspicious of the type, eventually expressed genuine regret at parting with the most 'kindly' aircraft they had flown. Captain R. Hartley, former Deputy Flight Manager of BOAC's Britannia 102 Flight, described the type as 'the best pilot's aircraft it has ever been my privilege to fly', and said that during the last few months of the Britannia's BOAC service the corporation had received 'widespread expressions of regret from the travelling public on its withdrawal from service'. Despite several mishaps the BOAC Britannia fleets had achieved an unblemished safety record, flying 5,000 million passenger miles without injuring a single passenger.

---

### The Freight Conversion Proposal

On several occasions the airline looked into the possibility of converting some of the srs 312s to an all-freight or cargo/passenger configuration, and in August 1959 Bristol produced a brochure on the Britannia 312 side-loading cargo-carrying conversion, intended for use by BOAC. This had two side-loading freight doors, the upper forward freight door on the port side being identical to that on the Britannia 252, and the aft upper freight door being identical to that on the Canadair CL-44 (see Chapter Six) and incorporating a passenger door similar to that on the all-passenger srs 312. The cabin floor would be strengthened to carry a 50,000lb (23,000kg) payload at a floor loading of 300lb per square foot (1,300kg per square metre). The timescale envisaged was seven months for design and initial manufacture and a further five months for installation. The price varied according to the number of conversions carried out, ranging from £500,000 for a single example, down to £200,000 per aircraft if ten conversions were ordered. In the end, BOAC did not proceed on cost grounds, although later operators such as British Eagle and British United were to undertake their own successful freight door conversions.

**BOAC Cargo Douglas DC-7F conversion G-AOIJ, used after a plan to convert BOAC Britannias to freighters was rejected as too costly.** Air-Britain

**A November 1961 BOAC advertisement for Britannia 102s for sale.** The late Dave Williams via Derek A. King

*(Above)* **Postcard of a BOAC srs 102 in the original 'white-tail' colour scheme.**
via Mrs M. K. Dixon

*(Above right)* **Postcard showing the later 'blue-tail' scheme adopted by the BOAC Britannia fleet.** via Mrs M. K. Dixon

*(Right)* **The A&AEE's srs 312F, XX367.** Keith Butler

*(Below)* **British Eagle srs 324 G-ARKB 'Equality' at Heathrow.** P.J.S. Pearson

*(Above)* Ghana Airways srs 319 9G-AAH at Heathrow in April 1963. P.J.S. Pearson

*(Right)* The original BKS Britannia colour scheme, worn by srs 102 G-ANBK at Heathrow in November 1964. P.J.S. Pearson

*(Below)* OK-MBA srs 318 of CSA at Heathrow in September 1962. P.J.S. Pearson

**(Top)** Air Spain srs 313 EC-BFJ landing at Palma in the late 1960s. Manfred Borchers

**(Middle)** Britannia Airways srs 102 G-ANBL at Palma in the late 1960s, with F-86s in the background. Manfred Borchers

**(Bottom)** Donaldson International srs 317 G-APNB at Palma in the early 1970s, with Grumman Albatrosses in the background. Manfred Borchers

**Britannia Airways srs
102 G-ANBJ.**
Tony Bryan

**BOAC srs 312 G-AOVH.**
Tony Bryan

**CF-CZW Canadian
Pacific srs 314 in the
later colour scheme.**
Tony Bryan

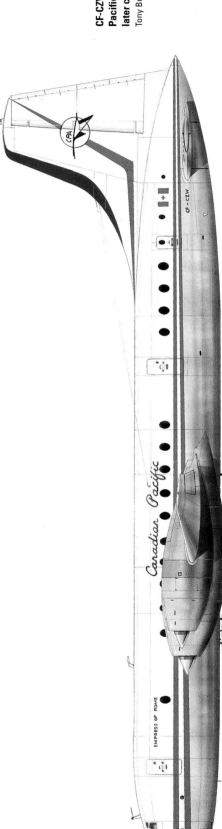

**Cubana srs 318**
**CU-P671.** Tony Bryan

**British Eagle srs 308F**
**G-ANCF.** Tony Bryan

**Caledonian Airways**
**srs 312 G-A0VJ.**
Tony Bryan

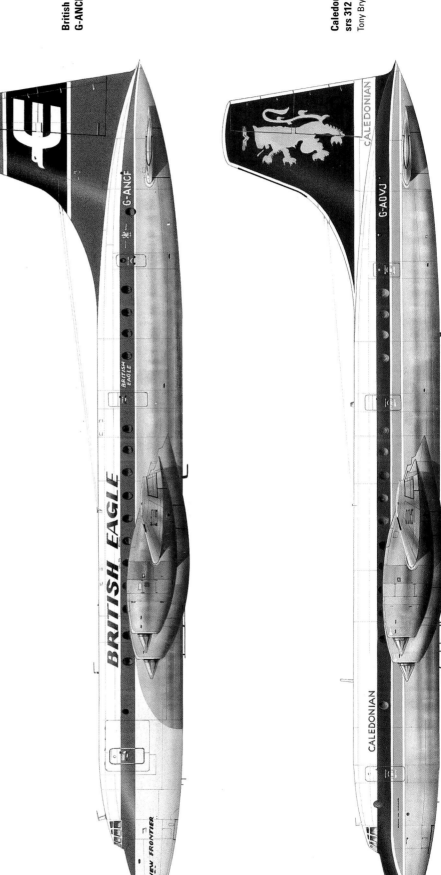

*(Top)* **Tellair srs 324 G-ARKA climbs out from Palma in the late 1960s.** Manfred Borchers    *(Middle)* **A Caledonian Airways Britannia landing at Palma in the late 1960s.** Manfred Borchers    *(Bottom)* **A Laker Airways srs 102 gets airborne from Palma in the late 1960s.** Manfred Borchers

(Above) RAF srs 253 C.1 XL657 refuelling at Mahé in the Seychelles whilst en route between Nairobi and Sharjah, 18 April 1973. John James

(Right) Srs 253 EL-WXA at Palma just before departure to Kemble on 14 October 1997. Toni Marimon

(Below) Aer Turas srs 253C EI-BBH on lease to Cyprus Airways at Basle on 7 July 1977. Eduard Marmet

**(Above)** Geminair srs 253F 9G-ACE at Luton in August 1977. Eduard Marmet

**(Left)** Srs 312 G-AOVF, preserved at Cosford Aerospace Museum in BOAC colours, May 1993. Author

**(Below)** Preserved Monarch Airlines srs 312 G-AOVT at Duxford in July 2001. Author

# CHAPTER FOUR

# Other Operators

Many airlines, large and small, operated Britannias over the years. They are presented here in alphabetical order.

## Aero Caribbean Britannia Operations

In July 1984 Cubana's last Britannia, srs 318 CU-T669, was retired and transferred to the newly formed Cuban airline Aero Caribbean. This veteran of over twenty-five years' Cuban service was ferried to Luton via Gander for overhaul and respray by Airline Engineering, and re-delivered to Cuba via Madrid on 6 July as CU-T114. In the summer of 1984 two former Afrek srs 252s, G-BDUP and G-BDUR, with freight floors and forward cargo doors, were also acquired. These, too, were sent to Airline Engineering at Luton for overhaul and respray, and on 8 August 1984 G-BDUP was ferried from Athens to Luton with her undercarriage locked down and using the nostalgic callsign 'Monarch 011'. G-BDUR followed three days later, using the callsign 'Monarch 013' – the very last Britannia to fly under a Monarch Airlines callsign. These two aircraft were the last two Britannias to be overhauled by Airline Engineering at Luton. They set off from Luton on delivery to Havana via Shannon on 6 September and 7 October as CU-T120 and CU-T121.

Once in service, one of their primary tasks seems to have been the carriage of Cuban troops and military equipment between Havana and Luanda. From June 1987 CU-T121 operated weekly livestock flights between Havana and Toronto, and in November of that year the same aircraft flew Havana–Gander–Brussels–Shannon–Gander–Havana on a cargo charter, flown by a Cubana crew. On 16 September 1989 CU-T120 flew Gander–Prague direct under flight number 'Aero Caribbean 176'. Two days later she flew from Prague to Shannon, and onwards to Toronto to collect a cargo of livestock to deliver to her home base at Havana. Due to a spares

shortage it eventually became impossible to keep all three Britannias airworthy, and the first to be retired was CU-T114, which was being used for spares by 1990. This machine had seen around thirty years of service and during that time it had only been used by Cubana and Aero Caribbean. The remaining two Britannias were retired in the spring of 1990. The final Aero Caribbean Britannia flight is believed to have been on 22 March, 1990 when CU-T120 was ferried on three engines from Guayaquil to Havana, having had to divert to Guayaquil with engine trouble the previous day during a flight from Peru to

**Aeronaves de Mexico srs 302 XA-MED.** Air-Britain

Havana. After retirement the Aero Caribbean Britannias were stored at Havana.

## Aeronaves de Mexico Operations

Aeronaves de Mexico was founded in 1934, with Pan American taking a 40 per cent stake, and in the late 1950s, after nationalization, embarked on an ambitious expansion programme, taking over many competing airlines. DC-6Bs and Constellations were used, but Aeronaves' fleet modernization programme was to lead to it becoming

the first airline in the world to operate scheduled services with srs 300 Britannias. The two srs 302s acquired were originally part of the batch of srs 300s ordered by BOAC and subsequently cancelled in favour of srs 310s. The airline's first Britannia, XA-MEC, was in fact the first production Britannia 300, and was delivered to Mexico City on 5 November 1957 after a 6,300-mile (10,000km) delivery flight from Filton via Prestwick, Goose Bay and Miami, commanded by Capt W. Daniel of Pan American World Airways. On the following day it inaugurated Aeronaves' prestigious and arduous 2,093-mile (3,370km) route between Mexico City and New York, making Aeronaves the first Britannia operator into New York, ahead of BOAC and El Al. Initially XA-MEC maintained the 6-times-weekly frequency single-handed, until XA-MED was delivered on 15 December 1957, entering service shortly afterwards. On 19 December this aircraft completed the Mexico City–New York run in 5 hours 25 minutes, a full 1 hour 20 minutes under the scheduled time, and this time was later to be reduced to 5 hours 8 minutes, an average of 401mph (645km/h).

The New York service was increased to a daily frequency, but the two Britannias

**AER srs 312 LV-JNL served the company for less than a year, being written off at Buenos Aires in July 1970.** Air-Britain

were still under-used and during 1958 they were also placed onto the airline's Mexico City–Los Angeles route. In November 1960 DC-8 jets replaced the Britannias on the New York service, but the crash of a DC-8 led to a temporary return of the Britannias, until 1 July 1962. At this time Aeronaves took over Guest Aerovias and the Britannias were placed onto the domestic service to Tijuana for the remainder of their time with the airline.

On 9 July 1965 XA-MEC was damaged beyond repair at Tijuana after a scheduled passenger flight from Mexico City. The main landing gear failed to lock into position and an emergency landing was made: there were no serious injuries to any of the nine crew members and seventy-three passengers, but the Britannia suffered damage to the engines, propeller blades, wings and fuselage. This machine was not replaced, and XA-MED maintained the Tijuana service alone until sold to Transglobe Airways in the UK in May 1966.

## Aerotransportes Rios Britannia Operations

Founded in 1962, this Argentinian operator specialized in the carriage of livestock, initially with a fleet of Constellations and Super Constellations. In October 1969 the

first production Britannia 312, G-AOVB, was bought from the receivers of British Eagle International Airlines, in whose hands it had been converted to a srs 312F freighter. The aircraft was initially registered as LV-PNJ (later changed to LV-JNL), and was used on non-scheduled cargo services from Buenos Aires to Miami with en route stops at Montevideo, Asuncion, Lima, Caracas and Panama City. However, on 12 July 1970 it was on final approach to Buenos Aires' Ezeiza Airport on a cargo flight when it came to grief. At the conclusion of the ILS/GCA approach to Runway 04 the visibility at the threshold was down to zero. Whilst attempting a go-around the Britannia veered to the left and struck the trailer of a mobile radar with its undercarriage. The aircraft struck the ground and slid for about 2,000ft (600m), fortunately without fatalities to the twelve people on board or anybody on the ground.

## Aer Turas Britannia Operations

Aer Turas Teoranta was formed in early 1962 to operate ad hoc passenger and freight charters from its base at Dublin Airport. The company's first aircraft was a De Havilland Rapide, and from this Aer Turas progressed onto DC-3, Bristol 170, DC-4,

DC-7CF and leased Argosy aircraft. With the advent of the larger types the airline began to specialize in the carriage of race-horses and other livestock. In March 1974 a DC-7CF was lost in an accident, leaving Aer Turas with just one DC-4.

The search for a replacement for the DC-7CF led eventually to a 42-month lease-purchase agreement with Monarch Airlines for a Britannia 307F, which entered Aer Turas service as EI-BAA on 29 May 1974 on a horse flight from Dublin to Milan via Luton. Further livestock flights were made in June 1974, and the following month charters were operated to Mauritania and Lagos, as well as the first two of a series of cattle-carrying services from Dublin to Greece. During August the Britannia operated its first transatlantic flight for Aer Turas, carrying a load of horses from Stansted to New York. This was followed at the end of that month by an even longer trip, a cargo charter from London via Brussels to Punta Arenas in Chile. During September another flight was operated to New York and a freight charter took EI-BAA from Liverpool to Khartoum. In mid-November the aircraft was positioned from Dublin to Abu Dhabi to begin a two-month contract with Pauling's Middle East, carrying building materials to the site of a new airfield at Midway. During this two-month period the Britannia transported nearly 2,000 tons of cargo in the course of 138 round trips. It returned to Dublin in February 1975 but was back in action at the end of the month on a series of sorties which saw it visiting Lourenço Marques, Frankfurt, Entebbe, Cairo, Rome and Kuwait. In early April it airlifted 190 tons of cigarettes from Southend to Rotterdam, and for the remainder of April and May it operated a series of seven cattle flights from Cork to Milan, as well as freight services to Khartoum, Addis Ababa, Benghazi, Sebha, Cairo and Kuwait.

Airways in 1976. A third Britannia was leased as EI-BDC in 1977, and another ex-RAF example, EI-BCI, was delivered from Airline Engineering on 29 April 1977. However, this aircraft had to return to Luton due to a technical fault, and, while parked there, 'undercarriage up' was inadvertently selected by someone. Only the nosewheel retracted, and the nose dropped onto a tow-truck, causing severe damage to the nose. After temporary repairs the aircraft was flown to Filton for more work,

retired in November 1981 and sold to Katale Aero Transport.

## Afrek Britannia Operations

Afrek was a company registered in Guernsey but operating out of Athens. Two former RAF Britannia 253s were delivered to the Athens base as G-BDUP and BDUR in June and July 1976, and were issued with restricted private Certificates of Airworthiness, as they were used in support of Afrek's own business activities. They carried cargo and personnel until February 1983, and then remained parked at Athens until they returned to the UK in 1984 for overhaul and eventual sale to Aero Caribbean.

## African Cargo Airways Britannia Operations

This airline commenced operations in 1973 and acquired the former African Safari Airways Britannia 313 5Y-ALT. It also leased Britannia 307F G-ANCD from IAS as 5Y-AYR between 1975 and 1977 and Britannia 308F G-ANCF from Invicta International as 5Y-AZP from June 1976 to January 1977. The Britannias were used on cargo charters within Africa and also to Europe, with visits being made to Luton and Manston, although some of these were for maintenance purposes. 5Y-ALT operated its last service on 22 May 1975 from Rotterdam to Stansted, where it was destined to remain and eventually serve with the fire school. African Cargo Airways ceased operations in 1977.

(*Top*) Aer Turas srs 307F EI-BAA at Manston in August 1970. Eduard Marmet

(*Above*) Aer Turas srs 253F EI-BDC, without titling and still with its former RAF fuselage stripe, at Luton in August 1977. Eduard Marmet

In September 1975 a second Britannia, a srs 253F, was acquired from the RAF, and after conversion by Airline Engineering at Luton it entered service as EI-BBH in late October, making several flights between Dublin and Venice in its first month with Aer Turas. It was also leased out to Cyprus

and returned to Airline Engineering in mid-June. The lease to Aer Turas eventually started on 31 March 1978. During 1979 EI-BBH was leased out to Gemini Air Transport, and by 1981 was the only one still operational, as DC-8-63 jets had been acquired. This machine was finally

## African Safari Airways Britannia Operations

African Safari Airways was founded in November 1967 by Karl Rudin, the founder of the now-defunct Globe Air, to operate flights to Entebbe, Mombasa and Nairobi for Swiss, Dutch and German tourists wishing to visit the African game reserves. Like Globe Air before it the new airline was based at Basle, and even used the former Globe Air headquarters building. The former Globe Air Britannia 313 was acquired in November, and was delivered from Gatwick to Zurich on 30 December as 5X-UVH (later to be re-registered as 5Y-ALT). In 1969 the former

**African Safari Airways srs 313 5X-UVH was re-registered 5Y-ALT in May 1970.** Air-Britain

**Srs 314 5Y-ALP of African Safari Airways, apparently at Biggin Hill after withdrawal in May 1971.** Air-Britain

Transglobe Britannia 314 G-ATGD was bought, and re-registered as 5Y-ALP, and Caledonian Britannia 314 G-ATMA was leased from October 1969 as 5Y-ANS. However, African Safari Airways suspended operations in 1971.

## Air Charter Ltd Britannia Operations

Air Charter had been founded by aviation entrepreneur Freddie Laker in 1947 as a charter operator based at Croydon, and was an associate company of Aviation Traders Ltd. Having previously acquired Avro Tudors built for, but now unwanted by, BOAC and successfully operated these on trooping contracts from Stansted, Mr Laker took advantage of the reduced prices being asked for the Britannia 305s and acquired his first, G-ANCE, in August 1958. Fitted with 115 rearward-facing seats and redesignated as a Britannia 307, this aircraft entered service in September 1958. On 1 October G-ANCE made the first of several trooping runs between Stansted and Christmas Island in the Pacific via Goose Bay, Vancouver and Honolulu, carrying up to 124 passengers on each trip. These flights were in connection with the use of Christmas Island as part of the British govern-

(*Above*) **African Safari Airways Britannia 314 5Y-ANS with a white tail fin.** Air-Britain

(*Right*) **Air Charter srs 307 G-ANCE at Heathrow.**
via author

(*Below*) **Air Charter srs 307 G-ANCE.** Air-Britain

ment's nuclear test programme, and the journey time was around twenty-nine hours. On 5 February 1959 G-ANCE left Stansted with 100 military passengers for Adelaide and Sydney. On the return leg 112 passengers were picked up at Christmas Island and the round-the-world flight of 26,100 miles (42,000km) was completed in seventy-two hours, with stops at Bahrain, Colombo and Singapore outbound, and San Francisco and Montreal inbound. On 18 February the Britannia was away on its travels again, leaving Stansted for Istanbul and the Far East, and returning via Brindisi on 23 February.

G-ANCD entered service on 27 May 1959 with a flight from Stansted to Lisbon, and on 26 June G-ANCE flew non-stop from Karachi to Stansted. The same aircraft left Stansted for Leopoldville in the Belgian Congo on 4 July to bring Europeans out of there to Brussels during the troubles, and returned to Stansted four days later. The Britannias were also used on Ministry of Defence trooping flights to the Gulf, Australia, Singapore, Ceylon, Canada and Hong Kong, but in June 1960 Air Charter Ltd became part of the British United Airways group and the two Britannias were transferred to BUA.

## Air Faisal Britannia Operations

Air Faisal, also operating as Air Faisel, had its base at Dubai, and in the mid-1970s acquired two former RAF Britannias, G-BDLZ (ex-XM490) and G-BEMZ (ex-XL660). These were delivered to Luton for conversion in November 1975 and February 1977, respectively. G-BDLZ operated its first service for Air Faisal on 24 December 1975, from Birmingham to the Middle East. The Britannias were used extensively on services from Dubai to points in India, especially Bombay. G-BDLZ was leased to Air Works India during 1976–77, and for part of 1978 Britannia 307F 5Y-AYR was leased in from Trans Gulf Cargo to cope with the demand for cargo charters in the region. To provide a source of spares former RAF Britannia 253 XN404 was bought, and was 'cannibalized' at Luton by Airline Engineering, who carried out maintenance there for Air Faisal and other Britannia operators. Operations to India and Europe continued until 1979, when the company ceased trading. G-BDLZ was scrapped at Luton and G-BEMZ went into open storage at Manston until purchased by Gaylan Air Cargo.

## Air Spain Britannia Operations

Air Spain was formed in May 1966, at a time when most Spanish charter airlines were using DC-6Bs and DC-7Cs, but had ambitions to operate more modern and faster equipment. Air Spain's headquarters was in Madrid but most of the flying was out of Palma. The purchase of two Britannia 312s was negotiated with British Eagle, who were also to provide crew training, and EC-WFJ (formerly G-AOVR) was handed over at Heathrow on 20 October 1966 and ferried to Spain the next day. EC-WFK (formerly G-AOVE) was delivered on 29 December 1966. Re-registered as EC-BFJ and EC-BFK, these aircraft entered service in May 1967 alongside srs 313 EC-BFL (formerly 4X-AGB with El Al).

The Britannias were able to carry a full load of holidaymakers from Helsinki to the Balearics or the Canary Islands without refuelling, and could also operate charters to Caribbean or African destinations, but entered service on a programme of inclusive-tour flights from Birmingham to Palma, Ibiza, Barcelona and Gerona. A large holiday flight programme was also undertaken from Gatwick that summer and this soon became Air Spain's major UK departure point, with services to Madrid, Palma, Malaga, Valencia and Barcelona. Holiday charters were also operated from Düsseldorf and Helsinki to Palma. At the end of the summer season the Britannias were used on ad hoc charters, including the carriage of tomatoes from Spain and the Canary Islands to the UK and West Germany. In this role they could carry up to 17 tons, and the UK destinations included Gatwick, Manston and Liverpool. During the winter of 1967–68 EC-BFJ and EC-BFK were overhauled at the Liverpool engineering base of British Eagle.

**Air Faisel srs 253 G-BDLZ in late 1975.** via author

**Air Faisal srs 253F G-BEMZ at Manston in August 1979.** Eduard Marmet

The summer 1968 inclusive-tour programme included only a few UK departures, as most of the services were operated out of Düsseldorf, Basle, Geneva and Helsinki. EC-BFL also operated a series of flights between Basle and Havana. During the winter the tomato flights to the UK resumed, with several flights each week from Alicante and Las Palmas to Gatwick, and other flights to Manston and Liverpool. The 1969 summer season saw a further reduction in Air Spain holiday charters out of the UK, with only one flight a week from Birmingham and Gatwick to Palma, and the main bulk of the programme being operated out of mainland Europe. On 2 December 1969 the former British Eagle

(*Above right*) **Air Spain srs 313 EC-BFL, formerly 4X-AGB with El Al.** Air-Britain

(*Right*) **Air Spain srs 312 EC-BFJ, probably at Biggin Hill after withdrawal from service.** Air-Britain

(*Below*) **An Air Spain Britannia at Algiers in the late 1960s.** Manfred Borchers

Britannia 312F G-AOVM was handed over to Air Spain at Luton as EC-BSY. The tomato flights resumed for the winter of 1969–70, and by the time the contract ended on 21 April 1970 a total of forty-nine round trips had been made to Liverpool from Las Palmas, Tenerife and Alicante. For the summer 1970 season a new UK departure point, Belfast, was introduced. The inaugural service to Palma was operated by EC-BFL on 17 May 1970 and services to Barcelona and Gerona were also flown from Belfast throughout the summer. Belfast departures were re-introduced for the summer of 1971 but on a much reduced scale, with only a fortnightly flight to Palma, and this was Air Spain's only regular service from a UK airport that summer.

The freighter Britannia, EC-BSY, only appeared on a handful of UK services and was the first of the type to be withdrawn when it was sold to the Aircraft and Armament Experimental Establishment at Boscombe Down in November 1971. By this time Air Spain had bought DC-8-21 jets, and two of the remaining three Britannias had been placed in storage by early 1973. The last operational Air Spain Britannia appears to have been EC-BFJ, which was still airworthy in early 1973. Eventually, all three were sold to International Aviation Services for spares. EC-BFJ was flown to Biggin Hill for scrapping in April 1973, and the other two were broken up at Palma and their remains transported by surface to the UK.

## AMAZ Britannia Operations

AMAZ (Agence et Mesageries Aerienne Du Zaire) acquired former RAF Britannia 253 XM517 in November 1975 and re-registered it as 9Q-CAJ. It arrived in Brussels on 15 November 1975 on its delivery flight from Luton to Zaire, but at this point the financing for the sale fell through and the aircraft never entered AMAZ service, returning instead to Luton where Airline Engineering registered it as G-BEPX and used it as an earthbound Proteus test-bed. The fuselage aft of the wings was removed, as were the outer wings and outboard engines. In this condition the remains of the Britannia were used for ground running of overhauled Proteus engines, including some taxying! Once the volume of Proteus overhauls declined, the contraption was withdrawn, being scrapped at Luton in the spring of 1980.

**AMAZ srs 253F wearing dual registrations 9Q-CAJ and G-BEPX at Luton in August 1977.** Eduard Marmet

## BCF Aviation Britannia Operations

In 1988 Business Cash Flow Aviation (BCF Aviation) acquired Britannia 253 9Q-CDT and Britannia 312 9Q-CHY from Katale Aero Transport. 9Q-CDT was used for spares, but srs 312 9Q-CHY was placed in service on the route from Kinshasa to Mbuji-Mayi. This took about two hours each way and was usually flown once daily. Seventeen passenger seats were fitted in the rear of the cabin, and cargo was also carried. The aircraft was repainted with a white fuselage top, a blue cheatline and a black, yellow and red tail motif. Ad hoc charters were also performed by 9Q-CHY, which became the world's only operational Britannia in March 1990. By this time it was suffering frequent technical delays and in-flight engine shut-downs. On 5 July 1991, whilst en route to Mbuji-Mayi, one engine was shut down due to a loss of oil pressure and it returned to Kinshasa. The journey was resumed the next day, when an oil leak developed in a different engine but the Britannia continued to its intended destination. During the return leg oil supply problems with all four engines were indicated but a safe landing was made at Kinshasa. The aircraft was then grounded pending further investigations into the problem and the owner of BCF Aviation, Dr Mayani, announced that a lack of serviceable Proteus engines had forced him to put the Britannia up for sale.

## BKS Air Transport Britannia Operations

BKS Air Transport was founded in February 1952 as BKS Aero Charter, a DC-3 operator based at Southend. The company took its initials from the surnames of its three founders, and changed its name when a network of scheduled services was built up. Airspeed Ambassadors were acquired and were also used on holiday charter flights on behalf of Airway Holidays. Worried by the increasing competition from Euravia and its Constellations, Airway Holidays decided that it needed bigger and faster aircraft for its Newcastle-based tour network. As a result, one of the BOAC Britannias that had been in store at Cambridge since December 1962 was leased for one year by Airway Holidays for operation on their behalf by BKS. This machine, registered, appropriately, G-ANBK, was ferried to Heathrow for overhaul and repainting, and flew again on 9 April 1964 in BKS colours. BKS was the first airline to buy former BOAC Britannia 102s, and was also to be the last operator of that series. The hire-purchase agreement between BOAC and Airway Holidays required an initial payment of £10,000 on signature of the contract on 17 March 1964, a further £20,000 on delivery and then monthly instalments of £544.9.0 for 36 months. The total purchase price of the aircraft and spares was £215,000. The contract also contained an option for Airway

(*Above*) BKS srs 102 G-ANBK, wearing British Air Services titling, at Heathrow North Side. Air-Britain

(*Right*) BKS Britannia 102 G-APLL was originally registered G-ANBG in its early days with BOAC. Air-Britain

(*Below*) BKS srs 102 G-ANBD at Heathrow North Side in the late 1960s. Air-Britain

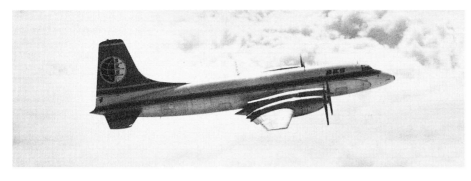

**Air-to-air studies of BKS srs 102 G-APLL.** David Jones

**An unusual view of a BKS Britannia 102 in the original colour scheme at Heathrow in 1964.** Captain Arthur Whitlock

Holidays to buy BOAC's last Britannia 102 for £160,000 if required.

After crew training at Shannon G-ANBK flew the inaugural BKS Britannia service on 24 April 1964, a scheduled service from Newcastle to Heathrow. It subsequently flew thrice-daily scheduled services between Newcastle and Heathrow on weekdays and inclusive-tour charters from Newcastle to Barcelona, Palma and Rimini at weekends. In order to gain maximum utilization on the holiday flights the cabin configuration was soon increased to 112 seats in a high-density layout. During the winter the inclusive-tour flights were suspended, but other work was found, including a series of leisurely 'aerial cruises' to Mediterranean and North African points such as Seville, Marrakesh and Tenerife. These services left Heathrow each Saturday morning throughout the winter and returned there the following Saturday, the aircraft and crew having stayed with the passengers throughout the trip.

On 11 March 1965 a second Britannia (G-ANBH) was delivered to Newcastle and that summer the inclusive-tour programme was expanded to include flights to Barcelona, Palma and Rimini from Heathrow, Newcastle and the newly-opened Teesside Airport. The frequency on the Heathrow–Newcastle scheduled service was increased to five flights each weekday, although some of these were still operated by Ambassadors. Britannias were also used occasionally on the Heathrow to Teesside route, which BKS had started with Ambassadors in November 1964. On 4 June 1965 BKS Britannias inaugurated a four-times weekly London–Biarritz service in association with BEA.

From 31 October 1965 to 1 April 1966 Woolsington Airport at Newcastle was closed for runway extension and servicing, and during this period RAF Ouston was used instead. This could only accommodate Ambassadors, so the Britannias were redeployed on a twice-daily Heathrow–Teesside service. With the reopening of Woolsington the Britannias returned, and were also used on services from Newcastle to Jersey and Belfast. In the meantime, two more Britannias, G-APLL and G-ANBD, had been delivered. 'Winter sun' flights were operated from Heathrow and Newcastle to Alicante, Gerona, Ibiza and Malaga, and for the winter of 1967–68 winter sports charters were operated to Turin, Zurich and Munich. On 17 December 1967 G-ANBK inaugurated a weekly departure to Munich, which involved no fewer than three Britannias, departing Heathrow each Sunday at twenty-minute intervals.

The summer of 1968 saw G-ANBD go on lease to Britannia Airways for the season, but the end of that summer also saw the first retirement of a BKS Britannia. During 1967 BKS had become part of the British Air Services Group, along with Cambrian Airways, and two Trident 1Es originally intended for Channel Airways were bought in 1968. On 25 October 1968 G-ANBH flew flight BK455 from Newcastle to Heathrow, its final revenue-earning flight, and was then ferried to Southend for scrapping. G-APLL was retired on 21 February 1969 after a Heathrow–Newcastle service, and was scrapped at Newcastle in April. G-ANBD had already been flown to Southend for storage on 1 October 1968, at the end of its Britannia Airways lease, but was placed back into service in British Air Services livery in February 1969, pending delivery of the Tridents. By April 1969 both of these had been delivered and the two surviving Britannias were relegated to off-peak scheduled services and lower-density inclusive-tour flights. In October 1969 G-ANBK was temporarily withdrawn at Newcastle, and on 12 January 1970 G-ANBD flew her last passenger-carrying flight, Heathrow–Newcastle, before being withdrawn and scrapped. However, G-ANBK was not quite finished. She was overhauled at Newcastle and re-entered service on 16 December 1970 carrying the operator's new name, Northeast Airlines. This aircraft was the last Britannia 102 flying anywhere in the world, but on 31 December 1971 she flew the airline's final Britannia flight, NS442 from Heathrow to Newcastle, before being withdrawn and scrapped.

## Britannia Airways Britannia Operations

During 1964 the holiday charter airline Euravia began to look for a turbine-powered replacement for its elderly Constellations and this search eventually led to the purchase of several of the retired BOAC Britannia 102s, which had spent some time in storage at Cambridge. Under the terms of the deal Euravia was able to buy six srs 102s for about £1m including 'special to srs 102' spares – less than the cost of a single new srs 310. In addition, about £100,000-worth of other spares were bought. The aircraft came equipped with

ninety-two seats, but were converted to 112-seaters by Scottish Aviation, who also removed the forward lavatories and fitted a new emergency exit door aft. The BOAC Gaby Schreiber-designed interior livery of turquoise, grey and lemon was retained. The aircraft were delivered with 'Check

(*Top*) **Britannia Airways srs 102 G-ANBO, with a Constellation in Euravia markings in the background.** Air-Britain

**Srs 102 G-ANBA served with Britannia Airways from March 1965 to November 1969.**
Air-Britain

Fours' overhauls carried out by BOAC, but the repainting was carried out by the airline itself. Two more Britannia 102s were to follow later from the same source, but before that, on 16 August 1964, the airline was renamed Britannia Airways in anticipation of the introduction of the new aircraft, and to reflect a perceived mood of pro-Britishness in the country at the time.

The first example, G-ANBB, was delivered to the airline's Luton base on 18 November 1964, and this machine flew the airline's first turboprop service on 6 December from Luton to Tenerife, the first time a Britannia had landed at the island's Los Rodeos Airport. In command of the flight was Britannia's Chief Pilot, Captain Derek Davidson, who had already amassed 1,600 flying hours on Britannias with El Al. On the Tenerife flight, and assigned to the airline throughout the Britannia conversion process, was one of the Ministry of Aviation's team of nine flight inspectors. All of Britannia's twenty-four pilots were converted onto the new type, with Constellation-

## Britannia Airways

The predecessor of Britannia Airways was Euravia, which was established in 1961 by Captain Ted Langton, the founder of the holiday company Universal Sky Tours. Several of the charter airlines he had been using, such as Falcon Airways and Air Safaris, had either collapsed or had a poor reputation for reliability, and he was worried about this reflecting on the reputation of his own business. He decided that the only way to control the air travel component of his holidays was to set up his own airline and so with his associate Jed Williams, a London aviation consultant, he paid £90,000 for three Constellations, fully overhauled, from El Al Israel Airlines. Another key figure in the new airline was Captain J. C. Harrington, a former Deputy Operations Director of BOAC, and later Service Manager of Bristol. Appointed Chief Pilot and Operations Manager was Captain Derek Davidson, formerly an El Al Britannia captain.

A base was established at Luton Airport, which at that time could not accommodate even a single Constellation-load of passengers in its tiny terminal building, but which offered great scope for expansion and good transport links to London via the new M1 motorway. Euravia operated its first commercial service on 5 May 1962, from Manchester to Palma via Perpignan. Three months later the independent airline Skyways folded and Euravia took over its three Constellations. By 1963 new departure points such as Newcastle had been added and the company was already looking to replace the Constellations. The redundant BOAC Britannia 102s provided the answer and the company name was changed to reflect the new equipment and the new image. The International Thomson Organisation conglomerate was seeking to enter the package

holiday market at the time and bought Universal Sky Tours and its airline subsidiary in 1965. The Britannias were replaced by brand-new Boeing 737-200s, but only after a protracted sales battle which almost saw Britannia Airways buying BAC One-Eleven srs 500s instead. It was hoped to have the 737s in service in time for the 1968 summer season, but production delays at Boeing meant that the first did not arrive at Luton until 8 July. As a result, Britannia had to lease Britannia 102s from other carriers, paid for by Boeing!

A total of thirty-one 737s were bought new from Boeing, with the last one being delivered on 23 March 1983. In addition to European inclusive-tour charters, they were also used on charters to Far East destinations such as Singapore, Kuala Lumpur and Hong Kong, and on trooping flights to Germany. During 1971 a short-lived boom in afffinity-group charters to North America saw the introduction of two leased Boeing 707-320s. By that time Britannia Airways was the second biggest independent airline in Britain, with a turnover in excess of £11.5 million. The search for a larger-capacity replacement for the 737s led eventually to the purchase of Boeing 767s, with the first example being delivered in February 1984. The last of the original 737s was retired in 1994. However, in 2001 the 'new-generation' Boeing 737-800 was being operated alongside 757s and 767s by Britannia in the UK and its subsidiaries in Germany and Scandinavia. In September of that year it was announced that Thomson Holidays and its airline subsidiary Britannia Airways were to be rebranded as TUI, the name of the leisure group's German parent company, and that the aircraft fleet was eventually to be repainted without the Britannia name or the trademark figure of Britannia on the tailfins

**Srs 102 G-ANBB, seen here at Luton, operated the first Britannia Airways service by the type, but was destroyed near Ljubljana in 1966.**
Britannia Airways

to-Britannia conversion taking up to ten hours, followed by 60–70 hours training 'on the routes'. Classroom training and some simulator time was bought from BOAC. By the summer of 1965 five 112-seat Britannias were in service, cutting over an hour from the flying time on most routes. Luton–Palma, for example, took six hours for the round trip, compared to eight hours with the Constellations.

Not all Britannia flights were uneventful. Captain Andre Jeziorski gained the distinction of being the only Britannia Airways pilot to have flown a Britannia on just two engines, both on the same wing. During a service to Venice, propeller trouble had developed on one of the outboard engines and he was eventually given permission to ferry the aircraft back to Luton on three engines. Unfortunately, just before Paris was reached, the adjacent inboard engine also developed problems, but he continued onwards on two engines to make a safe landing at Luton, in crosswinds and rain. The Britannias were also used on Haj pilgrimage flights on behalf of

Iran Air, returning pilgrims from Jeddah to Teheran, Shiraz and Abadan, and on similar work for Royal Air Maroc.

For the summer of 1966 the fleet had grown to eight aircraft, but one of these was lost in the early hours of 1 September 1966 when G-ANBB, operating flight BY105 from Luton, crashed shortly before touchdown at Ljubljana in Yugoslavia as a result of an incorrect altimeter setting. Out of the 110 passengers and seven crew aboard, only eighteen passengers and one crew member survived, making this the worst accident involving a British transport aircraft at that time.

For the 1968 summer season the capacity of the Britannias was increased to 117 seats and a programme of flights to Bulgaria, Greece, Italy, North Africa, Spain, Turkey and Yugoslavia was operated. Boeing 737 jets had been ordered, but because of their late delivery additional Britannias had to be leased from Laker Airways and BKS to meet the demand for flights. The Britannias were also to be seen on ad hoc charters to North America, affinity-group charters from Luton to the Far East and Ministry of Defence trooping flights to Germany and Northern Ireland.

At the end of the 1969 season the Britannias began to be withdrawn, but in the summer of 1970 four of them were still in service alongside the 737s. These were used for ad hoc charters, Ministry of Defence trooping flights and weekly services from many UK airports to Munich for the Oberammergau Festival. At the end of the 1970 season, however, the remaining Britannias were withdrawn. G-ANBL flew the last service, from Luton to Genoa and back on 29 December 1970, and all the surviving examples were broken up at Luton during 1970–71.

## British Eagle Britannia Operations

### Eagle and Cunard-Eagle

The first of many Britannias to be operated by Eagle Airways (and later Cunard-Eagle and British Eagle) was srs 318 G-APYY, which was delivered on a seven-month lease from Cubana on 5 April 1960. On the following day it went into service in a 104-seat configuration, operating a trooping flight from London to Christmas Island in the Pacific. On 28 July 1960 the airline was renamed Cunard-

Eagle Airways Ltd, following a buyout by the Cunard Steamship Co. For most of the summer G-APYY was used on Air Ministry trooping flights, although the occasional ad hoc sub-charter was operated, such as a Trans-Canada Air Lines sub-charter (flight EG419) from London to Gander via Manchester and Prestwick, returning via Halifax and Prestwick.

On 10 October 1960 G-APYY inaugurated Cunard-Eagle's low-fare, low-frequency 'Skycoach' service to Bermuda and Nassau. This was operated in conjunction with BOAC in alternate months, with BOAC Britannia 312s operating in between to complete a combined monthly frequency, although the two airlines operated in competition and did not pool their revenue from the services. The service was actually operated by Cunard-Eagle Airways (Bermuda) Ltd, who chartered the aircraft from the parent company, which also provided flight and cabin crews. This was followed on 15 October by a fortnightly London–Bermuda–Nassau–Miami service, also in conjunction with BOAC, but this time with the Britannia seating eighteen First Class and ninety-one Economy Class passengers. The service was upgraded to a weekly basis from 4 March 1961, when the seating arrangement was changed again, this time to accommodate fourteen First Class, sixty-six Economy Class and eighteen Skycoach passengers. The London–Nassau Skycoach

return fare was set at £162 and was restricted to British residents, but was in fact undercut by a seventeen-day offpeak excursion fare between Bermuda and London of £114.6.0 return, which was £40.1.0 cheaper than the normal economy return fare on propeller airliners and £85.1.0 cheaper than the return fare on jets.

The lease on G-APYY was extended until the end of the 1961 season and the hard-worked aircraft was joined in March and May 1961 by G-ARKA and G-ARKB, two srs 324s leased from Canadian Pacific. The Britannias were also used on a charter programme to New York via Montreal, as subsidiary Cunard-Eagle (Bermuda) held traffic rights between Montreal and New York, and the flights could thus be operated without the US Civil Aeronautics Bureau (CAB) permit that would otherwise be required. Cunard-Eagle's main aim, however, had been to become a North Atlantic scheduled service operator, and when this

**Cunard-Eagle's srs 318 G-APYY, leased from Cubana, and the first Eagle Britannia.**
Air-Britain

did not come to fruition Cunard entered into secret talks with BOAC, which led to the formation of BOAC-Cunard and left Cunard-Eagle with only a few European scheduled services and its charter flights with which to occupy its large fleet of various types. On 14 February 1963 Eagle Airways' founder, Harold Bamberg, bought back Cunard's shareholding in the airline and on 9 August it was renamed British Eagle International Airlines.

**Cunard-Eagle srs 324 G-ARKB in the early 1960s.** via author

(*Below*) **Cover of a British Eagle flight information brochure.** Author's collection

## British Eagle Appears

In August 1963 British Eagle achieved a breakthrough by becoming the first British independent airline to be granted a licence to operate scheduled passenger services in direct competition with the state airline BEA. Approval was granted for services from Heathrow to Glasgow, Edinburgh and Belfast, and on 3 November 1963 the Heathrow–Glasgow route was inaugurated by former BOAC Britannia 312 G-AOVT, configured to accommodate sixteen First Class and eighty-seven Tourist Class passengers, attended to by six cabin crew. 'Trickle loading' was introduced at Glasgow, allowing passengers to select their seat at check-in and then board the aircraft instead of waiting in a departure lounge. Full meals were served on flights at the appropriate times, and the airline's sales literature proclaimed that 'Plastic glasses and cutlery will not be used on any British

Eagle flights, only real glasses and attractive cutlery. Wedgewood china and fine quality glassware will be used in the First Class cabin'. On the following day Britannia 312 G-AOVT opened the route to Edinburgh, with Belfast services also being started by G-AOVB. In November 1963 British Eagle signed an initial co-operation agreement with Liverpool-based Starways, leading to a full take-over of that airline's route network (but not its fleet) on 31 December. A new subsidiary, British Eagle (Liverpool), was set up to operate the former Starways routes and an engineering base was established at Liverpool, where many of the Britannia overhauls were carried out. On 1 January 1964 srs 312 G-AOVT introduced a once-daily Britannia service on the Liverpool–Heathrow route, with the other daily services being operated by Viscounts. In February 1964 G-AOVO inaugurated a new scheduled service between Heathrow and Innsbruck.

During early 1964 work started on the conversion to convertible cargo/passenger configuration of the two former Transcontinental SA Britannia 308s, which had been bought in 1963. Both airframes were in excellent condition, despite their storage in the open, having been virtually non-operational for the previous two years. Only LV-GJC, which had stood at Idlewild Airport, New York, for almost three years, showed any sign of external corrosion, and this was purely superficial. The work on the first example, which became G-ANCF, took 67,000 man-hours in five and a half months to complete by British Eagle's own engineers, supported and supervised by the Bristol division of the British Aircraft Corporation. A 12 × 8ft (3.66 × 2.44m) section of the forward port-side fuselage was removed and replaced by a new section incorporating the new freight door. Two spare Britannia 252 cargo door panels were bought from an Air Ministry store and fitted, the crew entry door was repositioned, and a new freight floor, made from ordinary marine plywood, was fitted. When the work was completed, G-ANCF was the first Britannia to have the 6 × 7ft 4in (1.83 × 2.24m) cargo door. The work was estimated to have cost £150,000, but the experience gained enabled the same work to be carried out on G-ANCG for much less. After conversion these aircraft could carry up to 132 passengers or 36,000lb (16,300kg) of freight, or any combination of these. They replaced DC-6Cs, and later a Britannia 324 without a freight door, on London–Adelaide Ministry of Defence contract work, supporting the guided weapons test range at Woomera in Australia, with G-ANCF entering service on 2 July 1964. Several more srs 312s were acquired from BOAC, along with the unique srs 319 in April, bringing the total number of Britannias joining the British Eagle fleet between January and June 1964 to ten.

However, G-AOVO, the aircraft that had inaugurated the London–Innsbruck scheduled service in February, was lost whilst operating this route a few weeks later, hitting Mount Glungetzer whilst descending into Innsbruck on 29 February 1964, with the loss of all eighty-three on board. The Austrian investigation into the accident concluded that the primary cause of the accident was 'the erroneous decision on the part of the pilot in command, in the weather conditions obtaining, to descend below the stipulated minimum safe altitude, as a result of which he was unable to conduct the flight in accordance with visual flight rules'. At the time, Innsbruck had no instrument approach facilities and was generally regarded as one of the most difficult airports in Europe. Over the past seventeen months British Eagle had made ninety-one Britannia flights into Innsbruck, and in the past ten months there had been seven diversions, all to Munich.

During the summer of 1964 the Britannias flew inclusive-tour charters from Heathrow and Manchester to many destinations including Alghero, Palma and Rimini, and also appeared on scheduled services from Heathrow to Dinard and La Baulle, but that year trooping work became the backbone of British Eagle's year-round operations. The airline was awarded a two-year contract, formerly held by British United Airways, for five-weekly round trips to Singapore and Hong Kong. Rearward-facing seats were installed in the Britannias, which were then called 'Troopmasters' by the airline, and 28,000 personnel were carried

Srs 312 G-AOVE stands outside the BOAC engineering base at Heathrow in basic British Eagle colours but without titles. Air-Britain

British Eagle srs 324 G-ARKB at Luton. Air-Britain

British Eagle srs 312 G-AOVN. Air-Britain

annually on these services. The first left Heathrow on 10 May 1964, and the journey took 25 hours to Singapore or 26 hours to Hong Kong. Three Britannias were permanently allocated to Far East trooping flights. Other trooping contracts held at this time covered flights to Malta and Akrotiri, as well as the regular services to Adelaide.

A change of government in 1964 brought about a more restrictive approach to the independent airlines' participation

(*Top*) **British Eagle srs 312 G-AOVK outside the airline's Heathrow engineering base.** Air-Britain

(*Above*) **British Eagle's freighter Britannia srs 308F G-ANCF in late 1964.** Air-Britain

(*Right*) **British Eagle srs 312 G-AOVG 'Bounteous' at Liverpool in the late 1960s.** via author

(*Below*) **Former CPAL srs 324 G-ARKA at the British Eagle base at Heathrow in the late 1960s.** via author

in scheduled services, and as a result British Eagle abandoned its routes from London to Glasgow, Edinburgh and Belfast in February 1965. However, a few months later it returned to the Heathrow–Glasgow route with Britannias furnished with only eighty-seven seats. G-AOVL re-opened the route on the evening of 4 July 1965, with the airline's publicity promising 'free seat selection, high standards of personal attention and a delicious hot meals service'. The Edinburgh route remained suspended, but srs 324 G-ARKB re-started the Heathrow–Belfast service on 1 November 1965.

On the trooping flight front, G-AOVB had a lucky escape at Gan, in the Maldive

Islands, whilst inbound from Bahrain with 112 passengers and eight crew aboard on 10 October 1965. A heavy landing in poor weather conditions caused the aircraft to bounce back into the air, but the initial impact had caused the crash inertia switches to operate, shutting off the fuel supply to the engines. The Britannia landed to the right of Gan's main runway and the nosewheel collapsed on contact with the ground, but there were no injuries to anyone aboard.

The summer of 1965 also saw British Eagle return to transatlantic charter work, with seventy-eight flights being completed during the season. The following year this total was increased to 139 and an extensive inclusive-tour programme was also operated out of Heathrow with Britannias. An expanded fleet of seventeen aircraft was in service during 1966, and each aircraft logged over 1 million miles (1.6 million km) that year.

On 20 April 1967 Britannia 308F G-ANCG encountered problems after taking off from Heathrow for a government passenger charter to Adelaide via Kuwait. The undercarriage would not lock in the 'up' position and the crew tried recycling the gear a few times. On the third attempt the bogie, which was not rotating in the correct sequence, fouled the main hydraulic jack, fracturing the attachment bolt of the shuttle valve for the main and emergency 'down' hydraulic lines. All the hydraulic fluid escaped and the gear could not be extended any more. After circling for almost five hours to burn off fuel whilst attempting to cure the problem, Captain Chubb elected to make an emergency wheels-up landing on a bed of foam at Manston. There were no fatalities among the sixty-five on board, but after this incident the aircraft was withdrawn from use.

**A British Eagle Britannia on final approach.** via author

**British Eagle srs 312 G-AOVM 'Team Spirit'.** Air-Britain

## The Final Years

The transatlantic charters continued in 1967 and during the following winter the Britannias began flying tourists to East Africa, but 1968 was not to be a good year for British Eagle's Britannia fleet. On 31 March the trooping contracts to Singapore and Hong Kong were ended. Boeing 707s had been acquired for use on the transatlantic charters, and so new work had to be found for the Britannias. New inclusive-tour routes were opened from Heathrow and one aircraft was based in West Berlin on weekdays during the summer to carry

passengers for German tour operators. Many one-off charters were also sought out and flown. However, British Eagle was now in deep financial difficulties and in October 1968 the engineering base at Liverpool was closed down and all engineering work apart from routine turnaround checks was transferred to Heathrow. In the space of eighteen days, four Britannias were flown into storage at Liverpool. A last cargo charter into Liverpool, carrying tomatoes, was flown by G-AOVM on 2 November, but another consignment due to arrive on 5 November was diverted to Heathrow.

Finally, on the evening of 6 November 1968 British Eagle suddenly announced that all flying would cease at midnight.

This was not quite the end of British Eagle Britannia operations however. The last commercial movement was the arrival back at Heathrow on 7 November of G-AOVM with a cargo of oranges from Israel, but there was still one more Britannia to come home. On 4 November 'Bish' Bishop, one of British Eagle's training captains and a former RAF Britannia captain, had commanded G-AOVG on an empty ferry leg from Heathrow to Rotterdam to pick up passengers for flight EG4680 to Paramaribo in Suriname, South America. A refuelling stop was to be made at Santa Maria in the Azores in each direction, and for such a long trip an additional captain and flight engineer were carried, and crew rest bunks fitted. A nine-hour flight from Santa Maria

saw the Britannia arrive at Paramaribo at 1040hr on 5 November and the crew retired to a hotel in the town for some relaxation and a night's sleep before the return journey. After another day in town the crew took G-AOVG out of Paramaribo at 1915hr on 6 November, bound for Santa Maria, Rotter-

dam and London. After another nine-hour flight Santa Maria was reached and the crew went into the airport buildings to plan the next leg to Rotterdam. It was while they were in the handling agent's office that the first officer spotted a piece of paper which he stealthily passed to Captain Bishop. It was a telex from Pan American World Airways in New York, addressed to all their outstations, and read 'British Eagle International Airways ceased operations 1630 06 Nov 68 – all credit facilities withdrawn.' Fortunately, the handling agent had apparently not had time to read it, and so it was hastily disposed of before he could. The Captain signed the bill for the airport charges and the crew broke all records in starting the Britannia and taking off before permission was refused. Once over Northern France a radio call on the company frequency confirmed the bad news and advised the crew to drop their passengers at Rotterdam as planned and then proceed to Heathrow. On arrival at Rotterdam the airport manager padlocked the Britannia's throttles and announced that the aircraft was impounded pending settlement of outstanding bills totalling £3,000. Luckily, the aircraft charterer was still at Rotterdam Airport and Captain Bishop was able to persuade him to pay the bills, deducting that amount from the charter fee still owed to British Eagle. All the aggrieved parties were amenable to this apart from the Esso representative, who would only accept cash in hand, and so Captain Bishop finally paid him £108 in travellers cheques from the crew travelling allowance to secure 800gal (3,600ltr) of fuel – the minimum quantity needed to fly to Heathrow. The Britannia was released to the crew, but whilst taxying there came one final moment of anxiety. The tower radioed 'Victor Golf, there is a message from Amsterdam asking for you to return to the apron – you don't want to do that, do you?' On receiving a reply in the negative the tower radioed 'Roger, Victor Golf, you are clear to go'. At 2130hr on 7 November 1968 G-AOVG taxied onto its stand at Heathrow – the last aircraft movement of British Eagle International Airlines. During its history the airline had owned or leased twenty-three different Britannias.

**Srs 313 G-ARXA 'Liberty' was leased by British Eagle from El Al from May 1966 to November 1968.** Air-Britain

---

### British Eagle International Airlines

On 14 April 1948 Harold Bamberg registered Eagle Aviation as an air charter company with a capital of £100. He bought a fleet of Halifax freighter conversions and on 26 August 1948 began operations out of Wunsdorf on the Berlin Airlift. In October 1949 Avro Yorks replaced the Halifaxes and these carried out many notable long-distance passenger and freight charters. Regular contract flights on behalf of the Air Ministry started in August 1951, but in November 1952 the Yorks and the Air Ministry contract were sold to Skyways. A decision had been made to concentrate on short-haul work and DC-3s had been acquired. At first these were used for charters, but in March 1953 Eagle was awarded its first scheduled service licence, for passenger flights from its new base at Blackbushe Airport to Belgrade via Munich. This route was inaugurated on 6 June 1953 using Vickers Vikings, the first international scheduled passenger service to be operated by a British independent airline since the war. A new company, Eagle Airways, was set up to operate scheduled services, and a large fleet of Vickers Vikings was built up to fly both scheduled and charter flights. Turboprop aircraft followed on 23 December 1957 with the delivery of Eagle's first Viscount. After a few months of operations from the UK the Viscount was despatched across the Atlantic to open a new service between Bermuda and New York for subsidiary Eagle Airways (Bermuda).

A takeover by the Cunard Steamship Company, resulting in a change of name to Cunard-Eagle Airways, and a change of operating base to Heathrow, followed in 1960, and long-haul aircraft in the shape of DC-6Cs and Britannias enabled the airline to operate services throughout the world once more. In February 1962 Cunard-Eagle took

delivery of the first of two Boeing 707s that had been ordered in anticipation of a London–New York route licence being awarded. However, BOAC's objections to this licence were eventually upheld and on 15 May 1962 the first 707 inaugurated a London–Bermuda–Nassau service instead. This was to be short-lived, as Cunard joined forces with BOAC and formed BOAC-Cunard to operate long-haul services on 20 June 1962. The service to Bermuda and Nassau and the 707s were transferred to the new airline, leaving Cunard-Eagle with just some European scheduled services and charter flights.

On 14 February 1963 Harold Bamberg bought back control of the airline and severed all links with Cunard. The company was renamed British Eagle International Airlines on 9 August 1963 and that November opened scheduled services between Heathrow, Edinburgh, Glasgow and Belfast with ex-BOAC Britannia 312s. During the same month Liverpool-based Starways was acquired and a large fleet of Britannias and Viscounts was built up. In 1966 British Eagle became one of the first operators of the BAC One-Eleven, using them on both European scheduled services and inclusive-tour charters. Boeing 707s returned to the fleet in the summer of 1968 when two former QANTAS srs 138s were used on package holiday flights to the Caribbean, but 1968 was to be British Eagle's final year of operation. Trooping contracts had come to an end, as had a long-standing QANTAS sub-contract to fly emigrants to Australia. Much inclusive-tour work had been lost and in November the licences to Nassau and Bermuda were revoked. British Eagle ceased operations on the evening of 6 November 1968. As related in the main text, the last movements were operated by Bristol Britannias.

---

## British United Airways Britannia Operations

British United Airways was formed on 1 July 1960 by the merger of the Airwork group and Hunting-Clan Air Transport Ltd, and their subsidiaries. Among many other types, the combined fleet included two former Air Charter Britannia 307s and two ex-Hunting-Clan Britannia 317s. All four were initially based at Stansted for trooping flights to Hong Kong, Singapore, Nairobi, Aden, Cyprus, Malta, and several bases in West Germany including Gütersloh and Wildenrath.

Within a few weeks of the formation of British United one of the new airline's Britannias was involved in an incident when it was forced to land at Ankara after it had reportedly overflown a prohibited military zone. The Britannia was carrying 103 servicemen and their families, and eleven crew members, and was allowed to resume its journey after the pilot had been briefly questioned by the Turkish authorities. The pilot had reportedly said earlier that he had been unable to follow his assigned course because of bad weather.

In 1961 two Britannias were relocated to Gatwick for use on scheduled services to East Africa. This left BUA short of trooping capacity, so two srs 312s (G-AOVE and G-AOVI) were leased from BOAC from 1961 until 1964 for this purpose. G-AOVE was delivered to BUA just off a Check 4, with 8,811 flying hours, and repainted by BOAC in BUA colours. The interior had also been redecorated by BOAC, although BUA put their own seats in it. G-AOVI came with a Check One, with 8,888 hours flown, but without a respray or interior refurbishment.

The aquisition of the leased BOAC srs 312s for trooping flights released BUA's own two srs 317s, with their water-injection Proteus 765 engines, for use on African services, and after refurbishment the 87-seat Britannias replaced Viscounts on 2 October 1961 on BUA's low-fare 'Skycoach' services to East Africa and Central Africa in partnership with BOAC, while Viscounts took over from Britannias on the trooping flights to Germany. The Britannia 317s were also used to inaugurate non-stop services from Gatwick to Freetown on behalf of Sierra Leone Airways, on 16 November 1961. Unique in being the only civil Britannias with water injection, these machines had the necessary 'hot and high' performance to operate the 2,646nm (4,904km) leg nonstop. The Britannias were configured to carry sixty-four Economy Class and sixteen First Class passengers on the weekly service. Three Sierra Leone Airways stewardesses in national dress were carried, and the aircraft

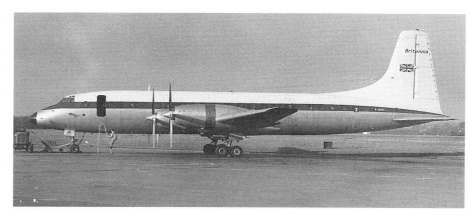

**British United srs 312 G-AOVI without fuselage titling.** Air-Britain

**Srs 317 G-APNB, seen in the original British United colour scheme at Gatwick.** Air-Britain

**Srs 309 G-ANCH was leased by British United from Ghana Airways from May 1964 to October 1966.** via author

wore the Sierra Leone Airways crest in addition to the BUA livery.

A long-running strike at El Al in 1961 led to BUA chartering two Britannias from El Al and operating them on the Israeli airline's behalf as G-ARWZ and G-ARXA. By the time the strike ended El Al had bought jet airliners and British United continued to hire the aircraft for use on its own services. Other Britannias were also

**Srs 307 G-ANCD BUA at Gatwick in the mid-60s.** The late Dave Williams

**Srs 317 G-APNA at Gatwick in the later, more colourful BUA markings.** Air-Britain

**Srs 314 CF-CZA, in British United markings but still wearing its original CPAL registration, was later to become G-ATGD.** via author

were available on the Britannia service to Freetown operated by BUA on behalf of Sierra Leone Airways. First Class and Tourist Class seats were offered to the Canary Islands, with Britannia flights to Tenerife and Las Palmas from Gatwick on Saturdays and Sundays. The low-cost 'Skycoach' services to Africa were operated in conjunction with BOAC, East African Airways and Central African Airways, with the various carriers each operating flights on specified dates only. Passengers were required to sign a form confirming that they were residing in and were travelling to UK territories, and that their travel did not form part of an onward international journey. The flights were very infrequent, and during the whole period of the winter timetable BUA only operated services on four dates in each direction. Three of these used DC-6s, and the only Britannia-operated Skycoach service was flight BR111 on 10 December 1963. This left Gatwick at 1500hr and flew via Benina to Nairobi, arriving there the following morning. After a lengthy stop-over in Nairobi the Britannia left on the evening of 12 December, arriving at Gatwick via Benina on the following morning.

On 21 April 1964 srs 312 G-AOVE was wet-leased to Middle East Airlines as a temporary replacement for a Caravelle lost at Dhahran earlier that month. On 1 October 1964 the last Britannia trooping flight was operated from Stansted and the

leased in at various times, including G-AOVA and G-ANCH from Bristol, and in total BUA operated eleven different examples, although not all at the same time.

During the winter 1963–64 British United Airways Britannias were in use on both BUA's normal scheduled services to Africa and also on the low-fare 'Skycoach' flights.

On Mondays and Wednesdays, flight BR101 was Britannia-operated from Gatwick to Entebbe and Nairobi, returning the following day as BR102. On Wednesdays Flight BR211 linked Gatwick with Salisbury via Entebbe, Ndola and Lusaka. These services were Economy Class only, but on Fridays First and Economy Classes

(*Right*) **A BUA srs 313 Britannia being readied for a sunset departure from Entebbe for London in May 1961.** Malcolm McCrow

(*Below right*) **A BUA srs 313 Britannia taxies out at Entebbe in 1961.** Malcolm McCrow

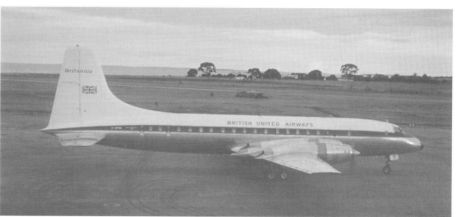

services were taken over by VC-10s flying from Gatwick, but the Britannia continued in service with BUA on the Africargo scheduled freight service, a few European scheduled services and on inclusive-tour charters. A typical holiday charter in 1965 was flight BR315 from Gatwick to Palma, which took 2 hours 15 minutes, cruising at 390mph (630km/h) at 19,000ft (6,000m). The passengers had each paid £50–60 for their two-week holiday (less than half the scheduled air fare), and the air travel portion accounted for only £18 of the total price.

The arrival of One-Elevens and VC-10s saw the withdrawal of the Britannias from passenger work, but they continued to earn their keep on the Africargo service, replacing DC-6Cs. The first Britannia service from London to Johannesburg was flown on 18 June 1966 by srs 307F G-ANCD, which had been the subject of a special cargo conversion by Aviation Traders. The modifications included the installation of a 10ft 3in × 6ft 7in (3.13 × 2.01m) freight door, large enough to load aboard a turbofan engine. To do this, a hole 25 × 12ft (7.63 × 3.66m) was cut in the port forward fuselage, and a pre-constructed panel containing the doorway was fitted into the cavity. The floor was strengthened and a bulkhead stressed to 9g was fitted behind the crew compartment. All this work increased the empty weight of the aircraft by 2,000lb (900kg), leaving a payload capacity of about 48,000lb (22,000kg). As a pure freighter the Britannia could accommodate eight 88 × 108in (2.24 × 2.74m) pallets, or up to 132 passengers, or any combination of the two; conversion from all-cargo to all-passenger configuration took about two hours. The cost of the work was £100,000, with interior modifications to the customer's requirements adding a further £20,000 or so. Further BUA Britannias were converted by Aviation Traders and, thus modified, the Britannias maintained the route until the beginning of 1969, when VC-10s took over. The final BUA Britannia service was operated by G-ANCE on 21–22 January 1969.

## British United Airways

The development of what was to become British United Airways really began in 1961, when a newly-elected Conservative government encouraged the major shipping companies of the day to invest in the independent airlines. This in turn stimulated the airlines to expand their activities in fields that complemented rather than competed with the services of the state airlines BEA and BOAC. These activities included trooping flights, all-cargo services and inclusive-tour charters. One of the best equipped of the independent airlines was Airwork Ltd, which took over several smaller carriers, including Air Charter, during 1958 and 1959. Then, in 1960 Airwork and its subsidiaries merged with Hunting-Clan Air Transport to form British United Airways, with Freddie Laker as its Managing Director.

At the time of its formation BUA inherited a fleet of more than fifty fixed-wing aircraft, including Viscounts, Britannias, DC-6As, DC-4s and Bristol 170s, plus fifty-four assorted helicopters. From its Gatwick base scheduled services were operated to many European points, and to East, Central and West Africa. Trooping flights were also operated from Stansted to Hong Kong, Singapore, Nairobi, Aden, Cyprus, Malta and Germany, and in 1961 BUA took over all the trooping movements to Germany, which had until then used the sea ferries from Harwich. By 1962 trooping contracts produced two-thirds of BUA's total revenue. BUA made history by becoming the first airline in the world to place an order for the BAC One-Eleven jet airliner, but the airline's first

regular jet services were in fact flown by VC-10s, on trooping flights and on scheduled services to Africa. In the spring of 1965, BUA VC-10s took over a package of routes to South America which BOAC had been forced to abandon as uneconomic, and in January 1966 One-Elevens started domestic schedules from Gatwick to Belfast, Edinburgh and Glasgow, in competition with both BEA and British Eagle out of Heathrow.

At the end of the 1960s an extensive inclusive-tour programme was operated by BAC One-Eleven srs 500s bought specifically for this purpose, but the trooping contracts had been dwindling and heavy start-up costs on new routes contributed to increasing losses during the period 1965–67. The report of the Edwards Committee on British civil air transport recommended the formation of a single, strong, independent 'second force' airline to provide effective competition for BEA and BOAC. Adam Thomson, the Chairman of Caledonian Airways, approached the BUA board with a merger proposal, and the BUA shareholders were anxious to dispose of the airline, but the government of the day was not in favour of such a move, and for a time it looked as if British United would be absorbed into BEA or BOAC instead. However, a change in government resulted in the takeover of British United by Caledonian Airways on 30 November 1970 for £6.9m. The new 'second force' airline was initially known as Caledonian/BUA, but before long the aircraft were being repainted again, this time with the name of British Caledonian Airways.

## BWIA Britannia Operations

On 29 April 1960 British West Indian Airways (BWIA) inaugurated its first transatlantic service, from London to Port of Spain via New York and Bridgetown, Barbados. Weekly services were operated by BOAC Britannia srs 312s with BOAC crews but wearing BWIA titles, the first flight being made by G-AOVB.

## Caledonian Airways Britannia Operations

Caledonian Airways (Prestwick) Ltd was founded in April 1961 and acquired its first aircraft, a former SABENA DC-7C, that November. The inaugural service was from Gatwick to Barbados on 29 November 1961. Caledonian specialized in long-haul charters and became the first non-American airline to be awarded a CAB licence for closed-group charters from the UK to the USA. This led to the acquisition of more DC-7Cs, and to the purchase of Britannias to replace them in late 1964 and the spring of 1965. These were the former BOAC srs 312s G-AOVH, G-AOVI and G-AOVJ. The hire-purchase agreement for G-AOVJ was for a total purchase price of £230,000, payable over fifty-five months. An initial amount of £5,000 was payable on signature of the contract on 27 April 1965. Six monthly payments of £6,000 were to follow, and then for the next six months the instalments reduced to £1,500. After that they increased again to £4,523.16.3 for the remaining forty-two months. The purchase price included

**BOAC srs 312 G-AOVL on lease to BWIA.** Air-Britain

**Srs 312 G-AOVL on lease to BWIA.** The late Dave Williams

delivery to Southend, and the engines and propellers were the subject of a separate hire-purchase agreement.

The first Caledonian Britannia commercial service was actually a sub-charter to Royal Air Maroc for a pilgrimage flight to Jeddah on 7 March 1965. By the summer of 1965 three Britannias and four DC-7Cs were in service, with the Britannias mainly handling the transatlantic charters and the DC-7Cs relegated to inclusive-tour flights to the Mediterranean. At the end of 1965 some of the Britannias were deployed on the Zambian airlift (see page 104), carrying drums of oil between Dar-es-Salaam and Lusaka, and it was at Dar-es-Salaam that Britannia 314 G-ATNZ was damaged on 27 March 1966 when its engines were started without chocks under the wheels, and it rolled forward and collided with a ground power unit and a tractor.

The Britannias returned to the UK in April 1966 and were used that summer on an intensive programme of transatlantic and Mediterranean charters from Gatwick, Manchester, Glasgow and Prestwick. By

**Caledonian Airways srs 314 G-ASTF in the late 1960s.** Air-Britain

**Caledonian srs 312 G-AOVI later served with Monarch Airways.** Air-Britain

**Srs 314 G-ATNZ in the basic Caledonian colour scheme, probably at Biggin Hill in 1971 after withdrawal from service.** Air-Britain

1967 they had completely replaced the DC-7Cs, but they were themselves soon displaced from front-line duties as Caledonian acquired Boeing 707s for transatlantic flights and One-Eleven srs 500s for European holiday charters. They were still used for sub-charters, however. In February–March 1968 Royal Air Maroc leased srs 312 G-AOVI for more Haj pilgrimage flights to Jeddah, and in April 1969 Caledonian began operating ex-British Eagle srs 324s G-ARKA and G-ARKB on behalf of the new Swiss airline, Tellair. Unfortunately, these services ceased in October 1969 and the Britannias were later flown back to Coventry, where they were scrapped. Britannias were still being used by Caledonian during the summer of 1970 for occasional inclusive-tour flights from Gatwick to Gerona, Ibiza, Munich and Palma, but the final Caledonian Britannia commercial service was a cargo charter from Las Palmas to Manston by G-ATNZ, on 9 March 1971.

## Canadian Pacific Air Lines Operations

Canadian Pacific Air Lines (CPAL) had originally planned to introduce the Britannia in 1957 on services from its Vancouver base to Amsterdam, Auckland, Hong Kong, Lima, Mexico City, Tokyo and Sydney, but delivery delays caused by the Britannia's engine icing problems meant that the first CPAL aircraft, srs 314 CF-CZA, did not fly until January 1958. The first example was eventually handed over in April 1958, with two more following the next month. On 1 June 1958 CF-CZA flew the first-ever scheduled turbine-powered air service over the North Pole, from Vancouver to Amsterdam via a refuelling stop at Frobisher on Baffin Island. The journey was scheduled to take 13 hours 30 minutes, a saving of about eight hours on the competing carrier's (KLM) time on this route. Ten round trips were operated each month, the Britannias completing the round trip, ramp to ramp, in an average time of 30 hours 33 minutes, and carrying eighty-eight passengers in a First and Tourist Class arrangement. On 16 July the westbound flight of 4,800 miles (7,700km) was made in just under fourteen hours at an average speed of 346mph (557km/h). Routes to Sydney, Auckland and Tokyo were also opened during the summer of 1958, with CF-CZA inaugurating the Tokyo service on 24 August. As with the Amsterdam route, the Britannias soon slashed journey times, and on 20 September a new record time for the 4,700-mile (7,600km) route was set, at 11 hours 44 minutes, an average of 400mph (640km/h).

On 4 May 1959 the Britannias began a daily transcontinental service on the route Vancouver–Winnipeg–Toronto–Montreal, carrying up to fifty-eight First Class and fifty-one Tourist Class passengers. On 11 September, following the completion of a new runway at Hong Kong, CF-CZX inaugurated an extension of the Vancouver–Tokyo service to that city. All this extra activity led to a need for extra aircraft, and two srs 320s, CF-CPD and CF-CPE, were leased for eighteen months from October 1959, with the new designation srs 324. These were the two srs 320s that had been speculatively built at Filton in the summer of 1958. The first left Filton on delivery to Vancouver on 16 October 1959, and the second followed a month later. These aircraft brought the CPAL Britannia fleet up to eight, and the President of CPAL, Grant McConachie, said at the time that the aircraft had been acquired 'because no other aircraft in the world today combines the same qualities of range, economy and airport capabilities with a speed well in advance of the types of aircraft it replaces. Passenger opinions of the Britannia have been particularly gratifying.'

(*Top*) **CPAL srs 314 CF-CZB was written off at Honolulu on 22 July 1962.** Air-Britain

(*Above*) **Srs 314 CF-CZA in the later CPAL colour scheme.** Air-Britain

**Britannia srs 314 CF-CZW in the final CPAL Britannia colour scheme.** The late Dave Williams

1960 saw the opening of another European route, to Lisbon and Rome, on 1 March, and by now the Britannias were also being employed on charter flights from Vancouver and Toronto to the UK. Services continued without serious incident until the night of 22 July 1962, when CPAL had the unhappy distinction of being involved in the first fatal Britannia accident involving fare-paying passengers. CF-CZB had arrived at Honolulu in the early hours of 21 July as Flight 323 from Vancouver. It was scheduled to continue on the night of 22 July as Flight 301 to Nandi in Fiji, then Auckland and Sydney. CF-CZB took off at 2238hr local time with twenty-nine passengers and eleven crew aboard. Approximately two minutes after becoming airborne a fire warning indication for No.1 engine was received in the cockpit. The No.1 propeller was feathered and the control tower was told that the aircraft was returning to Honolulu. As the gross landing weight would have been exceeded had the aircraft landed immediately, some 35,000lb of fuel was jettisoned and the Britannia flew west of the outer marker to intercept the ILS for Runway 08. The three-engined approach appeared normal until the aircraft had crossed the threshhold and started its landing flare at a height of around 20ft. At this point a go-around was attempted, but the aircraft banked and veered sharply to the left. The left wing-tip hit the ground and the Britannia progressively disintegrated, finally striking heavy earth-moving equipment some 970ft (296m) from the runway centreline. Twenty-seven people lost their lives in the accident and the the the crew were held responsible by the subsequent enquiry, for initiating a go-around with insufficient airspeed and altitude to maintain control.

The Britannias were phased out in favour of DC-8 jets between 1965 and 1967. What was probably the final CPAL Britannia service was a charter by CF-CZA from Vancouver to Prestwick on 3 January 1966, returning on 5 January as flight CP391.

## Cathay Pacific Britannia Operations

From 12 December 1960 this airline leased BOAC Britannia 102s for use on its Hong Kong–Singapore–Manila–Sydney route while its own Lockheed Electras were undergoing modifications. The first Bri-

---

### Canadian Pacific Airlines

Canadian Pacific Airlines Ltd was established on 30 January 1942 by Canadian Pacific Railways to take over and unify the operations of a group of ten small Canadian bush airlines. The airline's first large airliner was the Canadair Argonaut, and Convair 240s were also used on internal services. DC-6Bs were introduced in 1953, but before that an ambitious plan to enter the jet age had been put in motion with an order for Comet 1A jets. These were to be based at Sydney, but on 3 March 1953 the airline's first Comet, CF-CUN, crashed on take-off from Karachi during its delivery flight. Following this accident CPAL's second Comet 1A was sold to BOAC. Three Comet 2s were ordered in November 1953, but were never to be delivered. In the meantime the DC-6Bs were used on routes to Mexico City and Lima, and on 3–4 June 1955 they inaugurated Canadian Pacific's new Polar Route from Sydney to Vancouver and onwards to Amsterdam. The DC-6Bs were superseded by Britannias, and then in 1961 three DC-8 srs 40s arrived. These were used throughout the 1960s and early 1970s alongside the later 'stretched' DC-8 srs 63s, and Boeing 727s and 737s took over on the North American internal routes. The trading name CP Air was adopted in 1968. From 1979 DC-10-30s and Boeing 747-200s were used on transatlantic services, and in 1988, after a series of takeovers and mergers with smaller Canadian airlines such as PWA, Nordair and Eastern Provincial, Canadian Airlines International was formed. Wardair Canada was taken over in 1989 and Canadian Airlines International is now itself fully merged into Air Canada.

---

tannia service was operated by G-ANBO, and G-ANBB was also leased between 1961 and 1963.

## Centre Air Afrique Britannia Operations

Based in Burundi, Centre Air Afrique took delivery of former RAF Britannia 253 XL657 as 9U-BAD in 1976 and operated it briefly on freight work. In February 1977 the Britannia was impounded in Belgium for non-payment of landing and parking fees, and the airline was subsequently declared bankrupt.

## CSA Britannia Operations

In October 1961 the Czechoslovakian state carrier CSA leased Britannia 318 CU-T668 from Cubana, following its return from lease to Eagle Airways. Re-registered as OK-MBA it became the first Britannia to operate behind the Iron Curtain, maintaining a weekly service from Prague to Havana from 3 February 1962. The 6,040-mile (9,700km) route was scheduled to be completed in 23 hours 40 minutes, including refuelling stops at Shannon and Gander. In the event of bad weather the British government had authorized the use of either Manchester or Prestwick as alternates to Shannon, and OK-MBA had staged via Prestwick on two proving flights in January 1962 prior to the start of the service. Otherwise, visits to the UK were rare, although the aircraft made a precautionary landing at Heathrow on 25 February with flap trouble. At the expiry of the lease in May 1964 the aircraft was returned to Cubana but was replaced by CU-T671, re-registered as OK-MBB. This aircraft was sub-leased to Lot Polish airlines in the autumn of 1964 to carry out mass pilgrimage flights from Warsaw to Jeddah. At the completion of the flight series, about a week later, it returned to CSA at Prague. OK-MBB paid a two-month visit to Stansted between September and November 1966, for overhaul by Aviation Traders. Il-62 jets took over the route in January 1969.

**Centre Air Afrique srs 253 9U-BAD at Gosselies on 13 August 1977.** Colin Vangen

**CSA Britannia 318 OK-MBB, which was leased from Cubana from 1962 to 1969.**
The late Dave Williams

**Cubana srs 318 CU-P671 at Heathrow.** The late Dave Williams

## Cubana Britannia Operations

Cubana was formed by the Curtis Aviation Group in October 1929 as Compania Nacional Cubana de Aviacion Curtiss and began flights the next year using a Ford 4-AT aircraft. In May 1932 the airline was acquired by Pan American and renamed Compania Nacional Cubana de Aviacion. By 1945 the company name had been shortened to Compania Cubana de Aviacion and the first international services were flown, using DC-3 aircraft, to Miami.

In May 1957 Cubana ordered two Britannia 318s to replace the Super Constellations then in use. In August 1958 the order was doubled to four aircraft and the

first example, CU-P668 (later re-registered CU-T668), was delivered on 16 December 1958. This aircraft inaugurated Britannia services on the Havana–Mexico City route on 22 December 1958 and was also used on the Havana–Miami flights, but the most popular Cubana service was that linking Havana with New York. CU-P668 was introduced onto this route on 11 January 1959 and load factors soon rose to 80 per cent. During the period 17 December 1958 to 18 January 1959 this aircraft carried over 1,500 passengers during 112 flying hours on the services to Mexico City, New York and Miami, and on 17 January 1959 it established a new record for the Havana–New York distance, covering

the 1,317 miles (2,119km) in 3 hours 28 minutes at an average block speed of 380mph (611km/h).

Cubana's second Britannia, CU-T669, was delivered on 6–7 February 1959 and the third, CU-T670 followed on 15 May. In 1959, much publicity was devoted by Cubana to a 65-minute radio broadcast made to the people of Cuba by their President, Fidel Castro, while he was flying over Cuba at 19,500ft (6,000m) in a Cubana Britannia, en route from Houston to Buenos Aires. One of the motives given by Castro for his decision to visit Buenos Aires was 'because we have this formidable transport'. On 5 June 1959 the Britannias were placed onto the Havana–Madrid route, a route catering for the large number of rich people of Spanish descent in Cuba, but the political situation in Cuba made it uncertain for a time whether the option on the fourth aircraft would be taken up. This machine, CU-T671, was eventually delivered on 25 August 1959, but political uncertainty was deterring passengers and Cubana found it difficult to cope with falling load factors. In January 1960, CU-T668 was offered for sale at a price of $3,435,000 or for lease at a monthly rental of $65,000, the first srs 300 aircraft to come onto the second-hand market. Within a few weeks a deal had been concluded with Eagle Airways for the lease of CU-T668 as G-APYY.

By July the remaining trio of Britannias were operating three times weekly Havana–Mexico City, weekly Havana–Bermuda–Madrid, and daily Havana–New York. On 20 September 1960 Cubana had one of its Britannias impounded at New York for non-payment of landing fees. The aircraft was not released until November, and in 1961 the routes to New York and Miami were suspended, following a deterioration in relations between Cuba and the USA. On 28 February 1961, Cubana opened a new scheduled service linking Havana and Prague, with refuelling stops at Gander; either Shannon or Bermuda; and Santa Maria in the Azores. At the end of the Eagle Airways lease, CU-T668 was leased to CSA for use on a reciprocal Prague–Havana service. It returned to Cubana in November 1963 and was replaced on the CSA lease by CU-T671 until January 1969.

The Britannias were still being used as late as 1973 on the routes to Madrid, Prague and Mexico City, and on charter flights, but a shortage of spare parts and engineering personnel meant that rarely were more than two operational at a time.

The Britannia's career with Cubana was not without occasionally amusing incident. On 26 May 1963 a Cubana Britannia made an emergency landing at Heathrow when one engine failed during a flight from Madrid to Prague. There were thirteen passengers on board, including a second crew, and the immigration authorities allowed only the captain to disembark in order to engage an airline to effect repairs. BOAC were approached, but demanded cash for services rendered. Eventually the aircraft's own flight engineer made the repairs, and with the aid of a Cunard Eagle starter truck the Britannia was on its way again within five hours. Another unscheduled visit was paid, this time to Shannon, on 13 March 1965, when a Britannia carrying the Latin American revolutionary Che Guevera developed technical problems en route from Prague to Havana. The Britannia was flown to Filton for repairs and returned to Shannon the following day to pick up Guevera and the rest of the party of seventy-one passengers, and continue the journey to Havana. In 1967 Cuba bought a champion bull from Canada as part of a livestock improvement programme. A US embargo prevented the use of a Canadian carrier for transportation, and so a Cubana Britannia was sent to Canada to collect the animal. On 2 March 1968 CU-T670 had a lucky escape when it hit trees whilst on approach to Gander as a result of an incorrect altimeter setting. Fortunately the crew still managed to land safely.

## The Angolan War

The Britannias were also used on trooping flights to Angola as part of Cuba's support for the People's Movement for the Liberation of Angola (MPLA). Operation *Carlota* began on 7 November 1975 with the despatch of two flights from Havana to Luanda Airport, which at the time was still occupied by the Portuguese. Over a period of thirteen days, over 650 troops were to be sent, in the guise of holidaymakers. The first contingent of eighty-two special forces personnel left Havana at 1600hr on a special Cubana flight, attended to by two regular stewardesses and dressed as tourists. They carried ordinary passports and briefcases, but these contained machine-guns. The cargo hold was filled with light artillery and mortars, as well as personal firearms, and a

**Cubana srs 318 CU-P668 in flight.** Air-Britain

special floor hatch enabled the weapons to be removed via the passenger cabin in an emergency. The first stop was made at Barbados, in the middle of a tropical storm. Then a five-hour stopover was made at Guinea-Bissau to await nightfall before flying on to Brazzaville and then Luanda. Over the next nine months the three Britannias kept up a steady flow of supplies to Angola. Although the normal maximum payload was 185,000lb (84,000kg), on some flights they carried as much as 194,000lb (88,000kg). The pilots, who would normally be restricted to seventy-five flying hours per month, logged more than 200. As a general rule, each Britannia carried two full flight crews, who would change over midflight. However, one pilot recalled being on duty for the whole of a fifty-hour round trip, of which forty-three hours were spent in the air. The crews were unable to obtain accurate advance reports of the weather conditions awaiting them on arrival at Luanda and would often follow unknown flight

**Cubana srs 318 CU-T668 in the later colour scheme, at San Juan in June 1972. The aircraft had brought the Cuban national basketball team to compete in the World Cup Final, Cubana having been granted special permission for the flight by the US State Department.** William W. Sierra

paths, keeping to illegal heights to conserve fuel. On the most dangerous stretch, between Brazzaville and Luanda, there was no diversion airfield available. When the US government secured a ban on refuelling stops at Barbados the Cubans established a new route across the Atlantic, from Holguin in the far east of Cuba to Isla da Sal in the Cape Verde Islands. On the outward journey the aircraft arrived with barely two hours'-worth of fuel, whilst on the return leg adverse prevailing winds reduced their reserves to one hour. However, even this route had to be stopped in order not to expose the defenceless Cape Verde Islands to possible attack, and thereafter four extra fuel tanks were fitted in the cabin of the Britannias. These enabled non-stop flights to be made from Holguin to Brazzaville, but meant that thirty fewer passengers could be carried. In all, 101 flights were made during the course of the war.

### Final Years

In 1973 Cubana began using Il-62 jets on the transatlantic scheduled services. CU-T670 was withdrawn at Havana in the mid-1970s but the remaining three Britannias were still used for various duties, including occasional charters to Prague. They were also to be seen at Luton undergoing maintenance. The last Britannia passenger service took place on 16 September 1977, when CU-T669 passed through Shannon en route from Prague to Havana. In 1979 an irregular all-cargo service between Havana and Prague was launched using CU-T669, despite that aircraft's lack of a large cargo door. The fleet was gradually run down, and by 1984 only CU-T669 remained airworthy. This example was then transferred to a new Cuban carrier, Aero Caribbean, after twenty-five years of Cubana service.

# Donaldson International Britannia Operations

Donaldson International Airways Ltd was formed in 1964, and an associate company was Mercury Air Holidays, which operated inclusive tours from Glasgow to the Mediterranean, most of the flying being contracted to Lloyd International Airways. In October 1967 Donaldson acquired former BUA Britannia 317F G-APNA, but at first this was leased to Lloyd International. During 1968 it was announced that Donaldson would be launching its own Britannia operations in the spring of 1969, using two srs 317s based at Gatwick. Before then, the demise of British Eagle had placed many more Britannias on the market at reasonable prices, and Donaldson decided to buy some former British Eagle srs 312s. On 24 March another srs 317, G-APNB, was delivered

(*Above*) Donaldson International Britannia srs 317 G-APNA in the late 1960s/early 1970s. Air-Britain

Donaldson International srs 312 G-AOVC in 1969/70. Air-Britain

92

to Gatwick and four days later Donaldson carried out its first commercial operation under its own name, a sub-charter to its former owner British United Airways on the 'Silver Arrow' service from Le Touquet to Gatwick.

On 25 April 1969 the first commercial service under a Donaldson flight number was operated from Gatwick to Milan as DI1024. A base was established at Gatwick and on 3 May the summer inclusive-tour programme of Mercury Air Holidays from Glasgow commenced with a flight to Palma. On the Mediterranean routes the Donaldson Britannias were configured to seat 130 passengers at a 32in (81cm) seat pitch, and the programme was so intensive that the first weekend in July saw all three of their aircraft flying to and fro between Glasgow and Barcelona and Palma. Despite this, the airline still found time to operate transatlantic charters from Gatwick, Belfast and Prestwick as well. The inaugural transatlantic service was operated to Niagara Falls by G-APNB on 1 June 1969, and other destinations that summer included New York, Toronto, Los Angeles and Vancouver. Other long-haul charters were operated to Nairobi, Port of Spain, Kingston, Singapore and Hong Kong, and by the end of 1969 the Britannias had carried 40,598 passengers. During the winter of 1969–70 ad hoc charters to the Middle East and Far East were operated, and srs 312 G-AOVC carried out Haj pilgrimage flights between Accra and Jeddah in January 1970.

During 1970 Donaldson flights followed a similar pattern to 1969, with the addition of an inclusive-tour flight series out of Gatwick and some welcome extra revenue brought about by a national dock strike in the UK during the spring and summer. To meet the demand for freight flights a former British Eagle srs 312F with a cargo door was bought, and put to work on an intensive series of flights between Belfast and Liverpool, completing thirty-four round trips during the period 15 July–2 August 1970.

However, by now most of Donaldson's competitors were using jets on long-haul flights and so in December 1970 two ex-Pan American Boeing 707s were acquired to replace the Britannias on the Atlantic routes in 1971. G-AOVC flew Stockholm–Gatwick on its last commercial service on 27 September 1970, and was then retired. G-APNB followed it into retirement on 5 March 1971, but for the 1971 summer season G-APNA and G-AOVF

were still in service alongside the two 707s. They were used for inclusive-tour flights to Munich from Gatwick, Manchester, Edinburgh, Birmingham, Newcastle and Teesside, trooping flights to Germany, weekly Gatwick–Tel Aviv flights and holiday charters from Glasgow. The last of these was operated from Palma to Glasgow by G-APNA on 9 October 1971. Both Britannias were used for ad hoc charters during the winter of 1971–72 and the following spring,

project fell through. Donaldson International acquired two more Boeing 707s, but ceased operations on 8 August 1974.

## EAAC Britannia Operations

East African Airways Corporation (EAAC) began operating one of its Nairobi–London services – previously served by Canadair Argonauts – with a chartered BOAC

**British and Commonwealth srs 317 G-APNB on lease to EAAC.** Air-Britain

**A Lloyd International srs 307F while on lease to EAAC during 1969.** Air-Britain

but G-APNA was withdrawn at the end of May 1972, followed by G-AOVF in July. G-APNA was stored at Coventry and at one time in 1972 was earmarked for conversion to a restaurant for Bass Charington, but the

Britannia 312 from 8 October 1958. During 1959–60 the airline leased Hunting-Clan Britannia 317s until its own Comet 4s took over the route. Lloyd International Britannias were also used for cargo services.

**BOAC srs 102 G-ANBL at Heathrow North Side whilst on lease to EAAC.** Air-Britain

## El Al Britannia Operations

In order to replace its ageing Constellations El Al took delivery of three Britannia 313s in September, October and November 1957. 4X-AGA was damaged on 10 November 1957 and had to be returned to Filton for repairs to the rear fuselage, returning to El Al on 1 December. The Britannias were intended for use on services between Israel and the USA via cities in Europe, and on the night of 18–19 December 1957 4X-AGC made a spectacular non-stop proving flight from New York to Tel Aviv, a distance of 6,100 miles (9,800km), in 14 hours 56 minutes at an average speed of 401mph (645km/h); this ranked as a distance record for civil aircraft at that time.

Scheduled transatlantic services were inaugurated by 4X-AGB on 22 December 1957, just beating BOAC for the honour of being the first Britannia operator on the North Atlantic. Initially, one flight each week was operated from Tel Aviv to New York via London, increasing within six months to five flights per week via either London or Paris, the Paris service being inaugurated on 1 June 1958. The Britannias were fitted with seventy-two Tourist Class seats, and eighteen First Class seats and four sleeping berths.

El Al's transatlantic passenger total for the first six months of 1958 was 8,882, compared with 3,453 for the same period in 1957 with Constellations, an increase of 157 per cent. During the first six months of 1958 El Al carried 2 per cent of all airline passengers between Europe and the USA, compared with 0.09 per cent for the equivalent period in 1957. Since the round trip from Tel Aviv to New York and back totalled 12,000 miles (19,300km), this small fleet was averaging over 3,000 hours per annum each by June 1958, and a fourth srs 313 was ordered on 18 July. A Bristol-owned srs 305 was also operated on loan for about nine months until March 1959. In the meantime, taking advantage of favourable winds, 4X-AGB flew the 3,444 miles (5,540km) from New York to London on 8 January 1958 in 7 hours 44 minutes at a block speed of 445mph (716km/h).

The Britannias were operated on European services from Tel Aviv to Amsterdam, Athens, Brussels, London, Paris, Rome, Vienna and Zurich, and on a weekly flight to Teheran. Charters were also operated to Nicosia and Istanbul to bring Jewish emigrants to settle in Israel. In August 1960 El Al's Britannias achieved their peak utilization of eleven hours per day. This was a higher peak utilization and about the same average utilization as that achieved by El Al's Boeing 707s. In 1960 the Britannias recorded thirty defects per 100 flight hours, compared with twenty defects per 100 flight hours in the 707 fleet in 1962. At the end of 1960, commenting on the third anniversary of El Al's Britannia operations, the UK Commercial Manager for the airline, Mr M. Turel, said he hoped the Britannias would stay 'for many years to come because they deserve to stay with any major airline on their trunk routes. El Al cannot find terms too high to praise them.'

In 1961, however, El Al began to suffer the effects of a long strike. In order to overcome the industrial action by crew members, the three Britannias were chartered to British United Airways, who operated them on El Al flights with BUA crews. Once the strike was over BUA continued to hire these aircraft, as by then El Al had begun to receive Boeing 707 jets. In March 1964 4X-AGA was sold to the Swiss airline Globe Air, followed by 4X-AGD in 1965. At around this time 4X-AGB and AGC returned from their BUA lease and were then used for charters and for new scheduled services to Rhodes and Sofia. They were withdrawn at the end of the 1965 season, and eventually sold to British Eagle and Air Spain.

In 1962, Mr C. Pearlman, Chief Engineer of El Al, told an audience that before the Britannia El Al had been a second-class operator. 'In 1957 we became overnight a first-class operator.'

**Srs 313 4X-AGB operated the first El Al transatlantic Britannia service on 22 December 1957.** Air-Britain

(*Above*) **An artist's impression of a Britannia in an El Al colour scheme that was never applied to the type.** Bristol via Michael Harrison

(*Right*) **A night-time snow scene including El Al Britannia 313 4X-AGA.** Bristol via Michael Harrison

## El Al

El Al operations began after the founding of the state of Israel, using Israeli Air Force aircraft. Services to Paris, London and Switzerland were operated from 1949 using Douglas C-54s and Curtiss C-46s. Lockheed Constellations were used to start New York services in 1950. When Britannias were bought in 1957 the Constellations were sold to Euravia — which would become Britannia Airways — and in 1960 jet equipment in the shape of Boeing 707s entered service. Along with Boeing 720Bs these were to be the mainstay of the El Al fleet for another decade. In 1971 Boeing 747-200s were introduced, along with Boeing 737-200s for short-haul services. The 707s continued to soldier on, however, until the introduction of Boeing 767s in 1983. Today, El Al operates a fleet of Boeing 747s, 757s, 767s and 737s on services to the USA, Canada, Africa and Europe.

**El Al srs 313 4X-AGD at Heathrow North Side.**
Air-Britain

## Eurafric Britannia Operations

Eurafric was based at Lisbon, and in September 1976 bought ex-RAF Britannia XL640. The aircraft was placed on the Irish register as EI-BCI and probably did not actually fly any services for Eurafric, as over the next two years it was leased several times to Aer Turas. At the end of the Aer Turas leases it was sold to Redcoat Air Cargo. During the first half of 1978 the former RAF Britannia XL639 was leased as EI-BDC, and was probably used on charters between Europe and Africa. Eurafric ceased operations in June 1978, and this Britannia was also sold to Redcoat.

## Gaylan Air Cargo Britannia Operations

In April 1980 this company obtained Britannia 253 G-BEMZ and registered it in the United Arab Emirates as A6-HMS. The aircraft reverted to its former British registration in April 1981 and by the middle of 1981 the airline had ceased trading. The Britannia later returned to the UK and served briefly with Redcoat Air Cargo.

## Geminair Britannia Operations

Geminair was formed in September 1975 as a subsidiary of Gemini Air Transport (Nassau) Ltd, based in Ghana. Former RAF Britannia 253 XM520 was acquired as 9G-ACE and entered service on 7 May 1976 on a Redcoat Air Cargo service from Luton to Rotterdam and Accra. For the next five years it was used on cargo charters within West Africa and to Europe. It was a regular visitor to the UK, on services and also for maintenance at Luton. During the spring of 1979 Geminair also operated Britannia 253 EI-BBH on hire from Aer Turas, possibly while its own Britannia was away for maintenance. The company ceased operations in 1981.

## Ghana Airways Britannia Operations

Ghana Airways was founded on 4 July 1958 and started services on 16 July, using chartered BOAC Stratocruisers between Accra and London. From 14 April 1959 these were replaced by Britannia 102s,

Eurafric's Irish-registered srs 253F EI-BCI at Luton in August 1997. Eduard Marmet

Geminair srs 253 9G-ACE, the former RAF XM520. Keith Butler

again on hire from BOAC, the first Britannia service being flown by G-ANBL. G-ANBC was also used during 1960, but on 27 July Ghana Airways took delivery of the first of its own Britannias, srs 309 9G-AAG. A series of proving flights between London and Accra started on 17 August 1960, and following the handing over of Ghana Airways' second Britannia, srs 319 9G-AAH 'Osagyefo' (the last new Britannia to be handed over to a commercial operator) in a ceremony at Filton on 8 November 1960, a full twice-weekly

scheduled service on the route started on 2 December of that year. Twenty-eight First Class and forty-two Tourist Class seats were provided, and the aircraft were flown by BOAC flight crews, with two Ghanaian stewardesses among the cabin attendants. Initially the services routed via Barcelona, but on 25 June 1961 non-stop London–Accra services began, with a flight time of nine hours.

The two Britannias were also used on regional routes within West Africa, but 9G-AAH was returned to Bristol Aircraft

**Srs 102 G-ANBC on lease to Ghana Airways from BOAC in 1960.** The late Dave Williams

(*Below*) **A pre-delivery view of Ghana Airways srs 319 9G-AAH.** Bristol via Lester Stenner

(*Above*) **Ghana Airways srs 309 9G-AAG sporting a 'chequer-board' tail-fin scheme.** Air-Britain

**Ghana Airways advertisement for their Britannia services.** The late Dave Williams via Derek A. King

serving
Ghana

LONDON
TRIPOLI
BARCELONA
ROME
ACCRA

and
the world

\* LAGOS
\* TAKORADI
\* KUMASI
\* TAMALE
\* ACCRA
\* ABIDJAN
\* ROBERTSFIELD
\* FREETOWN
\* CONAKRY
\* BATHURST
\* DAKAR

Travelling by Ghana Airways Britannia, you fly the fastest and the most direct route between Accra and London.

Within West Africa too, Ghana Airways offers fast and comfortable flights serving points in Ghana, the Gambia and Guinea; Senegal and Sierra Leone; Liberia and Nigeria. Wherever you go —

*go* Ghana AIRWAYS

IN ASSOCIATION WITH B.O.A.C

Services at the end of 1963. 9G-AAG continued in service until replaced by a VC-10 in 1965. It was then leased out to a number of UK independent airlines including British United, Transglobe, British Eagle and Monarch, but returned to Africa each year for a few weeks' service on Mecca pilgrimage flights between Accra and Jeddah. It was placed into storage in 1972, and finally broken up at Biggin Hill in 1973.

## Globe Air Britannia Operations

Globe Air AG started operations from its Basle base in January 1961 with a former BEA Airspeed Ambassador on inclusive-tour charters to Las Palmas and Mediterranean holiday resorts. The Ambassador fleet was eventually built up to three examples, and these were later replaced by Handley Page Heralds.

A demand for long-range charters to destinations such as Entebbe, Addis Ababa and Nairobi resulted in the purchase and delivery to Basle on 2 April 1964 of an ex-El Al Britannia 313, re-registered as HB-ITB. This entered service on 4 April on flights to Athens, Cairo, Entebbe, Las Palmas, Nairobi and Palma. It made its first visit to the UK in Swiss markings on 11 April, on a student charter from Zurich to

**Srs 309 G-ANCH at Liverpool in Ghana Airways markings in summer 1968.** Author

**Globe Air srs 313 HB-ITB crashed at Nicosia on 20 May 1967.** The late Dave Williams

**Globe Air srs 313 HB-ITC.** Keith Butler

Bournemouth. During the coming summer it was to make more British appearances whilst flying into Gatwick from Basle and Geneva. However, it was mainly employed on long-haul work, and many charters were operated from Amsterdam, Basle and Zurich to Johannesburg and to Lourenço Marques in Mozambique, carrying European visitors to the African game parks. Other parts of the world visited by the Britannia included New York, Mexico City, Montego Bay, Jakarta and San Juan. On 8 March 1965 a second ex-El Al Britannia 313, HB-ITC, was delivered to Basle, and this entered service six days later carrying tourists from Basle to Nairobi. On several occasions during 1965 HB-ITB was leased to International Air for services from South Africa to Europe. The Globe Air Britannias were configured to seat up to 120 passengers in an all-tourist class layout and were supported by an extensive spares package from El Al.

On 20 April 1967 HB-ITB was flying from Bangkok to Basle via Colombo, Bombay and Cairo with a full load of 120 passengers and ten crew members when it was forced to divert from Cairo to Nicosia by bad weather. The aircraft was cleared to land on Runway 32 at Nicosia during a thunderstorm, but appeared to be a little high on the approach. This was abandoned, and a left-hand circuit was started in order to position for a new approach. Whilst making this circuit at low level the aircraft collided with a hillside near the airport and only three passengers and one stewardess survived the crash. At the time this was the worst ever accident involving a charter flight and the effect on the airline was devastating. The long-haul fleet was halved, and passengers were refusing to fly with the airline.

Ten days after the accident the West German authorities banned Globe Air from embarking passengers in that country. Operations did continue with the remaining Britannia and two Heralds throughout the 1967 summer season, but then the airline's founder, Karl Rudin, was arrested on embezzlement charges, and at a meeting of major creditors on 12 October 1967 Globe Air declared itself bankrupt. The final service had been operated from Basle to Luton by HB-ITC on 4 October and the aircraft was abandoned by its crew at Luton and later impounded there. However, in November 1967, Rudin re-acquired the Britannia and formed a new airline, African Safari Airways.

## Hunting-Clan Air Transport Britannia Operations

Hunting-Clan was founded in December 1945 as Hunting Air Travel. In October 1953 the Clan Line group of shipping companies bought an interest and the airline was renamed Hunting-Clan Air Transport Ltd. Vikings, Viscounts and DC-6As were used for a variety of purposes, and in September 1956 Hunting-Clan became the first British independent airline to order the Britannia when a single srs 310 was ordered, followed by an order for a second in December. The two orders were valued at £2.5m, with delivery scheduled for May 1958 for use on a planned new service to Central Africa, but a strike at Bristol delayed delivery by over six months. The plans for the Central Africa service were later dropped, but Britannia 317s G-APNA and G-APNB were finally delivered on 31 October and 11 December 1958. The two Britannias were unpainted at first, but were soon to wear the colours of the parent organization, the British and Commonwealth Shipping Group, co-owners of Hunting-Clan, whose crews operated the aircraft. The Hunting-Clan Britannias, like all subsequent examples, had round-tipped duralumin propeller blades, which were more efficient and less vulnerable to damage from stones thrown up in reverse pitch than the square-tipped hollow-steel blades originally specified by BOAC.

On 9 January 1959 a Britannia 317 was chartered by Bristol Aircraft Ltd to carry technicians and equipment out to Rangoon to carry out repair work on the stranded BOAC Britannia srs 102 G-ANBC. The Hunting-Clan Britannia set off from Filton with thirty people and 12,000lb (5,440kg) of spares aboard, and reached Bahrain 8½ hours later, an achievement that could not have been matched by any other transport aircraft in service at the time. Rangoon was reached after another eight-hour leg. On 31 January G-APNA set off from London Airport and for the next ten days transported 170 seamen of five nationalities from England to India, from Germany to Japan and from Hong Kong to England. A total distance of 20,000 miles (32,000km) was covered in sixty hours' flying time, and throughout the trip a Bristol team, comprising a test pilot, radio officer, flight engineer and maintenance engineers, was on board in case any unforeseen problems were encountered.

During the months that followed, Hunting-Clan Britannias made several UK–Far East charter flights. In April 1959 the airline was awarded an Air Ministry trooping contract for six flights each month between London and Singapore and Hong Kong carrying services personnel. The inaugural service left London on 15 May 1959, fitted with 114 rearward-facing seats. The interior decor was designed by Charles Butler Associates, and despite being a high-density layout was described as 'unusually luxurious' for a troop transport. The flights to Singapore were scheduled to take about twenty-four hours, with no overnight stops and only three refuelling stops, at Istanbul, Karachi and Bombay. This flight time compared extremely favourably with that of the previously-used Hermes aircraft of Airwork and Skyways, which took about 3½ days for the journey. The Far East trooping contract was followed by further ones for flights to Cyprus, Kenya and Aden, operated by Britannias and DC-6Cs. The Aden flights were scheduled to take fourteen hours by Britannia, with one stop at Benina, with the Nairobi services also calling there and taking one hour longer.

On 1 July 1960 a merger agreement between Hunting-Clan and the Airwork group of companies took effect and Hunting-Clan Air Transport became part of British United Airways. The Britannias were absorbed into the British United fleet, based at Gatwick

**One of British and Commonwealth's two srs 317s.** The late Dave Williams

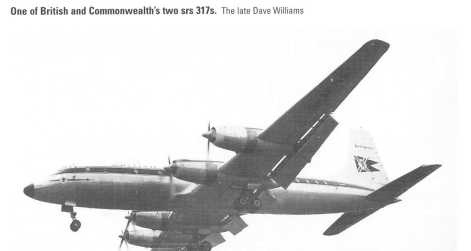

**Srs 317 G-APNA of British and Commonwealth Shipping on final approach.** Air-Britain

## IAC Airlines Britannia Operations

IAC Airlines leased Invicta International Britannia 312 G-AOVF as 9Q-CAZ between January and June 1981.

**Invicta International srs 312F G-AOVF in flight.** Keith Butler

**IAS Britannia 312F G-AOVS in the mid-1970s.** Air-Britain

**Britannia srs 312F G-AOVS of IAS.** The late Dave Williams

## IAS Cargo Airlines Britannia Operations

In the mid-1960s International Aviation Services was founded, and initially provided management and equipment services for African Safari Airways and their Britannia tourist services between East Africa and Europe. This contract came to an end in 1971, but in November 1971 the company bought Britannia 314 G-ATMA from Caledonian Airways and leased this aircraft to Nairobi-based associate company African International Airways, as 5Y-ANS, for use on cargo services between Africa and Europe, mainly carrying meat and machinery. In June 1972 International Aviation Services took over the operation of the Britannia in its own right and opened freight services from Gatwick to several points in Africa. A base was established in Nairobi and many contracts were acquired for cargo flights from Gatwick to the Middle East and Africa; one of the first of these was for the carriage of cattle from Gatwick to Khartoum.

On 17 November 1972 G-ATMA was damaged when a Twin Otter taxied into it at Khartoum, but it was returned to service. By the spring of 1973 G-ANCD and G-ANCH had joined the fleet, and a fourth example was added later in the year. Many other Britannias were purchased for spares. In 1975 the company name was changed to IAS Cargo Airlines, and in that year the first DC-8 jet was acquired. However, the Britannias were still in use and during 1975 one of them made several trips from Exeter to Italy carrying cattle. Also, Dave Sparrow recalls seeing G-AOVF arrive at Dubai on 10 June 1975 with a cargo of sheep, which scattered all over the apron while they were being unloaded! Many flights were also made carrying drilling and other oil-related equipment, with Tripoli often being visited on these services by the Britannias. During 1975 several freight contract flights were also operated from Belfast.

On 3 January 1976 one Britannia started flying freight services from Manston on behalf of the newly-reformed Invicta International Airlines, and it was later joined in this work by a second example. By the middle of 1978, however, the only Britannia left in service was G-AOVF. This was withdrawn after a flight from Nairobi to Gatwick on 28 October 1978.

## Indonesian Angkasa Civil Air Transport Britannia Operations

This Indonesian carrier (sometimes known as Indonesian Inckasa Civil Air Transport) acquired the two former Laker Airways Britannia 102s, which were delivered from Gatwick in February 1969 and re-registered as PK-ICA and PK-ICB. They were used for ad hoc charters around Indonesia and the Far East until the airline went bankrupt in May 1970. The Britannias were placed into store at Jarkarta and were eventually scrapped there.

## Interconair Britannia Operations

Interconair was the airline division of the Intercontinental Meat Company. It was formed in 1976 and acquired an ex-RAF Britannia 253, which was handed over as EI-BBY at Bournemouth in August 1976. The airline was granted a temporary operating licence by the Irish government for livestock carriage only, and EI-BBY was placed into service on cattle charters, with an inaugural service to Dublin on 7 January 1977. However, on 30 September the Britannia was approaching Shannon on a ferry flight with six persons aboard when severe vibration was experienced at a height of 300ft (90m). The approach to Runway 24 was abandoned and an overshoot was started. The Britannia continued to sink however, and collided with the ground short of and to the right of the runway. It bounced, and the right wing broke off. The aircraft skidded and caught fire, and was later declared a write-off. With this, Interconair ceased operations.

## Invicta International Britannia Operations

Invicta Airways Ltd was founded in November 1964 by Wing Commander Hugh Kennard, shortly after he resigned from the post of Managing Director of Air Ferry, another British independent airline of the time. A base was established at Manston Airport in Kent, and inclusive-tour operations began in March 1965, using Vikings and DC-4s. Invicta Airways went on to operate Vanguards and Boeing 720B jets, and to trade as Invicta Air Cargo for freight work and

Invicta International Airlines for passenger-carrying activities. However, in October 1975 the airline's owners since 1973, European Ferries, announced that flying would cease at the end of the month and the fleet would be disposed of. During November and December 1975 several of the former Invicta Air Cargo freight services from Manston to Rotterdam were operated by a British Air Ferries Carvair and by the African Cargo Airways Britannia 307F 5Y-AYR.

In December 1975 the assets and goodwill of Invicta were bought by Universal Air Transport Sales Ltd. In order to restart operations Invicta International leased Britannia 312s G-AOVF and G-AOVS from IAS Cargo Airlines, and commercial services resumed on 3 January 1976. G-AOVF was later bought, along with former Monarch Airways Britannia 308F, G-ANCF. One of the first Invicta Britannia charters was operated from Exeter to Milan by G-AOVS on 8 January 1976 with a load of cattle, and this was followed by another livestock charter, this time from Norwich to Venice on 17 January. The Britannias flew many livestock charters to Europe and were also used on a twice-weekly freight run between Manston and seventeen countries in Europe, the Middle East and North Africa.

During the winter of 1976–77 G-ANCF was leased out to African Cargo Airways. It completed its final service on 30 October 1980 and was moved to the Manston fire dump, but was rescued by a group of enthusiasts and is currently under restoration at Kemble. From January to June 1981 G-AOVF was leased out to IAC Cargo Airlines of Zaire, but at the end of this lease Invicta International ceased operations. The Britannia was flown back to Manston and stored, but this aircraft, too, was saved for posterity, being bought for the British Airways Museum collection at Cosford in 1984. It was delivered to Cosford from Southend on 31 May 1984, landing at 1610hr after one overshoot.

## Katale Aero Transport Britannia Operations

Katale Aero Transport was originally known as Domaine de Katale and was based in Goma, Zaire. It started flying Britannias in 1977, using aircraft leased from Zaire Aero Service, and gradually built up a large fleet of the type. In all, eight were acquired, making Katale the world's last operator of a

sizeable Britannia fleet, but not all of these were used commercially, several having been bought for spares. Britannias and Britannia spares were bought from many sources, including Aer Turas, Redcoat Air Cargo, Young Cargo, Gaylan Air Cargo and the Royal Aircraft Establishment.

The aircraft were used to fly coffee, fruit and other agricultural produce from Goma to various destinations in Zaire, and on the return legs consumer goods, machinery and even passengers were transported. By 1985 four Britannias were operational, three ex-RAF srs 253s (9Q-CDT, 9Q-CGP and 9Q-CHU) and the ex-RAE srs 312 9Q-CHY. Many of the services were operated for BCF Aviation, which initially bought space on the flights, but then chartered whole aircraft as the business expanded. The principal route was from Kinshasa to Mbuji-Mayi, and often one Britannia was fully utilized on this route alone. In May 1988 Katale acquired a mixture of Boeing 707 and DC-8 jet freighters. By then the operational Britannia fleet had been reduced to two examples, 9Q-CDT and 9Q-CHY, with the others used for spares. On 12 January 1988 9Q-CDT operated a service from Mbuji-Mayi to Kinshasa, the last undertaken by this aircraft and possibly the last Katale Britannia service. Later in 1988 both remaining Britannias were sold to BCF Aviation.

## Laker Airways Britannia Operations

Following his resignation from the post of Managing Director of British United Airways, Freddie Laker announced to the world in 1966 that he was starting his own airline. It was his intention to operate brand-new jets as quickly as possible, but as a short-term measure he paid £375,000 for two of the mothballed BOAC Britannia 102s stored at Cambridge. The first, G-ANBM, was delivered to the Gatwick base of Laker Airways in May 1966 and was leased to Air France from July to September 1966 for scheduled services out of Paris' Orly Airport. At the conclusion of this lease it was then hired to Britannia Airways to cover for the loss of G-ANBB, but it did inaugurate services under Laker's own name on 17 September 1966, when it operated a day-trip charter from Gatwick to Cologne. G-ANBN entered full-time service with Laker on 1 October 1966 and for the remainder of 1966 the two aircraft were mainly engaged on ad hoc

**Laker Airways srs 102 G-ANBN in the mid-1960s.** Air-Britain

**G-ANBM, a srs 102 of Laker Airways, at Liverpool in July 1968.** Author

**Liberia World Airways srs 253 OO-YCH, with a Beech Baron and a Beagle 206 in foreground.** Air-Britain

charter work out of Gatwick. By the end of the year almost 100,000 passengers had been carried.

On 29 April 1967 G-ANBM was leased to Treffield International Airways for a season of inclusive-tour work using Laker flight crews and Treffield cabin staff, but this came to an abrupt end on 11 June when Treffield collapsed and the aircraft was reclaimed. That winter G-ANBN was leased to Air Carriers of Zambia from November 1967 until January 1968, and in April 1968 it went on lease to Britannia Airways until October. In the meantime G-ANBM had become the first Bristol Britannia to visit Southampton Airport when it operated flight GK114 to Genoa on 28 May 1968. By the end of the year brand-new BAC One-Elevens had been delivered, and G-ANBM was retired in December. G-ANBN operated the final Laker Britannia revenue service on 5 January 1969, an inclusive-tour flight from Palma to Gatwick. In February 1969 both aircraft were sold to Indonesian Angkasa Civil Air Transport.

## Liberia World Airways Britannia Operations

This company intended to lease two of Young Air Cargo's Britannia 253s in 1977 and the aircraft were repainted in Liberia World livery as EL-LWG and EL-LWH. EL-LWH was never delivered, and it was restored to the Belgian register as OO-YCH in September 1977, but the lease of EL-LWG did go ahead until early autumn 1978.

## Lloyd International Britannia Operations

Lloyd International Airways was founded on 18 January 1961 by two shipbroking partners. Cambridge Airport was chosen as the operating base and in March 1961 a Douglas C-54A Skymaster was acquired to operate a low-cost service between the UK and the Far East, carrying ships' crews and spares. However, it was soon found that this type of work would not make full use of the aircraft, and it actually began service with Lloyd International on inclusive-tour charters out of Gatwick. The operating base was soon relocated to this airport and during 1962 and 1963 two DC-4s were used on holiday charters and Ministry of Defence trooping and freight contracts. A DC-6C was added to the fleet, and in 1965

**OO-YCG, srs 253 of Liberia World Airways at Gosselies on 13 August 1977.** Colin Vangen

### Lloyd International Wanderings

Bill Hickox goes back a long way in Britannia history. He was a member of the pre-delivery RAF team and was responsible for all the 'bits and pieces' needed by navigators – performance manuals, sector/fuel/payload tables etc. From the pages of the newsletter of The Britannia Association comes the story of the time in the summer of 1968 when he was serving with Lloyd International, as Chief Navigator and later as a Britannia First Officer. At the time, Fidel Castro was inviting European students to visit Cuba on working holidays. Castro was a bit of a Britannia 'fan', and perhaps because of this Lloyd International were awarded the contract for a series of flights staging via Gander. These were interspersed between Lloyd's transatlantic charters to the USA and Canada. The student flights all originated in Amsterdam and 'slipped' (changed) crews in Gander. Bill Hickox was on the final leg of the first of these. Having operated G-AOVP to Toronto via Glasgow, Manchester and Shannon, he flew as a passenger to Gander. On the next day he flew G-AOVP to Havana, an eight-hour leg. There the crew joined the passengers for a welcome reception, with glasses of Daiquiri. The next morning they flew the aircraft empty back to Gander, but on departure from Havana the Britannia seemed unaccountably tail-heavy. On handing over to the slip crew at Gander they discovered the reason why – the Cubans had taken the opportunity to stuff the rear holds with bundles of newspapers

containing a major speech by Castro. These had to be thrown out before the flight could continue. Three days later they flew G-AOVS to Kingston, Ottawa and back to Gander, and two days later they returned to their Gatwick base via Toronto.

For their next student trip they flew from Amsterdam to Gander and supplied crews there, taking the next aircraft through to Havana the next day. This was mainly a night flight, and to reach the toilets at the rear of the cabin they had to step over various writhing bodies in the aisle – students keen to join the 'Mile High Club'. On arrival at Havana they collected their return load of students. They were a far less enthusiastic bunch, having had to work hard in the sugar cane fields by day and listen to political lectures in the evenings. At Gander, an engine change was required, necessitating a five-day stopover. After a short time back at base they flew G-AOVP to Kingston and Trinidad, and, after a nightstop, back to Gatwick via Santa Maria. The busy tempo continued, with Gander, slip, Toronto, empty to Havana and back to Gander for another slip. The next trip was to Toronto and return, and their final Cuban trip was flown via Gander to Niagara Falls. After a slip, and a journey to Toronto by road, they flew empty to Havana, picked up a load for Gander, slipped crews there, flew to Ottawa and Niagara and transferred by road again to Toronto. Three days later they returned to Ottawa, slipped crews there and flew back to Gatwick.

**Lloyd International freighter srs 312F G-AOVS.** Air-Britain

two srs 312 Britannias, G-AOVP and G-AOVS, were lease-purchased from BOAC. G-AOVP operated Lloyd's inaugural Britannia service on 2 July 1965, from Stansted to Santa Maria in the Azores. The same aircraft also entered service on holiday charter flights for Mercury Air Holidays on 10 July, flying a programme of services from Glasgow to Palma, Valencia, Barcelona and Rimini, the first service being to Palma. Two days later G-AOVP operated the first of many long-haul charters from Gatwick to the Far East. G-AOVS was leased to British Eagle for the second half of 1965, and then went to Aviation Traders at Stansted for conversion to a srs 312F freighter during the winter. This work entailed the fitting of a 10ft 3in × 6ft 7in (3.13 × 2.01m) freight door and a strengthened floor. Once the job was completed the aircraft could accommodate up to 132 passengers in an all-economy layout, or could operate in a mixed passenger/freight configuration with up to eight standard freight pallets. The total payload was 18 tons and the conversion from one configuration to another could be accomplished in about two hours.

G-AOVS re-entered service on 14 June 1966, in time to ferry cargoes between Liverpool and Belfast during a national seamen's strike. Meanwhile, G-AOVP had joined Britannias of other independent airlines and the RAF on the Zambian oil airlift during early 1966, carrying up to fifty-five 44gal (200ltr) oil drums at a time between Dar-es Salaam and Lusaka or Ndola. It arrived back at Gatwick in May 1966 and spent the summer flying from Berlin to the Mediterranean resorts for a German tour operator during the week and Mercury Air Holidays charters from Glasgow at weekends. During that summer the Lloyd operating base was changed again, this time to Stansted. Both Britannias continued to fly throughout the winter, and in December G-AOVS carried the British polo team, comprising twenty-six ponies and seven grooms, from Stansted to Buenos Aires and back. A few days later, however, this aircraft suffered a nosewheel collapse during an attempted 'touch and go' landing whilst crew training, and was out of service for almost two months.

Whilst its companion was being repaired G-AOVP maintained services alone and in April 1967 operated a charter from Stansted to St John (New Brunswick) and return via Prestwick with forty passengers and six crew aboard. During the summer of 1967 both Britannias resumed inclusive-tour flights from Glasgow and Berlin and also undertook long-haul charters, including a series of Ministry of Defence flights to destinations as varied as Kinloss, Andoya (Norway) and Dubai. G-AOVS was to continue to be engaged on Ministry of Defence work for most of October and November 1967.

In the meantime Mercury Air Holidays had been engaged in setting up its own airline, to be known as Donaldson International. Until the new airline was ready to commence operations, its first aircraft, Britannia 317 G-APNA, was leased to Lloyd International for eighteen months from 26 October 1967, and the arrival of this aircraft released G-AOVP for its own freight-door conversion at Southend. During the winter of 1967–68 G-APNA was mainly used for long-haul passenger work out of Stansted, while G-AOVS flew Ministry of Defence flights and ad hoc charters. G-AOVP re-entered service on 21 April 1968 and three Britannias were in service for the summer of 1968, which was a very busy time for Lloyd International, with transatlantic charters and Mediterranean holiday flights from the UK but no longer from Berlin. In the autumn, once this work had wound down, a new weekly freight service from Stansted to Hong Kong via Rotterdam and Bangkok was launched. There were also many ad hoc freight flights on behalf of El Al from Tel Aviv to Paris, Heathrow, Amsterdam, New York and Frankfurt.

On 3 May 1969 G-APNA was withdrawn and returned to Donaldson International, but in the meantime Lloyd had bought British United Airways' two Britannia 307 freighters G-ANCD and G-ANCE, and so had four examples available for the summer of 1969. Inclusive-tour flying was dramatically reduced, with only a weekly Stansted–Gerona service, but the Britannia fleet was used on many services to the Far East. Ad hoc services to European destinations such as Brussels, Ostend, Hamburg, Maastricht and Athens were also operated, and many Ministry of Defence charters were undertaken, including one from Prestwick to Patrick Air Force Base, Florida, via Gander with 116 passengers in July. During November 1969 Lloyd Britannias began flying many cargo services for BEA while that airline's Vanguards were being converted to Merchantman freighters. Freight charters for Ford began on 11 May 1970 with flights from Liverpool and Stansted to Saarbrücken and Cologne, and other work that summer

**Lloyd International srs 312 G-AOVP.** The late Dave Williams

**A Lloyd International Britannia srs 300 at Gatwick.** via author

**A Lloyd International Britannia 312F takes on cargo at Liverpool in July 1968.** Author

included pilgrimage flights to Tarbes and charters from Stansted to Isfahan and Shiraz in Iran. By October 1970 G-AOVS and G-AOVP were being used almost exclusively on contract freight work for BEA and El Al, while the other two aircraft undertook Ministry of Defence flights from Brize Norton and Lloyd's own services from Stansted to the Far East. In January 1971 G-ANCD inaugurated a new weekly cargo service for East African Airways from Heathrow to Nairobi via Dar-es-Salaam, Entebbe and Lusaka, and in April G-ANCE began a series of day-trip passenger flights to the Dutch bulbfields for Clarksons Tours, flying from Bristol to Rotterdam and from Cardiff and Bristol to Beauvais. These flights continued daily for a period of five weeks.

The contract flights for El Al, East African and BEA continued throughout 1971, but by early 1972 Lloyd International's own services to the Far East had been considerably run down. The Clarksons Tours bulbfield flights resumed in the spring but on 16 June 1972 Lloyd International's parent company, Lloyd Aviation Holdings, announced the appointment of a Receiver for the airline. All flying was halted and the Britannia fleet returned to Stansted. The airline's Air Operator's Certificate was withdrawn on 19 June 1972,

but all four of the Britannias were to find work later, flying for other carriers.

## Lukum Air Services Britannia Operations

The former Geminair Britannia 252 9G-ACE was bought by Lukum Air Services as 9Q-CUM in September 1981, but was retired the following year after the carrier had acquired a DC-8 freighter.

## Malayan Airways Britannia Operations

This carrier leased several BOAC Britannia 102s from 1960, including G-ANBF, G-ANBG, G-ANBI, G-ANBJ, G-ANBM and G-ANBO. This last aircraft was in service with Malayan Airways in 1962, operating between Singapore, Kuala Lumpur, Hong Kong and Jakarta. The Singapore–Kuala Lumpur–Hong Kong service had previously been operated by chartered QANTAS Super Constellations, but was suspended in October 1960 and then reopened with Britannias. BOAC flight crews were used at first, but by the end of March 1962 they were replaced by UK-trained Malayan Airways pilots. Leased

BOAC srs 102s continued to operate for Malayan Airways between Kuala Lumpur and London until 1963, after BOAC had retired the type from its own services.

## Monarch Airlines Britannnia Operations

In January 1967 two former British Eagle directors, Don Peacock and Bill Hodgson, set up Airline Engineering Ltd as an aircraft maintenance organization. After talks with holiday company Cosmos Tours they became convinced that there was a shortage of good-quality charter aircraft capacity and as a result they founded Monarch Airlines Ltd on 1 June 1967. The initial plan was to operate from Stansted, but they were offered such good terms and facilities by Luton Corporation, including two superb hangars formerly used for production of the Hunting Pembroke and Jet Provost, that they changed their minds and set up their operating base at Luton Airport. Britannia 312s G-AOVI and G-AOVH were bought from Caledonian Airways and delivered to Luton on 15 February and 1 April 1968, and Monarch initially budgeted for a useful commercial life of five years for the Britannias, with jets then being introduced.

**BOAC srs 102 G-ANBM on lease to Malayan Airways in 1960.** Air-Britain

G-AOVI continued in service with Caledonian initially, though, on lease from Monarch until the end of March to complete a Mecca pilgrim flight contract.

The first Monarch Britannia revenue service took place on 5 April 1968, when G-AOVI left Luton for Madrid (arriving back forty minutes late on the round trip!), and during 1968 the 143-seat Britannias flew to Barcelona, Basle, Gerona, Ibiza, Madrid, Rimini and Valencia. They also undertook ad hoc charters, including occasional flights to the USA and Canada, and Ministry of Defence trips from Birmingham, Luton and Teesside to Aden, Gütersloh and Wildenrath. The collapse of British Eagle in November 1968 resulted in Monarch taking over five of that airline's Britannias during 1968 and 1969, and at the end of its first year Monarch Airlines had carried 122,873 passengers. On 29 April 1969 G-AOVH ran off the runway at Luton when its nosewheel collapsed on landing, but it was repaired and returned to service, and six Britannias were in service in time for the 1969 summer season. Also during that year Monarch was awarded a Ministry of Defence contract for regular freight flights to Perth, Australia, from Brize Norton and Lyneham (a contract formerly held by British Eagle). By the end of 1969 251,466 passengers had been carried aboard Monarch Britannias. For the 1970 season a greatly expanded programme of inclusive-tour flights was operated from Luton to seventeen destinations, and the fleet was also used on long-haul charters to the Far East, West Africa, Guyana and Suriname (from Rotterdam). In the springtime Clarksons Tours used the Britannias for day-trip charters from Manchester to Beauvais and Rotterdam for the delights of Paris and the Dutch bulbfields, and they were also chartered by Ghana Airways for Haj pilgrimage flights between Accra and Jeddah.

Boeing 720B jets were introduced from December 1971 and by the end of May 1972 four Britannias had been retired. However, the type was still in Monarch service at the end of the year, operating inclusive-tour flights, ad hoc charters, the Ministry of Defence freight run to Australia and trooping flights to Germany from Birmingham, Luton, Manchester and Teesside. Airline Engineering was also kept busy, overhauling Britannias belonging to African Safari Airways, Cubana, International Aviation Services and many other small operators. On inclusive-tour flights, the Britannia often had a distinct

**Monarch Britannia 312 G-AOVG had served previously with British Eagle.** Air-Britain

**Monarch Airlines srs 312 G-AOVH, with a British Eagle Britannia behind it.** The late Dave Williams

**Monarch srs 312 G-AOVI.** Air-Britain

advantage over the higher-flying jet types: although slower, the Britannia often made the journey in a shorter time, as the lower flight levels at which it cruised carried far less traffic. The Britannias also entered any 'stacks' for their arrival airports at a lower level, and so were cleared for approach before the jets.

(*Above*) Monarch Airlines srs 312 G-AOVT, possibly at Duxford after delivery for preservation. Note the collection of historic types in the background.
Air-Britain

**Monarch's ex-British Eagle srs 308F G-ANCF.** Air-Britain

**Monarch Airlines srs 309 G-ANCH was previously 9G-AAG of Ghana Airways.**
Air-Britain

In February 1974 G-ANCF was in Australia operating flood relief flights out of Darwin on behalf of Trans-Australia Airlines. Monarch's last passenger-carrying Britannia, G-AOVT, operated its last service under the Monarch name, a round-trip from Luton to Basle, on 9 October 1974, and on 13 October it was chartered by Northeast Airlines to replace a Trident on a Lisbon–Luton service. This was the last European passenger-carrying flight by a Britannia. The aircraft was then converted to a freighter and leased to Invicta International from December 1974 until March 1975, operating its last commercial services on 14 February 1975, from Dublin to Tripoli and Tripoli to Manston. At the conclusion of the Invicta lease G-AOVT was flown to Luton for storage and was then donated to the Duxford Aviation Society for preservation. Resprayed in Monarch colours, the aircraft was delivered to Duxford during an air display on 29 June 1975, and made one last low pass along the runway before landing. It was restored to passenger configuration during the winter of 1979–80 and is currently on show at Duxford in its Monarch colour scheme. Monarch's last serviceable Britannia, srs 308F G-ANCF, continued in service on the government freight run to

**Monarch Airlines srs 312 G-AOVB and a selection of period cars.** Air-Britain

**Former British Eagle srs 308F freighter G-ANCF in service with Monarch.** Air-Britain

**One-time BOAC srs 312 G-AOVL in Monarch colours.** Air-Britain

Adelaide until the end of 1975. It arrived back at Luton on 20 December 1975 at the conclusion of Monarch's last commercial Britannia service, and left Luton again on 27 January 1976 on delivery to African Safari Airways. Between 1968 and 1975, Monarch operated eleven Britannias.

## Nigeria Airways Britannia Operations

From 30 September 1958 WAAC (Nigeria) Ltd, trading as Nigeria Airways, began using BOAC Stratocruisers on the Lagos–London route under a revenue pooling agreement between the two carriers. On 16 April 1959 turboprop services were introduced onto this route, using chartered BOAC Britannia 102s. The first service from London was flown by G-ANBE, and G-ANBA, G-ANBB, G-ANBG and G-ANBK were also used at various times. Eventually the Britannias were replaced by VC-10s.

## Redcoat Air Cargo Britannia Operations

Based at Luton Airport, Redcoat Air Cargo bought Britannia 312F G-AOVS in 1977. This aircraft remained the sole member of the Redcoat fleet until 1979, when two former RAF Britannia 253s were bought as G-BRAC and G-BHAU. G-AOVS was withdrawn and stored at Luton in January 1979. It was donated to the Luton Airport Fire Service, but in February 1980 the registration G-BRAC was painted onto it, and it was given 'Redair' titles for filming the TV drama series *Buccaneer*, about a cargo charter airline. Its remains were still visible at Luton in 1994.

Back in the real airline world, the real G-BRAC was lost with seven of the eight people aboard, and some people on the ground, when it crashed at Billerica, USA, on 16 February 1980. The Britannia had taken off from Boston (Logan) a few minutes earlier as cargo flight 103 in conditions of snow, fog and moderate to severe icing. It reached an altitude of 1,700ft (500m) but then started to descend and crashed in a wooded area. Airframe icing was determined as the primary cause of the crash, with windshear, downdraughts and turbulence plus an inadequate weather briefing as contributing factors.

G-BHAU remained in service, mainly on cattle flights from Forli in Italy to Nigeria,

and also on occasional ad hoc charters, but Redcoat ceased operations in December 1981 and the aircraft was then sold to Katale Aero Transport in Zaire.

## Southern Cross International Britannia Operations

Southern Cross International was an Australian carrier that almost leased Britannia 312 G-AOVM from Air Spain in late 1969, but the deal did not go through. From 20 May 1970 srs 102 G-ANBL was leased from Britannia Airways for about a month. This was the only occasion on which a Britannia was operated by an Australian airline.

(*Top*) A BOAC srs 102 on lease to Nigeria Airways. The late Dave Williams

(*Above*) Srs 312F G-AOVS was operated by Redcoat Air Cargo from May 1977 to January 1979. Air-Britain

(*Right*) Southern Cross International leased srs 102 G-ANBL from Britannia Airways for just a month in 1970. Air-Britain

## Tellair Britannia Operations

Tellair was formed at Basle in March 1968 by a consortium of Swiss travel agencies and British Eagle International Airlines. The original intention was to use British Eagle Britannias on inclusive-tour flights out of Geneva and Zurich, but this was frustrated by the demise of British Eagle in November 1968. In the event, two members of the former British Eagle fleet, Britannia 324s G-ARKA and G-ARKB, under the new ownership of Caledonian Airways, were used when Tellair started operations in March 1969. However, in October 1969 the Swiss civil aviation authority told Tellair that it must buy and operate its own aircraft if it wished to continue flying. The company was unable to find the funds for this and services ended that month.

**Srs 324 G-ARKB of Tellair was operated on their behalf by Caledonian Airways from May to November 1969.** Air-Britain

**Tellair srs 324 G-ARKA.** Air-Britain

## Transair Cargo Britannia Operations

With the retirements of the Cuban Britannias in 1990 and those in Zaire in 1991, it seemed that the type's flying days were over. However, John Byrne, the Technical Director of BCF Aviation and a self-confessed Britannia enthusiast, had other ideas. He set up his own cargo airline, Transair Cargo, in Zaire with the intention of

buying and operating the retired BCF Britannia 313F 9Q-CHY. His original plan was thwarted when Dr Mayani of BCF refused to sell him either the Britannia or his inventory of spares because he did not want competition from a new Zaire carrier.

Byrne then travelled to Havana to inspect the Cuban Britannias. He made a successful bid for the former Aero Caribbean Britannia 253s CU-T120 and CU-T121, plus the remains of srs 318s

CU-T114 and CU-T671, and from these he decided to restore CU-T120 to airworthy condition. A new Proteus engine was acquired in the UK and despatched to Cuba to replace the one which had failed on the aircraft's last service. However, during ground runs the compressor of the number three engine failed and another Proteus was sent out from the UK and fitted. A test flight under the new registration 9Q-CJH was finally made on 25

August 1993, the first time a Britannia had been airborne in just over two years. All went well with the test flight until the time came for landing, and selection of 'undercarriage down' did not achieve the desired result. The gear was eventually lowered by using the emergency manual system, and the Britannia landed safely after a test flight lasting 1 hour 17 minutes.

After the undercarriage problem was rectified the cabin was filled with spares and the epic delivery flight to Zaire started on 10 September 1993. The flight went via Gander, Dublin, Filton, Ostend, Cairo, Goma and finally Kinshasa. The first leg to Gander was achieved in 7 hours 20 minutes, and the transatlantic flight from Gander to Dublin in only 6 hours 24 minutes, thanks to very favourable winds boosting the Britannia's ground speed to 370kt (686km/h). A stopover at Dublin had not been pre-planned, but the flight was behind schedule and Filton would have been closed by the time the Britannia arrived, so a few days were spent in Ireland. On departure from Dublin a steep take-off was followed by a high-speed low pass along Runway 16 before a course was set over the Irish Sea for Filton. The visit to Filton was really just a courtesy call, although some Britannia spares were offloaded there for overhaul elsewhere in the UK. During its time at Filton 9Q-CJH was visited by Sir Archibald Russell, the former head of the Britannia design team, and Walter Gibb, former Chief Test Pilot of Bristol. The delivery flight continued via Ostend, Cairo and Goma, with Kinshasa finally being reached at 1125hr on 26 September 1993.

The aircraft entered service on 4 October, carrying a full load of margarine from Kinshasa to Mbuji-Mayi. Dr Mayani was eventually persuaded to sell BCF's huge stock of Britannia spares, making the aircraft's future more secure, but just over a month later it landed at Kinshasa with its nosewheel retracted and sustained damage to the lower forward fuselage and propellers. After temporary repairs it was ferried to Johannesburg for more comprehensive work to be carried out, many of the replacement parts fitted being taken from the grounded BCF aircraft 9Q-CHY. The Britannia eventually returned to Kinshasa and re-entered service alongside Transair's DC-4 and DC-8 aircraft on cargo flights within Zaire, but by the summer of 1995 it appears to have been replaced by a Boeing 707-120B and either sold or leased to Trans Service Airlift.

# Transcontinental SA Britannia Operations

Transcontinental SA was founded in 1956 and began operations in 1957 with Curtiss C-46s. In 1958 it inaugurated a 6,240-mile (10,040km) route from Buenos Aires to New York via Rio de Janeiro and Caracas, using Super Constellations. The route was operated in competition with the Boeing 707 and DC-8 jets of Pan American, and in order to remain competitive Transcontinental needed turbine-powered aircraft. Two Britannia 305s from the frustrated Northeast Airlines order (G-ANCF and G-ANCG) remained unsold at Belfast in

1959, and on 24 August 1959 Transcontinental signed a contract with Bristol to buy these aircraft. Work went ahead to modify them to Transcontinental's requirements as srs 308s, fitted with just sixteen First Class and eighty-eight Tourist Class seats, instead of the maximum 132 seats that they could have fitted, and one of the other distinguishing features of the srs 308's spacious interior layout was a well-stocked cocktail lounge bar.

The first example, provisionally marked as G-14-1, made its first flight on 20 October 1959 from Short's airfield at Sydenham, Belfast, to Filton, where it was formally handed over to the airline.

A pre-delivery photo of Transcontinental SA srs 308 LV-PPJ before re-registration as LV-GJB. Air-Britain

Transcontinental SA srs 308 LV-GJC. Air-Britain

Provisionally re-registered LV-PPJ and LV-PPL, the two Britannias left on their delivery flights on 16 and 17 December 1959. Following their arrival in Buenos Aires they were re-registered as LV-GJB and LV-GJC, and placed into service on the Buenos Aires–New York route. This was operated three times weekly by the two Britannias, with stops northbound at Rio de Janiero, Sao Paulo, Paramaribo (Suriname) for refuelling, and Caracas. Southbound, the itinerary varied, with the technical stop at Paramaribo being dropped. The journey from New York to Buenos Aires took 21 hours 30 minutes, including around 18 hours' flying time. At Buenos Aires an extensive network of connecting flights to other Argentinian destinations, and to Paraguay and Uruguay, was provided by C-46s. In January 1960 the Britannias had succeeded in boosting the passenger load factor on the Buenos Aires–New York route to 46.2 per cent, compared to 38.2 per cent in January 1959, when L-1049H Super Constellations were in use. The Britannias were also used on the three-times weekly service to Santiago in Chile, covering the 700 miles (1,100km) in two hours.

Within eighteen months of the introduction of the Britannias, however, Transcontinental was encountering severe financial problems, and on 8 November 1961 all Transcontinental services were suspended following the impounding of LV-GJC at Idlewild Airport, New York, on 24 October for non-payment of fees and other debts. The aircraft was later released in April 1962 after payment of $83,000, but remained at a standstill. The other Britannia also remained idle at Buenos Aires, and later on in 1962 Transcontinental SA was declared bankrupt. The complicated state of the airline's finances meant that it was over two years before the two Britannias could fly again, but in January and February 1964 they were ferried to Heathrow to continue their careers with British Eagle.

## Trans Gulf Air Cargo Britannia Operations

This company commenced operations in 1977, having acquired a Britannia 307F on lease from Westwings Aviation Services. The aircraft was sub-leased to Air Faisal for part of 1978, and once the sub-lease was completed it was returned to Westwings and Trans Gulf ceased operating.

## Transglobe Airways Britannia Operations

Transglobe Airways began life on 21 August 1958 when an airline company named Air Links Ltd was founded with a share capital of £100. The airline remained dormant until May 1959 when a DC-3 was bought from Aer Lingus; charter work with DC-3s was carried out from July 1959. A Handley Page Hermes was bought in 1962 (the company was to be the last commercial operator of the type) and in 1963 Air Links began negotiations with BOAC for the purchase of several of the Britannia 102s then stored at Cambridge. However, the asking price proved too high and the sale was not proceeded with. Instead, in 1964 the first of a fleet of Canadair Argonauts was delivered to the airline's Gatwick base.

**Transglobe srs 302 G-ANCC, probably at Biggin Hill after withdrawal in 1970.**
Air-Britain

On 15 May 1965 the company's first Britannia was delivered to Southend for overhaul. This was not a srs 102, but the former CPAL srs 314 CF-CZA; sister-ship CF-CZC followed on 17 June 1965. Both these Britannias were converted to 125-passenger configuration and CF-CZA was delivered to Gatwick in full BUA livery, entering service on lease to that airline in mid-July. However, on 30 July 1965 this aircraft arrived at Gatwick from Southend as G-ATGD, repainted in the colours of Transglobe Airways, and on the following day Air Links officially changed its name to Transglobe Airways Ltd. For the next three months G-ATGD flew numerous scheduled services

and inclusive-tour charters on behalf of BUA to places such as Dubrovnik, Palma, Rimini and Tunis, but on 18 August it also operated its first service for Transglobe Airways, from Gatwick to Malta. This was followed on 25 August by its first long-haul charter, Gatwick–Belfast–Santa Maria (Azores)–Bermuda. In the latter part of 1965 charters were also operated on behalf of Caledonian Airways to New York via Gander, Baghdad and other airports in the Middle East and North Africa.

Transglobe's second Britannia, now re-registered G-ATLE, was handed over at Southend after overhaul on 12 December 1965 and flew its first service on 18 December 1965, from Gatwick to Khartoum. Following the Unilateral Declaration of Independence by Rhodesia G-ATGD joined many other Britannias on the airlift of barrels of oil between Dar-es-Salaam and

Lusaka in the winter of 1965–66. Despite having neither a reinforced floor nor a large cargo door, this aircraft carried fifty-five 44gal (200ltr) oil drums on each trip, and achieved turnaround times in the region of thirty-five minutes.

On 17 April 1966 inclusive-tour flying resumed, with G-ATLE opening a fortnightly Gatwick–Tunis service. That same month Transglobe acquired the Aeronaves de Mexico Britannia 302 G-ANCC (formerly XA-MED), and the remains of her sister-ship XA-MEC for spares. G-ANCC was delivered to Gatwick on 22 May and flew her first service for Transglobe on 13 July, from Gatwick to Benina.

**Transglobe srs 314 G-ATGD was formerly CF-CZA with CPAL.** Air-Britain

The Britannias were also used for transatlantic charters from overseas airports on routes such as Frankfurt–Toronto. By the beginning of the 1966 season Transglobe had secured bookings for some sixty-eight transatlantic charters from UK and European departure points. The final transatlantic flights of the 1966 season took place on 14 October, when G-ATGD flew New York–Gatwick and G-ANCC came home to Gatwick from Toronto via Gander. Mediterranean package-tour services were also operated by the Britannias that summer, to destinations such as Tunis, Catania, Dubrovnik, Pisa, Rimini, Malta and Malaga. The summer season closed with a round trip from Gatwick to Tunis by G-ATGD on 6 November. In September 1966 Transglobe had signed an agreement with the Flying Tiger Line for the lease-purchase of two Canadair CL-44s, but the US Civil Aeronautics Board embargoed the sale of these aircraft, and so on 9 December 1966 Britannia 309 G-ANCH was delivered to Transglobe on lease from the British Aircraft Corporation. Several charters were operated over the Christmas period, including one to Palma and a Toronto–Düsseldorf service, and with four Britannias available Transglobe was able to plan a far more extensive programme of transatlantic flights for the 1967 season.

In fact, during 1967 Transglobe carried more charter passengers between Canada and Europe than any other independent airline in the world. UK departure points

included Gatwick, Prestwick and Belfast, and on 16 July G-ANCH set off from Birmingham for Toronto on flight IK1041, the first-ever direct passenger service from that airport to North America. Transglobe had also started charters from Manchester to Toronto via Gander on 16 May, but Gatwick was still the airline's main departure airport, with flights to Toronto, Montreal, New York, Ottawa and Vancouver, usually with technical stops at Gander or Sondre Stromfjord in Greenland. Weekend inclusive-tour flights to the Mediterranean were also operated from Gatwick and Manchester.

The lease of G-ANCH ended in October 1967, but in May of that year Transglobe had finally secured a successful lease agreement for CL-44 aircraft, this time with Seaboard World Airlines, for six CL-44Ds for use on transatlantic charters during 1968. Throughout the first quarter of 1968 G-ATGD and G-ATLE were almost exclusively engaged on passenger charters to the Far East, East Africa and the West Indies. A new colour scheme was introduced during 1968 to coincide with the introduction of the CL-44s, with G-ANCC being the first Britannia to sport the new markings. The majority of the transatlantic services were now operated by CL-44s, but Britannias were still used for Mediterranean holiday flights during the summer, and also on sub-charters from Luxembourg to Johannesburg for Trek Airways. Time was running out for Transglobe

and the Britannias, however. G-ATLE was withdrawn on 13 October 1968, and in the early hours of 22 November G-ANCC arrived back at Gatwick from Montreal on the last transatlantic crossing by a Transglobe Britannia. She then flew a round trip to Tenerife on 24 November, arriving back at Gatwick on the 25th. This was to be her final service for Transglobe, as on the evening of 28 November the company announced that it was ceasing all flying immediately, being unable to raise further capital to continue operations. Transglobe management later attributed the failure to the use of uncompetitive turboprop airliners on the transatlantic routes, and the excessive £6.5m purchase price of the CL-44s. G-ANCC and G-ATLE were at Gatwick at the time of the collapse, and neither of them were to see further airline service, but G-ATGD was sold to African Safari Airways in 1969.

## Trans Service Airlift Britannia Operations

By the summer of 1995 Trans Service Airlift had either bought or leased Britannia 253 9Q-CJH from Transair Cargo. It was while it was in service with Trans Service Airlift, or possibly with Transair Cargo after return from lease, that the Britannia was mentioned in a January 1999 article in the *Washington Post*, titled 'The Illicit Gun Trade, Fanning Flames of Conflict', by

Kathi Austin. This contained the story of a February 1995 flight from Kalemie, in what was then eastern Zaire, to Kinshasa with a cargo of illicit weapons which the crew and the reporter, who was then a human rights investigator, believed to be small arms. The flight had to make an emergency return to Kalemie when the cargo turned out to be containers of toxic chloride which released a poisonous gas into the cabin once the air pressure dropped. The aircraft was landed with the use of oxygen masks by the crew, but the dozen or so Africans hitching a free ride in the back were not so lucky. These weapons-running flights originated in countries of the former Soviet Union or elsewhere in Eastern Europe, where the weapons and fictitious paperwork were picked up, and routed via Ostend or Bourgas in Bulgaria. False flight plans were filed to Cairo or Lagos, but the aircraft actually landed at clandestine airfields where the cargo was delivered to the UNITA rebels in Angola or the Hutu renegades in eastern Congo.

## The Return to the UK of the Last Britannia

By April 1997 srs 253 9Q-CJH was lying abandoned at Kinshasa with only three serviceable engines, its owners having been forced to leave their base by the imminent collapse of the Mabutu government. The Britannia was still awaiting a replacement engine when it departed on a three-engined ferry flight to Lanseria, near Johannesburg, on 4 May 1997, just twelve days before rebel forces invaded Kinshasa.

In August 1997 the aircraft was re-registered to Transair Cargo as EL-WXA and was fitted with a new engine at Lanseria. It was test-flown from there on 21 September, and on 12 October set off from Lanseria under the command of Captain Bob Sovek, with Captain Verveck assisting and John Byrne as Flight Engineer, on its long ferry flight to Kemble and preservation by The Britannia Aircraft Preservation Trust. Also on board was Tony de Bruyn, Britannia Aircraft Preservation Trust Joint Founder Trustee, the last-ever Britannia passenger.

Having routed via Doula it arrived at Palma late in the evening of 13 October and departed there on the 14th, arriving at Kemble that day and performing a very low flypast before making the very last (to date?) landing by a Bristol Britannia.

## Treffield International Airways Britannia Operations

In 1965 Treffield Aviation was founded and began life as a general charter operator using two Avro Nineteens. In late 1966 the airline won a major contract worth £500,000 for inclusive-tour flights out of Bristol and Cardiff on behalf of the local tour operator Hourmont Holidays. This was to start in the spring of 1967, and in order to carry out the work Treffield arranged for the lease of Viscount 812s from Channel Airways and Britannia 102 G-ANBM from Laker Airways, and changed its name to Treffield International Airways. The Britannia was handed over to Treffield on 5 May 1967 and the

**The last flying Britannia. Srs 253 EL-WXA at Palma on 13 October 1997 during its ferry flight to Kemble and preservation.** Toni Marimon

**G-ANBM, a Treffield International srs 102 on lease from Laker Airways, in 1967.** Air-Britain

programme of tour flights started, using Laker flight crews and Treffield cabin crews, but during June Treffield suffered a succession of problems leading to disputes with the tour operator. This resulted in the announcement that the airline would be ceasing its flights out of Bristol and Cardiff on behalf of Hourmont Holidays. The Britannia was handed back to Laker in the

middle of June and Treffield ceased operations on 23 June 1967.

## Young Cargo Services Britannia Operations

Young Cargo was set up by founder Edward Le Jeune on 9 September 1974 to operate

**Engineless srs 253F OO-YCA of Young Cargo at Stansted in August 1977.**
Eduard Marmet

worldwide cargo charters. Bases were established at Gosselies and Brussels, and the first revenue service was operated from Milan to Stavanger on 4 March 1975, using a CL-44 leased from Cargolux. During the mid-1970s eight former RAF Britannias were acquired. Four were used purely for spares but the other four (OO-YCC, OO-YCE, OO-YCG and OO-YCH) were operated on cargo charters between Belgium and Africa. OO-YCG was also leased out to Liberia World Airways. In 1977 Young Cargo bought two Boeing 707s and the Britannias were withdrawn. The last one in use on Young's own services was OO-YCH, which flew charters out of Ostend for a time in 1977 before being grounded there later in the year. On completion of the lease to Liberia World in September 1978, OO-YCG was flown into storage at Manston.

## Zaire Aero Service Britannia Operations

Ex-RAF Britannia 252 XN398 was purchased in February 1977 as 9Q-CPX, but spent most of its time on lease to Domaine de Katale before being sold to Katale Aero Transport in November 1977.

# CHAPTER FIVE

# Military Service

Though many Britannias were used for military transport flights, notably those chartered by the British Ministry of Defence for trooping flights, and the Cubana aircraft used for moving military supplies and personnel to Angola, only twenty-one, all in Great Britain, actually saw air force duty, twenty with the Royal Air Force and one with the Aircraft and Armament Experimental Establishment.

## RAF Britannia Operations

In February 1955 Bristol received an order from the Ministry of Supply for three mixed-traffic Britannias, which it at first hoped to lease to charter operators. The three aircraft, designated srs 252s, were built at Belfast, where Short Bros and Harland undertook the detail design of a large cargo door and strengthened freight floor for them. They were initially placed on the civil register as G-APPE, G-APPF and G-APPG, but were later assimilated into a fleet of twenty fully-developed Britannias ordered for RAF Transport Command and designated srs 253s by Bristol, although renamed Britannia C.1 by the Air Ministry. The Britannia was Transport Command's first turboprop aircraft type, and the decision to order was taken in November 1955, following the cancellation of the projected Vickers V.1000 jet transport. Six were ordered initially, the order later being increased to ten and eventually to twenty.

The first flight of a military Britannia took place on 13 October 1958, when G-APPE (later to become XN392), the first of the three srs 252s, began test flying from Belfast. The first flight of the Britannia 253 was made by XL635 from Belfast on 29 December 1958. The aircraft featured improved Proteus 255 engines of higher output and a full-length metal floor, fittings for aft-facing seats, stretchers or cargo, and RAF instruments and radios. RAF Britannias were equipped to carry a flight-deck crew of two pilots, navigator, signaller and engineer, although two engineers were

normally carried on route flying. Two Air Quartermasters/Loadmasters were also carried, and up to 117 troops could be accommodated, in six-abreast rearward-facing seats, which were stressed to 9g. These seats could be removed and stowed in the lower freight holds when the aircraft was required to operate in the freighter or casualty evacuation role. Alternatively, the aircraft could accommodate fifty-three stretcher cases and six medical attendants, or 37,400lb (17,000kg) of freight. There was also a VIP conversion unit designed and built by Bristol Aircraft that could provide accommodation for six VIPs and nine other passengers in the rear fuselage, leaving the rest of the cabin free for normal purposes. This unit could be installed in four hours and removed in two.

Delivery of the twenty C.1s to the RAF began with XL636 from Belfast on 4 June 1959. It was handed over to Wg Cdr Barnard, Commanding Officer of No. 99 Squadron, by Cyril Unwins, Deputy Chairman of the Bristol Aeroplane Company, in an informal ceremony at Royal Air Force Lyneham on 9 June 1959. Five were built at Filton (XM498 and XM517–20) and fifteen at Belfast (XL635–8, XL657–60, and XM496 and 497). These last two were also the last to be delivered, on 17 September and 2 December 1960.

**Srs 252 C.2 XN398 was originally registered to the Ministry of Supply as G-APPF.** Air-Britain

**Srs 253 C.1 XM520, with just 'Royal Air Force' titling.** Air-Britain

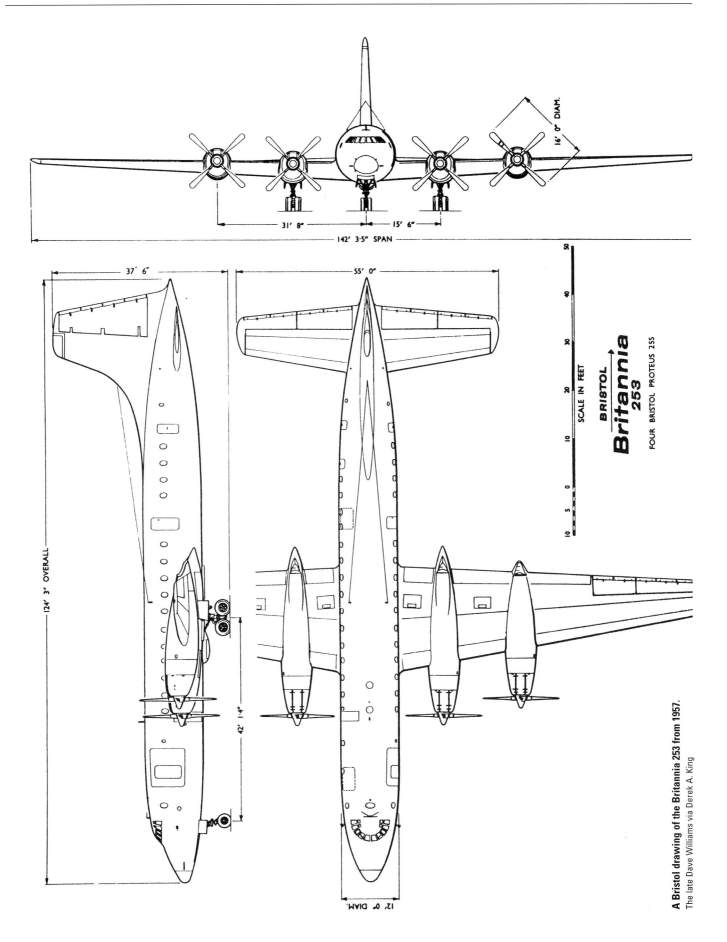

16′ 0″ DIAM.

31′ 8″   15′ 6″

142′ 3·5″ SPAN

37′ 6″   55′ 0″

124′ 3″ OVERALL

42′ 1·4″

BRISTOL
**Britannia**
253

FOUR BRISTOL PROTEUS 255

SCALE IN FEET

12′ 0″ DIAM.

**A Bristol drawing of the Britannia 253 from 1957.**
The late Dave Williams via Derek A. King

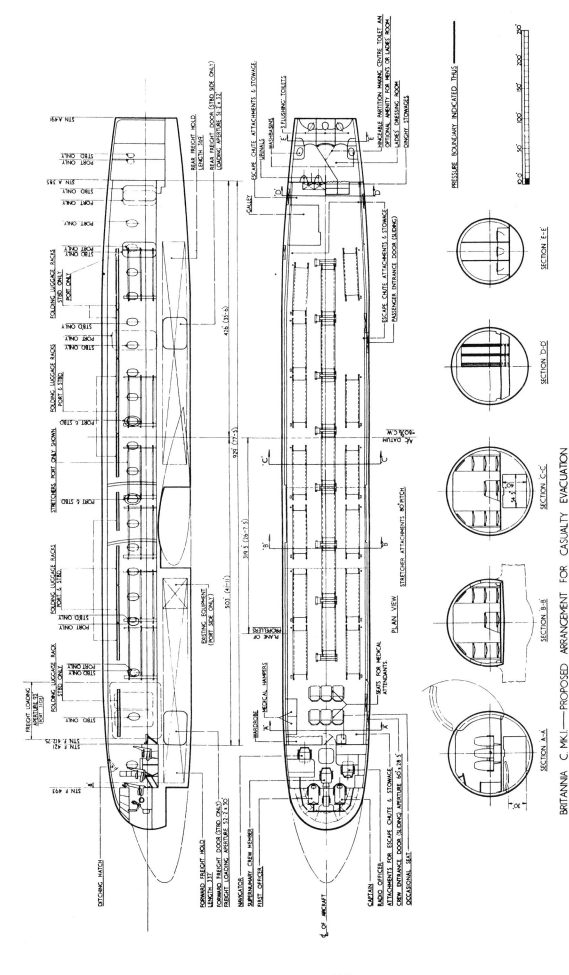

**Proposed Britannia C.1 cabin layout for casualty evacuation. From Bristol Type Specification for the Britannia 253 Military Transport Aeroplane, published by Bristol Aircraft Ltd on 1 December 1957.** The late Dave Williams via Derek A. King

BRITANNIA C.MK.I.—PROPOSED ARRANGEMENT FOR CASUALTY EVACUATION

The Britannias formed the basis for the rapid deployment of the Army's United Kingdom Strategic Reserve. No. 99 Squadron (at that time equipped with Hastings aircraft) was the first to receive Britannias, followed by 511 Squadron, which was re-formed as the RAF's second Britannia squadron on 14 December 1959. Both were based at Lyneham, where they served alongside the Comet C.2s of 216 Squadron. The fleet had regular detachments (known as 'Brit Det', 'Son of Brit Det', etc.) to the Far East, where they were engaged in transporting Ghurkas between Nepal and Hong Kong. Two aircraft at a time were based at RAF Kai Tak in Hong Kong for this work, flying Hong Kong–Singapore–Calcutta–Kathmandu and back.

In March 1960 four 99 Squadron Britannias joined with Hastings and Beverley transports in ferrying troops and stores to North Africa on the big Army/RAF mobility exercise code-named *Starlight*. This was the first Britannia participation in such an event, and about thirty sorties were operated from Lyneham. During the troubles in the Congo, aircraft were despatched to Ghana in July 1960 to assist the UN peacekeeping force, flying many trips into Leopoldville. Britannias were also used to transport troops from Nairobi to Kuwait during a crisis there in July 1960. In November 1961 Belize in British Honduras was devastated by Hurricane Hattie and six Britannias from 99 and 511 Squadrons flew medical teams and supplies to the scene, but were obliged to land at Kingston, Jamaica,

the nearest airport from which Britannias could operate. From there, a shuttle service to Belize was provided by Hastings and Shackleton aircraft. On the return legs, dispossessed British citizens were returned to the UK. Britannia XL636, piloted by Wg Cdr le Hardy, the Commanding Officer of 511 Squadron, established a new record by covering the 4,160 miles (6,690km) from Palisadoes Airport, Kingston to RAF St Mawgan in 12 hours 40 minutes, the longest ever non-stop flight by an RAF Britannia.

During the mid-1960s Southern Rhodesia declared unilateral independence from the United Kingdom. Sanctions were imposed by Britain and the Rhodesian government imposed a ban on British aircraft taking on fuel there. The oil pipeline route to Zambia was closed and, alongside chartered civil transports, the RAF Britannia squadrons undertook the airlift of oil in barrels into Zambia. The airlift from Nairobi to Lusaka and Ndola commenced on 19 December 1965, the less-distant supply base of Dar-es-Salaam having been ruled out by the refusal of the Tanzanian government to have British military personnel stationed on its territory. Initially, two RAF Britannias operated two return sorties each day, but this built up to a peak of eight sorties daily using eight aircraft in the weeks around Christmas 1965. Each flight took about three hours

**XN398 waits to depart from Heathrow North Side on 28 September 1961 as a Bristol Sycamore helicopter brings in its VIP passenger, Chief of the Air Staff Sir Thomas Pike.** Stan Roberts

(*Below*) **XL636 in RAF Transport Command markings.** Air-Britain

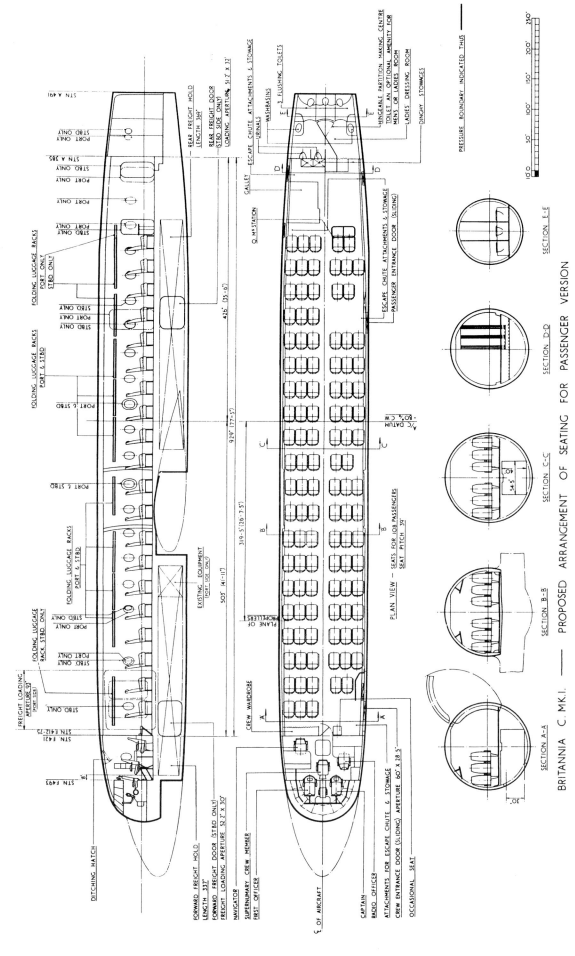

**Proposed Britannia C.1 cabin layout for passenger carrying. From *Bristol Type Specification for the Britannia 253 Military Transport Aeroplane*, published by Bristol Aircraft Ltd on 1 December 1957.**

The late Dave Williams via Derek A. King

BRITANNIA C. MK.I. — PROPOSED ARRANGEMENT OF SEATING FOR PASSENGER VERSION

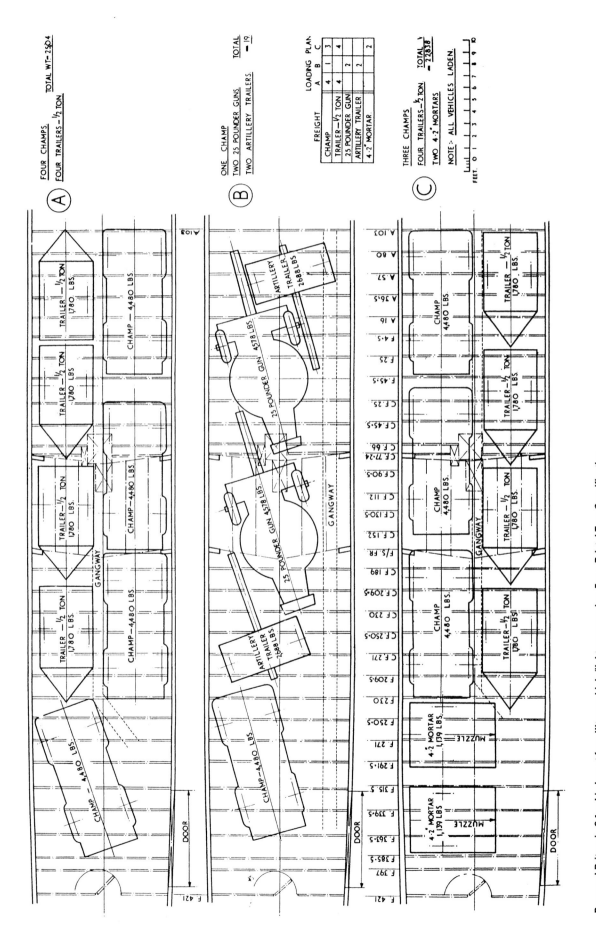

**Proposed Britannia C.1 cabin layout for military vehicle/light gun carrying. From *Bristol Type Specification for the Britannia 253 Military Transport Aeroplane*, published by Bristol Aircraft Ltd on 1 December 1957.**
The late Dave Williams via Derek A. King

and on each flight into Zambia the Britannias carried fifty-six oil drums of 44gal (200ltr) capacity. Following the arrival of a sizeable fleet of civil-registered transports (including several Britannias), the RAF participation in the airlift was terminated on 31 October 1966. By this time the RAF Britannias involved had made 1,563 sorties in over 10,000 flying hours.

In May 1966 a Britannia made an emergency aeromedical flight to Ascension Island, where a road accident had resulted in eleven casualties, all of them British. As

it was anticipated that emergency treatment would be needed during flight the aircraft was fitted out as a mobile operating theatre, but in the event only normal patient handling was required.

At midnight on 31 July 1967 RAF Transport Command officially became RAF Air Support Command, but Britannia C.1 XL660 was noted wearing the new titles at Lyneham as early as 21 July. At the end of 1967 the United Kingdom withdrew its military presence from Aden, and RAF Britannias were among the many transport aircraft involved in the biggest

**An unidentified RAF Britannia climbs out.** Air-Britain

(*Below*) **A busy scene at Lyneham in the heyday of the RAF Britannias. XL520 'Arcturus' prepares to depart on the Singapore run, while in the background can be seen four more Britannias, a Comet C.2 and a Hastings.** Rolls-Royce Heritage Trust

(*Above*) Srs 253 C.1 XL658 wearing RAF Air Support Command titles.
Air-Britain

(*Left*) XL636, with one of its VC-10 replacements behind.
The late Dave Williams

(*Below*) After RAF retirement, Britannias XL658, XL660 and XL637 await their fate at Kemble in early 1976. Graham Salt

## Navigation Testing at the North Pole

During 1971 Britannias participated in flights to the North Pole, organized by the Royal Air Force College of Air Warfare to evaluate the Smiths Flight Navigation System, and former Flt Lt A. J. S. (John) James recalls one such flight in XM496 that left Brize Norton on 6 August 1971. On board were no fewer than twenty-one navigators, including two from his 99 Squadron. The flight from Brize Norton to Thule in Greenland took 9 hours 10 minutes, and on the following day the Britannia flew from Thule to the North Pole, where 20 minutes were spent circling at 20,000ft (6,000m). A maximum altitude of 35,000ft (11,000m) was reached before commencing the descent into Brize Norton from overhead Scotland. The whole flight took 11 hours 25 minutes. The cabin was crammed with navigation equipment placed on tables laid out pullman style. He recalls that there were several LORAN installations that caused a lot of head scratching among the specialist navigators, and a 'spaghetti' of wires taped to the floor. A very laid-back American, an employee of Litton Inc, had a Litton 41 Inertial Navigation System (INS) unit on one table. He spent his time reading Playboy magazines and smoking, confident of his position to the nearest 20 miles! The British INS unit came from Farnborough and was usually fitted in a test Harrier. Apparently, it did not work very well. The aircraft compasses had to be checked every 20 minutes. After careful analysis at Manby the Smiths Flight System was declared to have performed better than expected.

John James left the RAF in 1974 and went on to fly Britannias for IAS Cargo Airlines. After joining Air Europe in 1979 and flying for them until they ceased operations in 1991, he finally retired from flying as a Lauda Air Boeing 767-300ER Captain.

**RAF srs 253 C.1 XM496 night-stopping at Thule in Greenland as part of a Polar navigation exercise, 7 August 1971.** John James

airlift to be undertaken by the RAF since the Berlin Airlift. This culminated in the last British High Commissioner for Aden being flown home via Bahrain in an Air Support Command Britannia in January 1968. As part of a general rationalization programme within the RAF, the Britannia squadrons were relocated to Brize Norton in June 1970, joining their eventual replacements, the VC-10s of 10 Squadron, as well as the Belfasts of 53 Squadron. The only loss of an RAF Britannia occurred on 14 October 1967 when XL638 overran the runway whilst landing at RAF Khormaksar, Aden, and sustained damage serious enough for the aircraft to be written off.

Without doubt the oldest and most valuable cargo to be carried by the Britannia fleet was the solid gold death mask of King Tutankhamun, which was displayed with other priceless antiquities at the British Museum in 1972. As the cargo was uninsurable it was decided to use military transport for added security, and so on 24 January a 99 Squadron aircraft left Brize Norton for Cairo via Akrotiri to pick up the precious load.

At the end of 1973 two RAF Britannias joined civil airliners on charter to the United Nations on the airlift of 210,000 refugees from Pakistan to Bangladesh and vice versa, an operation described by the UN High Commissioner for Refugees as 'the biggest ever airlift of human beings'. By January 1974 the two Britannias had carried 5,896 refugees on the 1,400-mile (2,250km), 3½-hour flight from Karachi to Dacca, and 3,270 in the opposite direction.

Following the latest round of defence cuts the Britannia fleet was retired on the disbandment of 99 and 511 Squadrons in January 1976. The first example to go (XL658) was actually withdrawn in January 1975 and the final Britannia to be ferried into storage was XL660. At the time of their retirement the fleet still had low airframe hours and were offered for sale by the Ministry of Defence to commercial operators. They were all still serviceable, but before they could be accepted for civil use a Certificate of Airworthiness needed to be issued and this entailed determining the design standard (i.e. modification state, drawing registers, and so on) at the time of build. The machines involved in the first applications had been built at Belfast and the records had lain undisturbed in the archives since 1960 or thereabouts. A similar search was also necessary for the records relating to the engines. These were located at the Coventry division of Roll-Royce. A flight manual had to be prepared, as this was mandatory for civil operations but had not been an RAF requirement, and all the RAF modifications had to be cleared as acceptable by the CAA. Just before Christmas 1975 the first civil Certificate of Airworthiness was granted to the former XM490, and it became srs 253F G-BDLZ of Air Faisel.

**XL660 at Kemble in early 1976, awaiting disposal after retirement.** Graham Salt

### The RAF Britannia Fleet

*C.1s*

XL635 'Bellatrix'
XL636 'Argo'
XL637 'Vega'
XL638 'Sirius'*
XL639 'Atria'
XL640 'Altares'
XL657 'Rigel'
XL658 'Adhara'
XL659 'Polaris'
XL660 'Alphard'
XM489 'Denebola'
XM490 'Aldebaran'
XM491 'Procyon'
XM496 'Regulus'
XM497 'Schedar'
XM498 'Hadar'
XM517 'Avior'
XM518 'Spica'
XM519 'Capella'
XM520 'Arcturus'

*C.2s*

XN392 'Acrux'
XN398 'Altair'
XN404 'Canopus'

*The sole casualty – written off at
Aden in 1967.

## Aircraft and Armament Experimental Establishment Britannia Operations

In November 1971 the Aircraft and Armament Experimental Establishment bought the former Air Spain Britannia 312F EC-BSY and secured for it the military serial XX367. In its past this machine had also seen service with BOAC and British Eagle, and it was to be used for development flying from Boscombe Down until 1984. During this period it made occasional appearances at airshows and special events, and in April 1983 it visited Filton to commemorate its 25th anniversary. It was retired in early 1984 and flown to Cranfield for storage, and was sold to Katale Aero Transport in March 1984 as 9Q-CHY.

**The Britannia Preservation Society's srs 253, XM496, being restored to its original RAF markings at Kemble in March 2001.** Author

# CHAPTER SIX

# Derivatives

## The Canadair CL-28 Argus

Although Britannia production in Britain ended earlier than had been hoped, its descendants continued in production in Canada. The first of these was the Canadair CL-28 Argus. As early as 1952 discussions had begun between Bristol, the Royal Canadian Air Force, the Canadian Department of Defence and Canadair Ltd, regarding both maritime reconnaissance and transport versions of the Britannia for the RCAF. Canadair had previously suggested to the RCAF that a version of their North Star airliner would make a suitable replacement for its ageing Lancasters, but when the detailed RCAF requirements were published in 1952 it became clear that the North Star would not do. Instead, the RCAF was offered versions of both the Lockheed Super Constellation and the Britannia 100. The Constellation was discarded as it was considered unable to manoeuvre safely at low speeds and low altitudes, and the Britannia was favoured as it was thought possible to build just one variant that could carry out both maritime patrol and anti-submarine warfare (ASW) missions. In March 1954 a licence agreement was reached with Canadair, and on 27 May the Canadian government awarded

(*Top*) RCAF CL-28 Argus Mk 1 10718. Air-Britain  (*Above*) CL-28 Argus Mk 2 10736. Air-Britain

Canadair a contract to produce thirteen maritime patrol/ASW aircraft based on the Britannia and designated the CL-28 Argus. This design retained the wings, tail and control systems of the Britannia, but had a redesigned unpressurized fuselage containing two large weapons bays and a transparent nose. For maximum fuel economy at low altitudes four 3,700hp Wright Turbo-Compound R-3350 piston engines, capable of conferring a maximum patrol endurance of twenty-four hours, were selected.

The conversion of a fast, high-flying pressurized turboprop airliner into a slow, low-altitude, unpressurized piston-engined patrol aircraft was a major challenge, and entailed the conversion of some 9,000 Bristol drawings to Canadian and US standards, materials and processes. However, the first Argus Mark 1 made its maiden flight on 28 March 1957 and then started a prolonged flight test programme, which eventually involved seven examples. In early 1956, Canadair received another contract, this time for twenty of a slightly modified version, the Argus Mark 2, the most obvious difference between the two marks being the size and shape of the nose radome. The first Mark 1 was delivered to the RCAF on 30 September 1957 and Arguses served with 404 and 405 Squadrons at CFB Greenwood, Nova Scotia, 415 Squadron at CFB Summerside, Prince Edward Island, and 407 Squadron at CFB Comox, British Columbia. For many years it was the most advanced anti-submarine warfare aircraft in the world. The first Mark 2 flew on 27 August 1958 and the last Argus was rolled out on 13 July 1960.

During the type's twenty-four years of service two examples were lost. No. 20727, of 404 Squadron, crashed near Puerto Rico during night exercises on 25 March 1965 and No. 10737 crashed on landing at Summerside on 31 March 1977. The last Argus operational flight took place on 10 November 1980, after which twenty-four of the survivors were sold for scrap. Arguses are preserved at the National Aviation Museum, CFB Greenwood, CFB Comox, and the former CFB Summerside.

## The Canadair CL-44

### The Yukon

The CL-44 came about as the result of an RCAF requirement for a replacement for its ageing C-54GM North Stars, which were providing personnel and logistics support for Canadian forces in Europe. Since Canadair had already acquired a licence for the Bristol Britannia design, plans were announced in January 1957 for a fleet of long-range transports based on that type. A contract was awarded for eight aircraft initially, later increased to twelve. They were given the RCAF designation CC-106 Yukon (Canadair designation CL-44-6).

The CL-44 was a further lengthened variant of the Britannia 253. It used the modified Argus wings and controls, but the fuselage was almost identical to that of the Britannia srs 300. It was originally intended to have four Bristol Orion engines, but the design was revised as the CL-44D to incorporate Rolls-Royce Tyne turboprops. The CL-44 had large cargo doors on the port side, both fore and aft of the wing. The roll-out of the first prototype suffered an embarrassment when it was found that the tail was too tall for it to be pushed out of the hangar! The first CC-106 made its maiden flight on 15 November 1959, but deliveries to the RCAF were hampered by problems Rolls-Royce were encountering with delivery of Tyne engines. The last Yukon was delivered to the RCAF in 1961.

The Yukon could accommodate 134 passengers and a crew of nine, or in the casevac role it could carry eighty patients and a crew of eleven. In December 1961 a CC-106 set a new world record for aircraft of its class by covering the 6,750 miles (10,900km) from Tokyo to Trenton, Ontario, in 17 hours 3 minutes at an average speed of 400mph (644km/h). Later, another aircraft established another record by staying airborne for 23 hours 51 minutes. These records were to remain unbroken until 1975, when they were bettered by the new Boeing 747SP. The Yukons were operated by 437 Squadron of the RCAF, and in the VIP transport role by 412 Squadron.

The Yukon was replaced in RCAF service by Boeing 707s and retired in March 1971, whereupon the whole fleet began new lives as commercial freighters. The Yukon's service life with the RCAF might have been longer but for two factors: the RCAF needed an aircraft that could double as an in-flight refuelling tanker; and serviceability was marred by a chronic shortage of spares, resulting from the fact that the CL-44 had never gone into large-scale production.

### The Civilian CL-44s

The CC-106s were followed in production by twenty-seven examples of a new version intended specifically for the civil market, the CL-44D-4. This had a swing-tail, for easy rear loading of palletized or bulky freight loads, but could also be used as an economical large-capacity passenger airliner. While the first prototype was being built a major problem arose when the American FAA refused to certify the type, because its Britannia-type windshields did not comply with its latest vision standards.

**The prototype Canadair CL-44 CF-MKP-X.** Air-Britain

**Canadair CC-106 Yukon 15921.** Air-Britain

**RCAF CC-106 15929 at Heathrow North Side.** Air-Britain

However, the windscreen of the Convair 880/990 jet airliners was compatible, and was adapted for the CL-44.

The prototype, CF-MKP-X, made its first flight on 16 November 1960, but by then most passenger airlines wanted the new jets coming into service on the world's main routes. However, cargo airlines found the CL-44's initial purchase price and projected costs very favourable in comparison to the high operating costs of the elderly DC-6Bs and Super Constellations they were using at the time, and it was calculated that the fuel burn was approximately half that of a Boeing 707.

In July 1961 the first of an order for seven entered service with Seaboard World Airlines, followed by twelve for the Flying Tiger Line and four for Slick Airways. A fourth customer for the type was Iceland's Loftleidir, which initially bought three in an all-passenger layout with the swing-tail feature deleted. These were used in a 178-seat configuration on low-cost transatlantic services via Iceland. They were joined in 1966 by a fourth example, which had been modified to accommodate 214 passengers by means of a 15ft (4.58m) fuselage stretch. In this form it was known as the CL-44J, or Canadair 400. After it entered Loftleidir

service the other three machines were also retrospectively modified to this standard. Other potential customers included Pakistan, Saudi Arabia, Japan Cargo Airlines, the USAF Military Air Transport Service and BOAC, but these deals all fell through, mainly for political reasons.

A total of twenty-seven civil CL-44s was built, and production continued into 1964. One CL-44D, N228SW, was leased by Seaboard World Airlines to BOAC, in whose livery it could often be seen at London Airport on all-cargo services. Seaboard World also leased three CL-44Ds to British independent operator Transglobe Airways

(**Above**) Seaboard and Western Airlines
CL-44D-4s were regular visitors to Heathrow.
N124SW is pictured here. Air-Britain

The ultimate Britannia derivative, Conroy CL-44-0
N447T whilst serving with Transmeridian Air Cargo.
Air-Britain

for use on low-cost transatlantic passenger charters. Deliveries started in April 1968 and all three examples were in Transglobe service for the height of the summer season. They enabled Transglobe to offer very low whole-aircraft group charter rates in a 165-seat configuration, including a lead-in fare of £37 return from either London, Manchester or Prestwick to New York, Toronto or Montreal.

A final version of the CL-44 was the CL-44-0. This was a CL-44D-4 which was bought from the Flying Tiger Line by the Conroy Aircraft Corporation in the USA for conversion to a large volume cargo transporter. It had its upper fuselage removed and replaced by an enlarged section, which raised the cabin height by 4ft 11in (1.5m). It first flew in its new form on 26 November 1969 and had a maximum internal height of 11ft 4in (3.46m) and a maximum width of 13ft 11in (4.24m), whilst retaining the

swing-tail loading facility. A total of thirty-nine CL-44s of all versions was built, and thirteen (including former RCAF CC-106s) remained in service in 1983.

## Unbuilt Britannia Derivatives

### Srs 350

This was the designation of a proposed developed version of the Britannia powered by four Bristol Orion twin-spool turbo-props. BOAC ordered sixty Orions, which were to be fitted to the Britannia 312s, with appropriate strengthening of the wing mountings, in the 1960s. It was expected that the Orion would extend the service life of the Britannias by several years, whilst keeping them competitive with more modern designs. The Britannia 350 would have had a range of 6,500 miles (10,500km) at a

cruising speed of 430mph (690km/h). However, despite the promise shown by the engine when test-flown in the prototype Britannia, G-ALBO, government support for the Orion was withdrawn at the beginning of 1958 (*see* page 33).

### Srs 400

This version was announced in the summer of 1956 and was intended to be available for commercial operation in the spring of 1959. It was to have had a fuselage 10ft (3m) longer than previous models, and a thinner wing to permit higher operating weights. Power was to be supplied by four 6,000bhp Orion srs II turbo-props. It was to have had a range of 6,900 miles (11,100km), cruising at 443mph (713km/h), and a service ceiling of 40,000ft (12,000m). A typical route considered ideal for this version was London–

Sydney, via either Aden and Singapore, or Nairobi and Cocos Island.

### Britannia Rear-Loading Freighter

This was a direct development of the Britannia 250, with Proteus 770 engines. It featured a number of improvements to better suit it for the long-range strategic freighter role. The Britannia 250 fuselage, complete with side-loading door, was retained, but aft of the wings the floor was lowered to cater for an increase in freight volume. The rear fuselage was completely redesigned and incorporated a hydraulically operated rear freight-loading door, which enabled cargo to be easily loaded. The Rear-Loading Freighter was to be capable of transporting any type of guided weapon in service or projected, or a wide range of Army trucks or trailers. The standard Britannia wing was developed and fitted with integral fuel tanks with a capacity of 9,750gal (44,320ltr), instead of the bag type. The undercarriage was strengthened and more powerful Proteus engines fitted. With a 40,000lb (18,000kg) payload, a stage length of 3,000nm (5,600km) could be covered with full fuel reserves. An alternative 126-seat passenger version was also envisaged.

### Srs 600

Also known as the Bristol 187, the srs 600 was the subject of a joint design study with Convair of San Diego for a 'double-decker' Britannia with thinner and more slender wings, and Orion engines. Up to 200 passengers were to be carried.

### Types 189 and 195

Two other projects derived from the Britannia were examined in the early months of 1955. The first was the Bristol Type 189, corresponding in layout and role to the Canadair CL-28 Argus, but designed around the requirements of RAF Coastal Command for a Shackleton replacement. The second was the Type 195, a high-wing, rear-loading heavy-cargo carrier. This used the Britannia wing, in common with the first layout of the Shorts S.C.5, which in its final, enlarged, form later went into limited production at Queen's Island as the Belfast (known initially as the Short Britannic). The wings for the Belfast were designed and manufactured at Filton under contract to Short Bros and Harland.

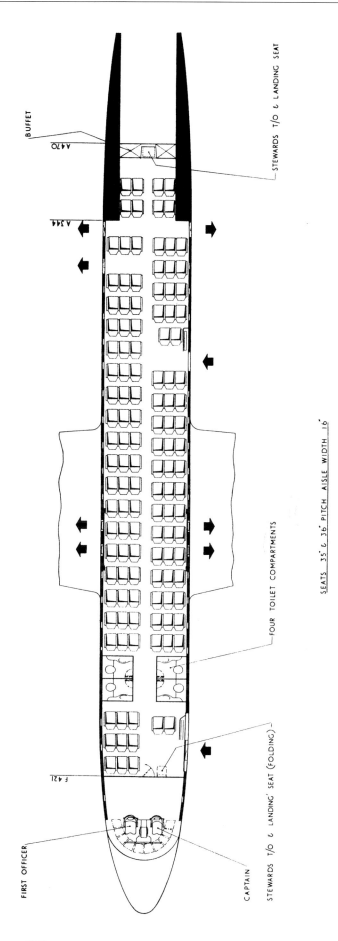

**Rear-Loading freighter.**

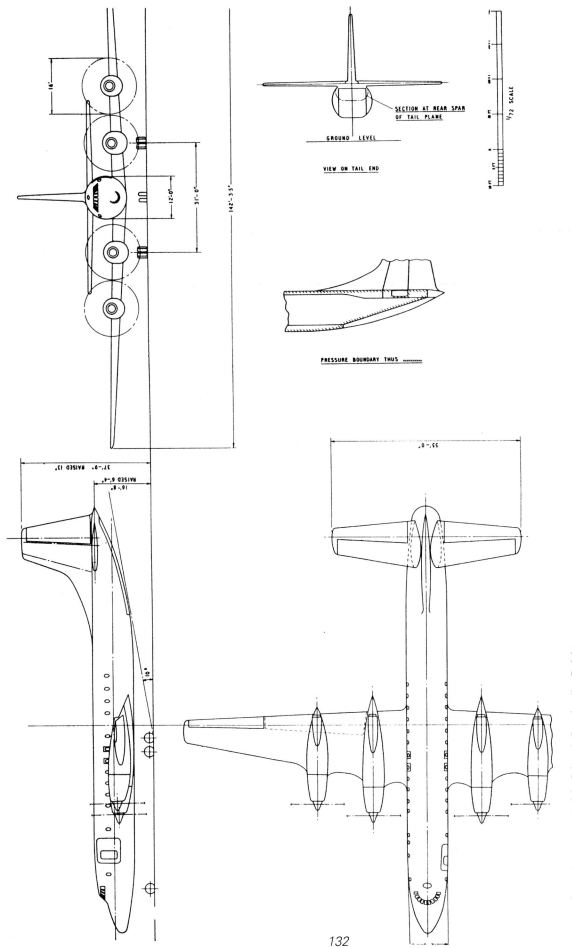

SECTION AT REAR SPAR
OF TAIL PLANE

GROUND LEVEL

VIEW ON TAIL END

1/72 SCALE

PRESSURE BOUNDARY THUS

**General arrangement of the Britannia Rear-Loading Freighter.**

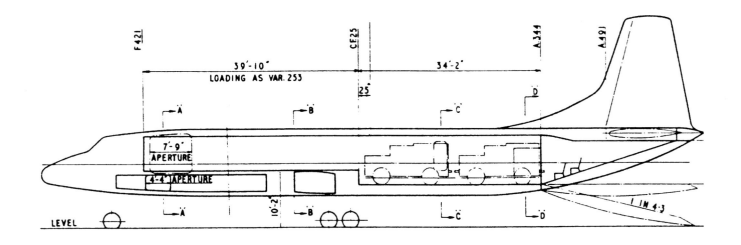

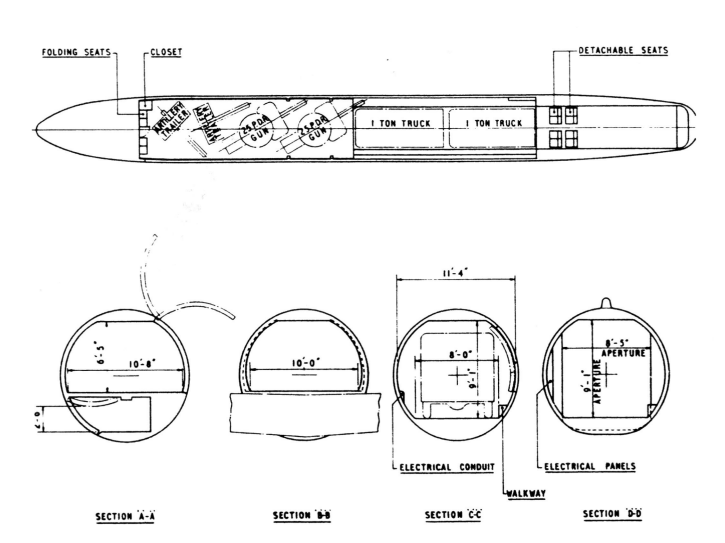

**Interior layout views of the military vehicle/light-gun configurations of the Britannia Rear-Loading Freighter.** The late Dave Williams via Derek A. King

# Individual Aircraft Histories

## Preserved Britannias

Britannia preservation is an exclusively British affair, and the UK is fortunate in having at least pieces of seven examples preserved in various states of completeness.

**c/n 12873 G-ALBO** srs 100. This was the first prototype, which was broken up at St Athan in June 1968. The Bristol Aero Collection at Kemble hold the only surviving piece of this aircraft, a wing aileron balance tab.

**c/n 12874 G-ALRX** srs 101. This was the second prototype, which suffered turbine failure and an in-flight fire in 1954, resulting in a forced-landing on the mud-banks of the River Severn. The flight-deck section was recovered and used for crew training for many years at Filton and later at Boscombe Down. It is now preserved at Kemble.

**c/n 12922 G-ANCF** srs 308F. Constructed as a srs 308 at Belfast. First flew in 1958 and used by Transcontinental SA and later British Eagle, who fitted it with a cargo door and used it on government contracts to the rocket-testing ground at Woomera in South Australia. After use by other operators it was retired at Manston and dismantled. All the components are preserved at Kemble, and a programme of partial or complete re-assembly is under discussion.

**c/n 13237 G-AOVF** srs 312. Delivered to BOAC in January 1958. The last operator was Invicta International. Preserved at Cosford museum in BOAC colours.

**c/n 13427 G-AOVT** srs 312. Delivered to BOAC in January 1959. Last operated by Monarch Airlines, who retired it in March 1975. Preserved at Duxford museum in Monarch colours.

**c/n 13430 G-AOVS** srs 312F. Delivered to BOAC in October 1958. Last operated by Redcoat Air Cargo. Withdrawn from use 1979 and broken up at Luton. Fuselage used for fire training and still visible on fire dump at Luton in July 2001.

**c/n 13508 XM496** srs 253. Originally delivered to RAF Transport Command. Constructed at Belfast and first flown in 1960. After varied history became the last airworthy Britannia. Was ferried as 9Q-CJH of Transair Cargo from Lanseria, near Johannesburg, to Kemble, and landed there on 14 October 1997. In the care of the Britannia Aircraft Preservation Trust, who run the engines regularly and are in the process of re-painting it in original RAF markings.

## Individual Britannia Histories

**c/n 12873** srs 100, Filton-built. Registered to Ministry of Supply as VX442 (not taken up). Registered to Ministry of Supply as WB470 (not taken up). Registered to Bristol Aeroplane Co Ltd as G-ALBO 11.6.48. Transferred to Ministry of Supply 25.6.51. First flight 16.8.52. Last flight as G-ALBO 31.3.60. Transferred to Air Ministry as 7708M and flown to RAF St Athan 31.11.60. Used as ground instruction airframe. Broken up at 12.6.68. Parts remained until 4.74.

**c/n 12874** srs 101, Filton-built. Registered to Ministry of Supply as VX447 (not taken up). Registered to Ministry of Supply as WB473 (not taken up). Registered to Ministry of Supply as G-ALRX 25.6.51. First flight 23.12.53. Damaged beyond repair in forced landing Severn Estuary 4.2.54. Fuselage to Company Service School as training aid. Nose section to RAF Lyneham and then to Brize Norton in 1971. Transferred to A & AEE at Boscombe Down in 1976 for aeromedical and safety training. Nose section currently preserved at Kemble by Britannia Aircraft Preservation Group.

**c/n 12875** srs 101, Filton-built. Registered to Ministry of Supply as VX454 but not taken up. Not completed. Used as functional mock-up. Nose later used in rebuild of G-ANBC (c/n 12904).

**c/n 12902** srs 102, Filton-built. Registered as G-ANBA to Bristol Aeroplane Co Ltd 7.1.54. First flight 5.9.54. Transferred to Bristol Aircraft Ltd 9.3.56. Delivered to BOAC 22.8.57. Leased to Nigeria Airways 13.4.59–1960. Leased to Malayan Airways 19.12.61–17.1.62. Withdrawn from use and stored Cambridge 11.62. Ferried to Heathrow and stored 6.63. Leased to Britannia Airways 25.3.65. Withdrawn from use and stored Luton 11.69. Broken up at Luton 6.70.

**c/n 12903** srs 102, Filton-built. Registered as G-ANBB to Bristol Aeroplane Co Ltd 7.1.54. First flight 18.1.55. Transferred to Bristol Aircraft Ltd 9.3.56. Delivered to BOAC 18.6.57. Leased to Nigeria Airways 6.59–1960. Leased to Cathay Pacific 1961–1.63. Withdrawn from use and stored Cambridge 1.63. Leased to Britannia Airways 18.11.64. Crashed near Ljubjana 1.9.66.

**c/n 12904** srs 102, Filton-built. Registered as G-ANBC to Bristol Aeroplane Co Ltd 7.1.54. First flight 29.6.55. Delivered to BOAC 30.12.55. Registered to BOAC 31.12.55. Seriously damaged Rangoon 9.9.58. Shipped to Filton and rebuilt using nose of static test airframe 12875. First flight after repair 15.8.59. Delivered back to BOAC 20.8.59. Leased to Ghana Airways 1960–1960. Damaged beyond repair Khartoum 11.11.60.

**c/n 12905** srs 102, Filton-built. Registered as G-ANBD to Bristol Aeroplane Co Ltd 7.1.54. First flight 14.11.55. Delivered to BOAC 30.12.55. Withdrawn from use and stored Cambridge 1.63. Leased to BKS 16.11.65. Sub-leased to Britannia Airways 27.4.68–1.10.68. Withdrawn from use and stored Southend. Transferred to Newcastle and stored 22.1.70. Broken up at Newcastle 5.70.

**c/n 12906** srs 102, Filton-built. Registered as G-ANBE to Bristol Aircraft Ltd 18.1.56. First flight 17.1.56. Delivered to BOAC 2.3.56. Leased to Nigeria Airways 4.58–1959. Leased to Ghana Airways 1960. Leased to Malayan Airways 1962–3.4.63. Withdrawn from use and stored Cambridge 4.63. Leased to Britannia Airways 1.2.66. Sold to Britannia Airways 3.70. Withdrawn from use and stored Luton 16.11.70. Broken up at Luton 7.72.

**c/n 12907** srs 102, Filton-built. Registered as G-ANBF to Bristol Aircraft Ltd 18.1.56. First flight 23.2.56. Delivered to BOAC 14.3.56. Leased to Malayan Airways 10.61–14.11.61. Withdrawn from use and stored Cambridge 1.63. Leased to Britannia Airways 12.2.65. Withdrawn from use and stored Luton 10.69. Broken up at Luton 4.70.

**c/n 12908** srs 102, Filton-built. Registered as G-ANBG to Bristol Aircraft Ltd 18.1.56. First flight 29.3.56. Delivered to BOAC 8.5.56. Re-registered as G-APLL 19.3.58. Leased to Nigeria Airways 1959–1960. Leased to Malayan Airways 10.5.62–6.6.62 and 3.7.62–1.8.62. Withdrawn from use and stored Cambridge 1.63. Leased to BKS 16.11.65. Withdrawn from use 21.2.69 and stored at Teesside. Moved to Newcastle 4.69. Broken up at Newcastle 2.70.

**c/n 12909** srs 102, Filton-built. Registered as G-ANBH to Bristol Aircraft Ltd 18.1.56. First flight 9.5.56. Delivered to BOAC 24.7.57. Withdrawn from use and stored Cambridge 11.62. Leased to BKS 10.3.65. Sold to BKS 30.9.65. Withdrawn from use and stored Southend 10.68. Moved to Newcastle. Broken up at Newcastle 9.69.

**c/n 12910** srs 102, Filton-built. Registered as G-ANBI to Bristol Aircraft Ltd 18.1.56. First flight 24.5.56. Delivered to BOAC 29.6.56. Leased to Ghana Airways 1960. Leased to Malayan Airways 12.4.62–9.5.62. Withdrawn from use and stored Cambridge 1.63. Leased to Britannia Airways 3.2.66. Withdrawn from use 27.9.69. Broken up at Luton 10.69.

**c/n 12911** srs 102, Filton-built. Registered as G-ANBJ to Bristol Aircraft Ltd 4.3.56. First flight 5.8.56. Delivered to BOAC 22.11.56. Leased to Malayan Airways 8.2.62–7.3.62 and 6.62–4.7.62. Withdrawn from use and stored at Cambridge 11.62

Transferred to Heathrow and stored 6.6.63. Leased to Britannia Airways 16.4.65. Sold to Britannia Airways 29.7.70. Withdrawn from use and stored Luton 10.70. Broken up at Luton 2.71.

**c/n 12912** srs 102, Filton-built. Registered as G-ANBK to Bristol Aircraft Ltd 4.3.56. First flight 14.9.56. Delivered to BOAC 12.2.57. Leased to Nigeria Airways 1961–2. Withdrawn from use and stored Cambridge 12.62. Leased to BKS 17.3.64. Withdrawn from use and stored Newcastle 10.69. Sold to BKS 24.4.70. Company name changed to Northeast Airlines 2.11.70. Re-entered service after overhaul 16.12.70. Withdrawn from use again 31.12.71 and stored Newcastle. Broken up at Newcastle 3.72.

**c/n 12913** srs 102, Filton-built. Registered to Bristol Aircraft Ltd as G-ANBL 4.3.56. First flight 24.2.57. Delivered to BOAC 2.3.57. Leased to Cathay Pacific 12.12.60–31.1.61. Withdrawn from use and stored at Cambridge 11.62. Ferried to Heathrow and stored 19.7.63. Leased to Britannia Airways 26.6.65. Sub-leased to Southern Cross International 20.5.70–6.70. Sold to Britannia Airways 29.7.70. Withdrawn from use and stored Luton 29.12.70. Broken up at Luton 7.72.

**c/n 12914** srs 102, Filton-built. Registered as G-ANBM to Bristol Aircraft Ltd 4.3.56. First flight 8.3.57. Delivered to BOAC 11.3.57. Leased to Nigeria Airways 10.59–1960. Leased to Malayan Airways 15.11.61–18.12.61, 18.1.62–7.2.62 and 25.9.62–24.10.62. Withdrawn from use and stored Cambridge 12.62. Ferried to Heathrow and stored 26.7.65. Leased to Laker Airways 8.4.66. Sub-leased to Air France 29.7.66–6.9.66. Sub-leased to Britannia Airways 9.9.66–25.9.66. Sub-leased to Treffield International 29.4.67–11.6.67. Sold to National Aero Leasing 19.1.69. Sold to Indonesian Angkasa Civil Air Transport as PK-ICA 2.69. Withdrawn from use and stored Jakarta 6.70. Broken up at Jakarta 12.71.

**c/n 12915** srs 102, Filton-built. Registered as G-ANBN to Bristol Aircraft Ltd 4.3.56. First flight 11.4.57. Delivered to BOAC 4.5.57. Leased to Nigeria Airways 1.10.60–1961. Leased to Malayan Airways 8.3.62–11.4.62, 28.8.62–26.9.62 and 23.10.62–15.1.63. Withdrawn from use and stored Cambridge 1.63. Leased to Laker Airways 21.4.66. Sub-

leased to Air Carriers of Zambia 16.11.67–23.1.68. Sub-leased to Britannia Airways 16.4.68–17.10.68. Sold to National Aero Leasing 21.1.69. Sold to Indonesian Angkasa Civil Air Transport as PK-ICB 2.69. Withdrawn from use and stored Jakarta 6.70. Broken up at Jakarta 12.71.

**c/n 12916** srs 102, Filton-built. Registered as G-ANBO to Bristol Aircraft Ltd 4.3.56. First flight 17.5.57. Delivered to BOAC 31.5.57. Leased to Cathay Pacific 24.1.61–1961. Leased to Malayan Airways 2.9.61–10.61 and 31.7.62–29.8.62. Withdrawn from use and stored Cambridge 12.62. Leased to Britannia Airways 4.1.65. Sold to Britannia Airways 16.3.70. Withdrawn from use and stored Luton 15.10.70. Broken up at Luton 5.71.

**c/n 12917** srs 301, Filton-built. Prototype srs 300 aircraft. Registered to Bristol Aeroplane Co Ltd as G-ANCA 11.3.55. Transferred to Ministry of Supply 26.3.56. First flight 31.7.56. Crashed during test flight at Downend, near Bristol, 6.11.57.

**c/n 12918** srs 302, first Belfast-built Britannia. Registered to Bristol Aircraft Ltd as G-ANCB 20.1.56. Re-registered as G-18-1 6.57. First flight 21.6.57. Delivered to Aeronaves de Mexico as XA-MEC 1.11.57. Damaged beyond repair Tijuana 9.7.65. Broken up at for spares Tijuana 4.66. Parts reported to be sold to Transglobe Airways.

**c/n 12919** srs 302, Belfast-built. Registered to Bristol Aircraft Ltd as G-ANCC 8.1.57. Re-registered as G-18-2 7.57. First flight 24.7.57. Delivered to Aeronaves de Mexico as XA-MED 15.12.57. Sold to Transglobe Airways as G-ANCC 12.5.66. Delivered to Transglobe 23.5.66. Sold to International Aviation Services for spares 1968, but not used. Withdrawn from use and stored Biggin Hill 3.70. Broken up at Biggin Hill 8.70.

**c/n 12920** srs 305, Belfast-built. First flight 1.6.57 as G-18-3 for flight from Belfast to Filton. Registered to Bristol Aeroplane Co Ltd. Re-registered to Bristol Aircraft Ltd as G-ANCD 3.1.58. Allocated registration N6595C for Northeast Airlines, but not taken up. Converted to srs 306 and leased to El Al as 4X-AGE 17.7.58–6.3.59. Re-registered to Bristol Aircraft Ltd as G-ANCD 20.3.59. Leased to Air Charter Ltd 24.3.59. Converted to srs 307 6.59. Sold to

Air Charter Ltd 23.8.61. Transferred to BUA on merger 1.7.60. Converted to srs 307F by Aviation Traders 2.66. Sold to Lloyd International 1.69. Leased to East African Airways during 1969. Withdrawn from use and stored at Stansted after Lloyd International ceased operations 6.72. Sold to Shackleton Aviation 7.73. Sold to Aivex Holdings Ltd 27.7.73. Leased to International Aviation Services-IAS Cargo Airlines 9.73. Sold to Gemini Air Transport (Ghana) Ltd 22.11.74. Withdrawn from use and stored Luton 12.74. Leased to African Air Cargo as 5Y-AYR 13.5.75. Sold to Westwings Aviation Services 1.2.77. Sold to Black Arrow Finance 5.77. Leased to Transgulf Air 11.77–1978. Leased to Air Faisal during 1978–15.12.78. Leased to All-cargo AL 15.12.78–8.79. Leased to Gaylan Air Cargo 8.79–12.79. Withdrawn from use and stored Bournemouth 10.12.79. Broken up at Bournemouth 10.82.

**c/n 12921** srs 305, Belfast-built. Allocated registration N6596C for Northeast Airlines but not taken up. Registered as G-ANCE to Bristol Aircraft Ltd 3.1.58. First flight 3.9.58. Converted to srs 307 9.58. Leased to Air Charter Ltd 12.9.58. Transferred to BUA on merger 1.7.60. Converted to srs 307F 10.65. Sold to Lloyd International 26.2.69. Withdrawn from use and stored Stansted after Lloyd International ceased operations 16.6.72. Sold to Monarch Airlines 22.6.73. Leased to International Aviation Services 1.74–5.74. Sold to Aer Turas as EI-BAA 20.5.74. Leased to Pauling Construction Co 17.11.74–17.1.75. Leased to Eurafric 4.79–5.79. Withdrawn from use and stored at Manston 5.79. Flown to Dublin for spares use 24.10.79. Broken up for spares at Dublin 5.81.

**c/n 12922** srs 305, Belfast-built. Allocated registration N6597C for Northeast Airlines but not taken up. Registered to Bristol Aircraft Ltd as G-ANCF 3.1.58. Re-registered as G-18-4 11.58. First flight 19.11.58. Stored at Belfast after first flight until 8.59. Converted to srs 308 10.59. Re-registered as G-14-1 for ferry flight to Filton 24.10.59. Delivered to Transcontinental SA as LV-PPJ 16.12.59. Re-registered as LV-GJB 12.59. Withdrawn from use and stored Buenos Aires 11.61. Sold to British Eagle International and delivered 1.64. Re-registered as G-ANCF 2.3.64. Converted to srs 308F 7.64. Transferred to British Eagle (Liverpool) 13.11.64. Transferred to British Eagle International 5.7.67. Sold to

Monarch Airlines 6.12.68 after collapse of British Eagle in 11.68. Leased to African Cargo Airways as 5Y-AZP 4.2.76. Sub-leased to Invicta International 14.6.76. Sold to Invicta International 7.1.77. Re-registered as G-ANCF 10.1.77. Withdrawn from use after heavy landing at Cherbourg 1.2.80. Stored at Manston 30.10.80. Dismantled at Manston by Proteus Aero Services and components stored temporarily at Brooklands Museum. Components acquired by Britannia Aircraft Preservation Trust and taken to Bristol Aero Collection at Barnwell. Transferred to Kemble for possible partial or complete re-assembly in future.

**c/n 12923** srs 305, Belfast-built. Allocated registration N6598C for Northeast Airlines but not taken up. Registered to Bristol Aircraft Ltd as G-ANCG 3.1.58. First flight 20.11.59. Ferried to Filton as LV-PPL 21.11.59. Converted to srs 308 12.59. Delivered to Transcontinental SA as LV-PPL 17.12.59. Re-registered as LV-GJC 12.59. Withdrawn from use and stored Idlewild Airport, New York, 10.61–2.64. Sold to British Eagle International and delivered 23.2.64. Re-registered as G-ANCG 6.4.64. Converted to srs 308F 1964. Transferred to British Eagle (Liverpool) 13.11.64. Damaged beyond repair Manston 20.4.67. Broken up at Manston.

**c/n 12924** srs 305, Belfast-built. Allocated registration N6599C for Northeast Airlines but not taken up. Registered to Bristol Aircraft Ltd as G-ANCH 3.1.58. Converted to srs 309. First flight 19.2.60. Re-registered as 9G-AAG 28.5.60. Delivered to Ghana Airways on lease 16.8.60. Re-registered as G-ANCH. Leased to BUA 31.5.64–7.10.66. Leased to Transglobe Airways 6.12.66–30.9.67. Leased to British Eagle 13.2.68. Restored to Bristol Aircraft 12.3.68 but remained at Liverpool in Ghana Airways colours. Not used by British Eagle. Leased to Monarch Airlines 28.9.68. Withdrawn from use and stored Lydd 30.4.72. Sold to International Aviation Services for spares 12.72 and flown to Biggin Hill. Broken up at Biggin Hill 8.73.

**c/n 12925** srs 312, Filton-built. First flight 29.1.58. Delivered to BOAC as G-AOVH 11.2.58. Leased to British Eagle International 6.11.64–2.65. Leased to Caledonian 7.3.65–4.68. Sub-leased to Royal Air Maroc 14.3.65–5.5.65. Sold to Monarch Airlines 1.4.68. Withdrawn from use

11.71 and used as a cabin staff trainer at Luton. Broken up at Luton 6.72.

**c/n 12926** srs 312, Filton-built. First flight 15.2.58. Delivered to BOAC as G-AOVI 26.2.58. Leased to BUA 21.9.61–1.7.64. Leased to Caledonian 18.12.64. Sold to Caledonian 4.65. Leased to Royal Air Maroc 4.66. Sold to Royal Air Maroc 14.2.68 and chartered to Monarch Airlines for Haj pilgrimage flights until 15.2.68. Leased to Caledonian 17.2.68–29.3.68 for completion of Haj flights. Returned to Monarch under lease 5.4.68. Withdrawn from use and stored Luton 1.72. Broken up at Luton 4.72.

**c/n 13207** srs 200. Registered to Bristol Aeroplane Co Ltd as G-AMYK 25.2.52. Cancelled as withdrawn from use 11.3.55 but not in fact built as such.

**c/n 13207** srs 300LR. Registered to Bristol Aeroplane Co Ltd as G-AOFA 21.11.55. Cancelled as withdrawn from use 1.1.56 but not in fact built as such.

**c/n 13207** srs 311, Filton-built. Registered to Bristol Aeroplane Co Ltd as G-AOVA 21.11.55. Transferred to Bristol Aircraft Ltd 9.3.56. Converted to srs 312 3.56. First flight 31.12.56. Leased to BOAC 15.7.57–30.7.57. Converted to srs 319 10.60. Delivered to Ghana Airways as 9G-AAH 9.11.60. Returned to Bristol Aircraft Services as G-AOVA 31.12.63. Withdrawn from use and stored Filton 31.12.63. Leased to BUA 12.2.64–19.4.64. Leased to British Eagle 25.4.64. Sold to British Eagle 29.12.67. Leased to Caledonian 18.4.68–11.68. Withdrawn from use and stored Liverpool 11.68. Sold to CCT (Aircraft Leasing) 25.3.69. Leased to Caledonian 25.3.69–11.69. Leased to Lloyd International 13.12.69. Sub-leased to Caledonian 13.12.69. Returned to CCT (Aircraft Leasing) 2.70. Withdrawn from use and stored Gatwick 2.70. Moved to Coventry 5.70. Sold to Airline Engineering 5.71 for spares. Broken up at Coventry 10.71.

**c/n 13208** srs 200. Registered to Bristol Aeroplane Co Ltd as G-AMYL 25.2.52. Cancelled as withdrawn from use 11.3.55 but not in fact built as such.

**c/n 13208** srs 300LR. Registered to Bristol Aeroplane Co Ltd as G-AOFB 21.11.55. Cancelled as withdrawn from use 1.1.56 but not in fact built as such.

**c/n 13230** srs 312, Filton-built. First flight 5.7.57. Delivered to BOAC as G-AOVB 10.9.57. Leased to British Eagle 15.10.63. Converted to srs 312F. Returned to BOAC on collapse of British Eagle 6.11.68. Sold to Aerotransportes Entres Rios as LV-PNJ 3.10.69. Re-registered as LV-JNL 15.10.69. Damaged beyond repair Buenos Aires 12.7.70. Broken up at Buenos Aires.

**c/n 13231** srs 300LR. Registered to Bristol Aeroplane Co Ltd as G-AOFC 21.11.55. Cancelled as withdrawn from use 1.1.56 but not in fact built as such.

**c/n 13231** srs 312, Filton-built. First flight 22.10.57. Delivered to BOAC as G-AOVC 15.11.57. Leased to British Eagle 15.5.64–11.68. Leased to Donaldson International 20.5.69. Withdrawn from use 16.11.70. Ferried to Stansted and donated to fire school 17.11.70. Destroyed by fire at Stansted 1973.

**c/n 13232** srs 313, Filton-built. First flight 28.7.57. Delivered to El Al as 4X-AGA 12.9.57. Leased to BUA as G-ASFV 19.3.63–1.4.63. Sold to Globe Air as HB-ITB 3.4.64. Leased to International Air several times in 1965. Damaged beyond repair after undershooting at Nicosia 20.4.67.

**c/n 13233** srs 313, Filton-built. First flight 2.9.57. Delivered to El Al as 4X-AGB 19.10.57. Leased to Bristol Aircraft Ltd as G-ARWZ 13.2.62. Sub-leased to BUA same day. Transferred to Bristol Aircraft Services Ltd 12.3.64, but BUA sub-lease continued. Returned to El Al as 4X-AGB 26.3.65. Sold to Air Spain as EC-WFL 3.67. Re-registered as EC-BFL 3.67. Withdrawn from use and stored Palma 72. Sold to International Aviation Services for spares 9.73. Broken up at Palma 74.

**c/n 13234** srs 250. Registered to Bristol Aeroplane Co Ltd as G-ANGK 23.11.53. Cancelled as withdrawn from use 11.3.55 but not in fact built as such.

**c/n 13234** srs 313, Filton-built. First flight 4.10.57. Delivered to El Al as 4X-AGC 29.11.57. Leased to Bristol Aircraft Ltd as G-ARXA 12.3.62 and sub-leased to BUA same date. Transferred to Bristol Aircraft Services 12.3.64 but BUA sub-lease continued. Returned to El Al as 4X-AGC 13.10.64. Leased to British Eagle as G-ARXA 22.4.66–6.11.68. Re-registered to

El Al as 4X-AGC 8.11.68 but withdrawn from use and stored at Liverpool. Sold to Monarch Airlines for spares 11.70. Broken up at Luton 11.70.

**c/n 13235** srs 300LR. Registered to Bristol Aeroplane Co Ltd as G-AOFD 21.11.55. Cancelled as withdrawn from use 1.1.56 but not in fact built as such.

**c/n 13235** srs 312, Filton-built. First flight 13.11.57. Delivered to BOAC as G-AOVD 6.12.57. Crashed in fog at Sopley Farm, near Christchurch, Dorset, 24.12.58.

**c/n 13236** srs 300LR. Registered to Bristol Aeroplane Co Ltd as G-AOFE 21.11.55. Cancelled as withdrawn from use 1.1.56 but not in fact built as such.

**c/n 13236** srs 312, Filton-built. First flight 8.12.57. Delivered to BOAC as G-AOVE 21.12.57. Leased to BUA 27.9.61–21.5.64. Sub-leased to Middle East Airlines 21.4.64–21.5.64. Leased to British Eagle 6.6.64. Sold to British Eagle 30.11.66. Sold to Air Spain as EC-WFK 12.66. Re-registered as EC-BFK 12.66. Withdrawn from use and stored Palma 9.71. Sold to International Aviation Services for spares 9.73. Broken up at Palma 74.

**c/n 13237** srs 300LR. Registered to Bristol Aeroplane Co Ltd as G-AOFF 21.11.55. Cancelled as withdrawn from use 1.1.56. but not in fact built as such.

**c/n 13237** srs 312, Filton-built. First flight 18.12.57. Delivered to BOAC as G-AOVF 2.1.58. Leased to British Eagle 4.3.64. Converted to srs 312F 1968. Withdrawn from use and stored Liverpool 6.11.68. Repossessed by BOAC 27.11.68. Sold to Monarch Airlines 22.1.70. Withdrawn from use and stored Luton 1.70. Leased to Donaldson International 21.4.70. Sold to Donaldson International 24.7.72. Withdrawn from use and stored Coventry 7.72. Sold to International Aviation Services (UK) 31.10.72. Leased to African Safari Airlines 1.11.72. Returned to IAS for operation by IAS Cargo Airlines 19.12.72. Leased to Invicta (1976) Ltd 4.76–78. Sold to Invicta International Ltd 2.11.78. Leased to Redcoat Air Cargo 3.8.79 and returned. Leased to IAC Cargo as 9Q-CAZ 6.1.81–4.6.81. Re-registered as G-AOVF. Withdrawn from use and stored at Manston 5.82. Sold to Merchant Air Ltd 21.2.84. but not delivered. Donated to

Cosford Aerospace Museum and delivered to Cosford 31.5.84. Preserved at Cosford in BOAC colours.

**c/n 13238** srs 300LR. Registered to Bristol Aeroplane Co Ltd as G-AOFG 21.11.55. Cancelled as withdrawn from use 1.1.56 but not in fact built as such.

**c/n 13238** srs 312, Filton-built. First flight 10.1.58. Delivered to BOAC as G-AOVG 19.3.58. Leased to BEA 4.61–5.61 Leased to British Eagle 3.4.65. Repossessed by BOAC 27.11.68. Sold to Monarch Airlines 10.10.69. Withdrawn from use and stored Luton 1.74. Used as cabin staff training aircraft. Broken up at Luton 8.74.

**c/n 13393** srs 314, Belfast-built. First flight 11.1.58. Delivered to Canadian Pacific as CF-CZA 9.4.58. Leased to BUA 15.5.65. Sub-chartered to Air Links and re-registered as G-ATGD 9.7.65. Sold to Transglobe Airways 9.8.65. Sold to African Safari Airways as 5X-UVT 4.9.69. Re-registered as 5Y-ALP 4.70. Withdrawn from use and stored Biggin Hill 5.71. Broken up at Biggin Hill 5/6.72.

**c/n 13394** srs 314, Belfast-built. First flight 14.4.58. Delivered to Canadian Pacific as CF-CZB 29.4.58. Damaged beyond repair during attempted overshoot at Hickham Field, Honolulu, 22.7.62.

**c/n 13395** srs 314, Belfast-built. First flight 13.5.58. Delivered to Canadian Pacific as CF-CZC 20.5.58. Sold to Air Links 17.6.65. Re-registered as G-ATLE to Transglobe Airways 30.11.65. Leased to Trek Airways 6.68–7.68. Sold to IAS(UK) Ltd for spares 30.12.69. Remains to BAA at Gatwick for fire training 1970. Broken up at Gatwick 3.84.

**c/n 13396** srs 314, Belfast-built. First flight 13.6.58. Delivered to Canadian Pacific as CF-CZD 27.6.58. Sold to Caledonian Airways 1.66. Re-registered as G-ATNZ 31.1.66. Transferred to Caledonian/BUA 17.5.66. Leased to IAS 10.3.71. Sold to IAS 20.4.71 for spares. Broken up at Biggin Hill 5/6.72.

**c/n 13397** srs 253 C.1, Belfast-built. First flight 29.12.59. Delivered to 99 Squadron RAF as XL635 29.1.60. Transferred to 99/511 Squadrons 22.12.60. Withdrawn from use and stored St Athan 6.75. Sold to Young Cargo 5.9.75. Re-registered as

OO-YCA 11.9.75. Withdrawn from use and stored Stansted. Broken up at Stansted 7.77.

**c/n 13398** srs 253 C.1, Belfast-built. First flight 23.4.59. Delivered to 99 Squadron RAF as XL636 4.6.59. Transferred to 99/511 Squadrons 2.11.60. Withdrawn from use and stored Kemble 9.1.76. Re-registered as OO-YCE 23.2.76. Sold to Young Cargo 6.5.76. Withdrawn from use and stored Ostend 12.77. Broken up at Ostend 8.80.

**c/n 13399** srs 253 C.1, Belfast-built. First flight 12.5.59. Delivered to 99 Squadron RAF as XL637 28.6.59. Transferred to 99/511 Squadrons 26.9.60. Withdrawn from use and stored Kemble 9.1.76. Sold to Captain J. de Bruy 8.3.76. Sold to Young Cargo as OO-YCH 8.76. Delivered to Brussels 7.9.76. Leased to Liberia World Airways 8.77–9.77 but not actually delivered. Withdrawn from use and stored Manston 12.78. Sold to Domaine de Katale as 9Q-CKG 4.79 but ferried to Goma in full Liberia World Airways colours as EL-LWH and used for spares. Broken up at Goma 1.92.

**c/n 13400** srs 253 C.1, Belfast-built. First flight 22.6.59. Delivered to 99 Squadron RAF as XL638 4.8.59. Transferred to 99/511 Squadrons 30.9.60. Damaged beyond repair after over-running runway RAF Khormaksar, Aden, 12.10.67.

**c/n 13418** srs 300LR. Registered to Bristol Aeroplane Co Ltd as G-AOFJ 21.11.55. Cancelled as withdrawn from use 1.56, but not in fact built as such.

**c/n 13418** srs 312, Filton-built. First flight 27.2.58. Delivered to BOAC as G-AOVJ 23.4.58. Leased to BWIA 11.60–61. Leased to Caledonian 28.4.65. Sold to Caledonian 12.11.69. Withdrawn from use and stored Stansted 4.10.68. Moved to Southend 15.10.68. Returned to service 10.1.69. Sold to Donaldson International 16.11.70. Withdrawn from use at Stansted for spares 12.70. Remains to Stansted Fire School 22.12.70. In use until 31.1.80.

**c/n 13419** srs 312, Filton-built. First flight 18.3.58. Delivered to BOAC as G-AOVK 11.5.58. Leased to British Eagle 30.4.65. Sold to British Eagle 1.12.67. Sold to CCT (Aircraft Leasing) 11.4.69. Sold to Airline Engineering Services for spares 5.69. Broken up at Luton 2.70 (still in British Eagle colours).

**c/n 13420** srs 312, Filton-built. First flight 9.4.58. Delivered to BOAC as G-AOVL 20.5.58. Leased to British Eagle 30.4.65. Sold to British Eagle 18.4.68. Leased to Monarch Airlines 17.2.69. Sold to Monarch Airlines 31.7.69. Withdrawn from use and stored Luton 4.71. Used as cabin trainer. Broken up at Luton 7.71.

**c/n 13421** srs 312, Filton-built. First flight 29.4.58. Delivered to BOAC as G-AOVM 10.6.58. Leased to British Eagle 29.3.64. Converted to srs 312F at Liverpool 12.67–2.68. Sold to Air Spain 6.3.69. Re-registered as EC-BSY 1.12.69. Sold to Ministry of Defence (Procurement Executive) as XX367 11.71. Transferred to Aircraft & Armament Experimental Establishment, Boscombe Down, 3.5.72. Withdrawn from use and stored 5.83. Sold to Katale Aero Transport as 9Q-CHY 3.84. Sold to Business Cash Flow Aviation (Zaire) 4.89. Retired 6.7.91 and stored Kinshasa. Used for spares and broken up.

**c/n 13422** srs 312, Filton-built. First flight 16.5.58. Delivered to BOAC as G-AOVN 4.7.58. Leased to British Eagle 2.6.64. Converted to srs 312F in 1968. Sold to Monarch Airlines 6.3.69. Leased to African Safari Airways 28.9.72–2.11.72. Withdrawn from use and stored Luton 11.73. Broken up at Luton 2.74. Nose section to Laker Airways at Gatwick as crew trainer, then to Orion Airways at East Midlands Airport.

**c/n 13423** srs 312, Filton-built. First flight 3.7.58. Delivered to BOAC as G-AOVO 4.9.58. Leased to British Eagle 17.1.64. Crashed into Glungezer Mountain on approach to Innsbruck 29.2.64.

**c/n 13424** srs 312, Filton-built. First flight 22.7.58. Delivered to BOAC as G-AOVP 15.9.58. Leased to BEA 4.61–5.61. Leased to Lloyd International 15.4.65. Converted to srs 312F 12.67–4.68. Sold to International Aviation Services (UK) Ltd 10.7.73. Withdrawn from use and stored Biggin Hill 8.75. Broken up at Biggin Hill 1975.

**c/n 13425** srs 317, Filton-built. First flight 10.10.58. Delivered to British and Commonwealth Shipping Co Ltd 11.12.58. Transferred to Hunting-Clan Air Transport Ltd 31.5.60. Transferred to BUA on merger 1.7.60. Sold to Donaldson International 2.10.67. Leased to Lloyd International 10.67–5.69. Withdrawn from use

and stored Coventry 5.72. Sold to International Aviation Services for spares use 10.72. Broken up at Coventry 7.73.

**c/n 13426** srs 317, Filton-built. First flight 10.11.58. Delivered to British and Commonwealth Shipping Co Ltd 30.4.59. Transferred to Hunting-Clan Air Transport Ltd 31.5.60. Transferred to BUA on merger 1.7.60. Sold to Donaldson International 10.67. Leased to Lloyd International 10.67–3.71. Withdrawn from use and stored Luton 3.71. Sold to Airline Engineering Services for spares 6.10.71. Broken up at Luton 11.71.

**c/n 13427** srs 312, Filton-built. First flight 17.12.58. Delivered to BOAC as G-AOVT 1.1.59. Leased to BEA 4.61–5.61. Leased to British Eagle 13.9.63. Sold to Monarch Airlines 18.8.68. Leased to Invicta International 13.12.74–10.3.75. Withdrawn from use and stored at Luton 10.3.75. Donated to Duxford Aviation Society 29.6.75 and flown to Duxford for preservation. Preserved there in Monarch colours.

**c/n 13428** srs 314, Filton-built. First flight 19.6.58. Delivered to Canadian Pacific as CF-CZX 3.7.58. Leased to Caledonian 28.11.65–31.10.69. Re-registered as G-ATMA 28.12.65. Leased to African Safari Airways as 5Y-ANS 10.69–4.71. Sold to International Aviation Services 4.71. Leased to African Safari Airways 4.71–2.72. Leased to African International 2.72. Returned to IAS (UK) Ltd as G-ATMA 18.5.72. Withdrawn from use and stored Gatwick 6.73. Flown to Biggin Hill. Broken up at Biggin Hill spring 1974.

**c/n 13429** srs 312, Filton-built. First flight 4.8.58. Delivered to BOAC as G-AOVR 3.10.58. Leased to British Eagle 22.2.63. Sold to British Eagle 17.10.66 and sold to Air Spain as EC-WFJ same date. Re-registered as EC-BFJ 20.10.66. Sold to IAS Cargo 4.73 for spares. Withdrawn from use at Palma and flown to Biggin Hill. Broken up at Biggin Hill 8.75.

**c/n 13430** srs 312, Filton-built. First flight 5.9.58. Delivered to BOAC as G-AOVS 29.10.58. Leased to Lloyd International 4.7.65. Sub-leased to British Eagle 8.65–11.65. Converted to srs 312F 6.66. Sold to Lloyd International 1.69. Withdrawn from use and stored Stansted. Sold to IAS (UK) Ltd 2.73. Sold to Aivex Holdings Ltd

28.12.73 and leased to IAS same date. Sold to Westwings Aviation Services 14.10.75 and leased to IAS same date. Sub-leased to Invicta Airways (1976) Ltd 1.1.76–13.6.76. Withdrawn from use and stored Luton 1.77. Sold to Aivex Holdings Ltd 21.3.77. Leased to Redcoat Air Cargo Ltd as 5.77. Withdrawn from use and stored Luton 31.1.79. Sold to Redcoat Air Cargo Ltd 4.4.79. Fictitious registration G-BRAC applied 2.80 for filming purposes. Broken up at Luton 1980. Fuselage still on fire dump at Luton in 2001.

**c/n 13431** srs 313, Filton-built. First flight 21.2.59. Delivered to El Al as 4X-AGD 7.3.59. Leased to BUA as G-ASFU 18.3.63–8.4.63. Sold to Globe Air as HB-ITC 8.3.65. Leased occasionally to International Air on behalf of African Tourist Development Co. Abandoned by crew at Luton 17.10.67 when company went bankrupt. Sold to African Safari Airways as 5X-UVH 12.67. Re-registered as 5Y-ALT 5.70. Reported impounded at Basle in 12.71. Sold to African Cargo Airways 11.73. Withdrawn from use and used for spares Stansted 5.75. Remains to Stansted Fire School 6.75. Destroyed by fire.

**c/n 13432** srs 318, Filton-built. First flight 24.11.58. Delivered to Cubana as CU-P668 16.12.58. Re-registered as CU-T668 12.58. Leased to Eagle Airways as G-APYY 4.60. Transferred to Cunard-Eagle 1.9.60. Returned to Cubana as CU-T668 15.9.61. Leased to CSA as OK-MBA 10.61–5.64. Withdrawn from use and stored at Havana by 1983. Broken up at Havana.

**c/n 13433** srs 318, Filton-built. First flight 19.1.59. Delivered to Cubana as CU-P669 6.2.59. Re-registered as CU-T669 2.59. Sold to Aerocaribbean as CU-T114 7.84. Withdrawn from use and stored Havana 1990. Later broken up at Havana.

**c/n 13434** srs 253 C.1, Belfast-built. First flight 7.4.60. Delivered to 511 Squadron RAF as XM489 5.5.60. Transferred to 99/511 Squadrons 19.4.61. Withdrawn from use and stored Kemble 9.75. Sold to Young Cargo as OO-YCC 1.76. Used as spares source. Broken up at Gosselies, Belgium 2.78.

**c/n 13435** srs 253 C.1, Belfast-built. First flight 16.5.60. Delivered to 511 Squadron RAF as XM490 9.6.60. Transferred to 99/511 Squadrons 7.11.60. Withdrawn from

use and stored Kemble 8.75. Sold to Euroworld 29.10.75 as G-BDLZ. Sold to Air Faisel as G-BDLZ 17.11.75. Leased to Air Work India 1976. Impounded Luton 11.78. Withdrawn from use and stored Luton 11.78. Broken up at Luton 9.79.

**c/n 13436** srs 253 C.1, Belfast-built. First flight 16.6.60. Delivered to 511 Squadron RAF as XM491 7.7.60. Transferred to 99/511 Squadrons 7.11.60. Withdrawn from use and stored St Athan 6.75. Sold to Aer Turas as EI-BBH 8.9.75. Leased to Cyprus Airways 9.9.76–12.4.78. Leased to Gemini Air Transport 23.3.79–23.5.79. Sold to Domaine de Katale as 9Q-CMO 30.11.81. Withdrawn from use and stored. Broken up at Goma 1.92.

**c/n 13437** srs 318, Filton-built. First flight 2.4.59. Delivered to Cubana as CU-P670 15.5.59. Re-registered as CU-T670 5.59. Leased to CSA as CU-T670 during 1963 and returned. Withdrawn from use and stored by 1978. Broken up at Havana.

**c/n 13448** srs 253 C.1, Belfast-built. First flight 28.8.59. Delivered to 99 Squadron RAF as XL639 8.10.59. Transferred to 99/511 Squadrons 12.10.61. Withdrawn from use and stored Kemble 2.11.75. Sold to Guinness Peat Aviation 10.2.76. Withdrawn from use and stored Stansted 2.76. Sold Airline Engineering Ltd 2.77. Re-registered as EI-BDC 24.5.77. Leased to Aer Turas 17.6.77 and sub-leased to Cyprus Airways 19.6.77–8.7.77. Withdrawn from use and stored Luton. Leased to Cyprus Airways 10.77–7.11.77. Sold to Eurafric 20.1.78. Sold to Redcoat Air Cargo as G-BRAC 8.6.78. Crashed near Boston, USA, 16.2.80.

**c/n 13449** srs 253 C.1, Belfast-built. First flight 8.10.59. Delivered to 99 Squadron RAF as XL640 2.11.59. Transferred to 99/511 Squadrons 12.10.61. Withdrawn from use and stored Kemble 9.75. To Monarch Airlines 31.12.75, then to Aer Turas at Coventry and withdrawn from use and stored Coventry 13.1.76. To Airline Engineering at Luton for conversion 2.9.76. Re-registered as EI-BCI 4.4.77. Leased to Aer Turas 31.3.78–10.4.78 and also 25.5.78–10.11.78. Leased to SATA-Air Acores 13.11.78–26.11.78. Withdrawn from use and stored Luton 26.11.78. Leased to Redcoat Air Cargo as G-BHAU 13.8.79. Sold to Swordvale Aviation 2.12.81. Withdrawn from use and stored

Manston 3.12.81. Sold to Katale Aero Transport as 9Q-CHU 16.4.82. Withdrawn from use and stored Kinshasa. Broken up at Goma 1986.

**c/n 13450** srs 252 C.2, Belfast-built. First flight 13.10.58. Registered to Ministry of Supply as G-APPE 28.11.58. Delivered to Aircraft & Armament Experimental Establishment, Boscombe Down, as XN392 19.3.59. Transferred to 99 Squadron RAF 18.9.59. Transferred to 99/511 Squadrons 5.61. Withdrawn from use and stored St Athan 7.75. Sold to Aer Turas for spares 18.12.75. Broken up at Coventry 5.76.

**c/n 13451** srs 252 C.2, Belfast-built. Registered to Ministry of Supply as G-APPF 28.11.58. First flight 7.12.58. Delivered to 99 Squadron RAF as XN398 19.3.59. Transferred to 99/511 Squadrons 17.5.61. Withdrawn from use and stored Kemble 4.75. Sold to Euroworld 11.9.75 and withdrawn from use and stored at Stansted. Sold to Zaire Aero Service 2.77. Re-registered as 9Q-CPX 11.77. Leased (later sold) to Katale Aero Transport 11.77. Withdrawn from use by 3.84. Broken up at Goma, Zaire.

**c/n 13452** srs 252 C.2, Belfast-built. Registered to Ministry of Supply as G-APPG 28.11.58. First flight 3.3.59. Delivered to Aircraft & Armament Experimental Establishment, Boscombe Down, as XN404 8.4.59. Transferred to 99 Squadron RAF 1959. Transferred to 99/511 Squadrons 27.2.61. Withdrawn from use and stored St Athan 7.75. Sold to Shackleton Aviation 17.12.75. Moved to Luton 7.5.76 for spares use for Air Faisel. Sold to F & H Aircraft/Euroworld 8.5.76. Sold to Air Faisel 1.2.76. Broken up at Luton 11.76.

**c/n 13453** srs 314, Belfast-built. First flight 22.7.58. Delivered to Canadian Pacific Airlines as CF-CZW 7.8.58. Leased to British Eagle as G-ASTF 20.5.64–15.10.64 and returned to CPAL as CF-CZW. Leased to Caledonian Airways 23.1.66. Re-registered as G-ASTF again 14.2.66. Withdrawn from use and stored Gatwick 17.11.69. Broken up at Gatwick 10.70.

**c/n 13454** srs 253 C.1, Belfast-built. First flight 23.11.59. Delivered to 511 Squadron RAF as XL657 23.12.59. Transferred to 99/511 Squadrons 24.2.61. Withdrawn from use and stored St Athan 8.75. Sold to F & H Aircraft/Euroworld 9.75. Sold to Monarch Airlines 31.12.75. Sold to Centre

Air Afrique as 9U-BAD 10.3.76. Parked at Bujambiru, Burundi, in late 1976. Withdrawn from use and stored Charleroi 2.77. Broken up at Gosselies 4.81.

**c/n 13455** srs 253 C.1, Belfast-built. First flight 3.12.59. Delivered to 511 Squadron RAF as XL658 5.2.60. Transferred to 99/511 Squadrons 24.3.61. Withdrawn from use and stored Kemble 6.12.75. Sold to Airline Engineering Ltd 26.5.76 for conversion. Sold to Interconair as EI-BBY 6.76. Withdrawn from use and stored Hurn 10.8.76. Returned to service 1.1.77. Damaged beyond repair near Shannon 30.9.77.

**c/n 13456** srs 253 C.1, Belfast-built. First flight 1.2.60. Delivered to 511 Squadron RAF as XL659 4.3.60. Transferred to 99/511 Squadrons 30.11.60. Withdrawn from use and stored St Athan 5.75. Sold to Young Cargo 5.9.75. Re-registered as OO-YCB 11.9.75. Withdrawn from use and stored Ostend 8.76. Broken up at Ostend 6.80.

**c/n 13457** srs 253 C.1, Belfast-built. First flight 4.3.60. Delivered to 99 Squadron RAF as XL660 23.4.60. Transferred to 99/511 Squadrons 1.5.60. Withdrawn from use and stored Kemble 12.1.76. Sold to Air Faisel 14.5.76. Sold to Transgulf 5.76. Returned to Air Faisel as G-BEMZ 11.2.77. Sold to T.F. Richter & Co 13.9.79. Sold to Black Arrow Leasing Ltd 14.2.80. Leased to Gaylan Air Cargo as A6-HMS 9.4.80. Withdrawn from use and stored Hurn 26.1.81. Re-registered to Gaylan Air Cargo as G-BEMZ 3.4.81. Leased to Redcoat Air Cargo 22.9.81. Sold to Swordvale Aviation 2.12.81. Withdrawn from use and stored Manston 3.12.81. Sold to Katale Aero Transport as 9Q-CGP 11.82. Withdrawn from use and stored. Broken up at Goma by 1.92.

**c/n 13508** srs 253 C.1, Belfast-built. First flight 24.8.60. Delivered to 99/511 Squadrons RAF as XM496 19.9.60. Withdrawn from use and stored Kemble 2.11.75. Sold to Monarch Airlines 6.1.76. Re-registered as G-BDUP to Airline Engineering Ltd 31.3.76. Sold to Afrek Ltd 21.5.76. Withdrawn from use 13.9.82 and stored at Athens. Sold to Monarch Aircraft Engineering Ltd 30.7.84. Sold to Aerocaribbean as CU-T120 8.84. Withdrawn from use 29.3.90 and stored at Havana. Sold to Transair Cargo as 9Q-CJH 1.93. Sold to Trans Service Air Lift. Ferried to Lanseria, near Johannesburg, on

three engines 4.5.97. Re-registered as EL-WXA to Transair Cargo 8.97. Test-flown Lanseria 21.9.97 and ferried to Kemble. Currently preserved at Kemble by Britannia Aircraft Preservation Trust.

**c/n 13509** srs 253 C.1, Belfast-built. First flight 17.11.60. Delivered to 99/511 Squadrons RAF as XM497 5.12.60. Withdrawn from use and stored Kemble 9.1.76. Sold to Young Cargo 23.4.76. Re-registered as OO-YCF 5.5.76. Delivered to Stansted for overhaul by ATEL. Not delivered to Young Cargo. Withdrawn from use and stored Stansted 5.76. Broken up at Stansted 7.77 and remains to Civil Aviation Authority Fire School at Stansted. Burnt out by 5.81.

**c/n 13510** srs 253 C.1, Belfast-built. First flight 30.9.59. Delivered to 99/511 Squadrons RAF as XM498 19.10.59. Withdrawn from use and stored Kemble 9.1.76. Sold to Young Cargo as OO-YCG 11.6.76. Leased to Liberia World Airways as EL-LWG 11.7.77–9.78. Withdrawn from use and stored Manston 4.12.78. Sold to Domaine de Katale 5.79. Re-registered as 9Q-CDT 7.80. Withdrawn from use early 88 and stored at Kinshasa. Sold to BCF Aviation 7.88 for spares. Broken up at at Kinshasa by 1.92.

**c/n 13511** srs 253 C.1, Belfast-built. First flight 24.11.59. Delivered to 99/511 Squadrons RAF as XM517 3.12.59. Withdrawn from use and stored St Athan 4.75. Sold to Monarch Airlines 21.10.75. Sold to AMAZ as 9Q-CAJ 8.76, but not taken up. Withdrawn from use and stored Luton 8.76. Sold to Airline Engineering as G-BEPX 14.4.77 but not used. Withdrawn from use 5.78 and used as engine test-bed at Luton. Broken up at at Luton 3.80.

**c/n 13512** srs 253 C.1, Belfast-built. First flight 18.12.59. Delivered to 99 Squadron RAF as XM518 30.12.59. Transferred to 99/511 Squadrons 28.11.60. Withdrawn from use and stored Kemble 9.1.76. Re-registered to Young Cargo as OO-YCD 23.2.76. Withdrawn from use and stored 3.76. Broken up at at Gosselies 1978.

**c/n 13513** srs 253 C.1, Belfast-built. First flight 28.1.60. Delivered to 511 Squadron RAF as XM519 8.2.60. Transferred to 99/511 Squadrons 28.11.60. Withdrawn from use and stored Kemble 9.1.76. Sold to Airline Engineering Ltd 13.2.76. Re-regis-

tered as G-BDUR 31.3.76. Sold to Afrek Ltd 2.7.76. Withdrawn from use and stored Athens 13.9.82. Sold to Monarch Airline Engineering Ltd 30.7.84. Sold to Aerocaribbean as CU-T121 8.84. Withdrawn from use and stored Havana 1990. Sold to Transair Cargo for spares 1.93. Broken up at at Havana 11.95.

**c/n 13514** srs 253 C.1, Belfast-built. First flight 9.3.60. Delivered to 511 Squadron RAF as XM520 21.3.60. Transferred to 99/511 Squadrons 1.5.60. Withdrawn from use and stored St Athan 8.75. Sold to Gemini Air Transport 16.9.75. Re-registered as 9G-ACE 4.76. Leased to Redcoat Air Cargo 5.76–5.77. Withdrawn from use and stored Manston 5.3.81. Sold to Lukum Air Services as 9Q-CUM 9.81. Sold to Katale Aero Transport for spares. Broken up at at Kinshasa 7.86.

**c/n 13515** srs 318, Filton-built. First flight 29.4.59. Delivered to Cubana as CU-P671 22.8.59. Re-registered as CU-T671 8.59. Leased to CSA as OK-MBB 7.5.62–5.69. Returned to Cubana as CU-T671 5.69. Withdrawn from use and stored by 1979. Broken up at at Havana.

**c/n 13516** srs 324, Filton-built. Registered to Bristol Aircraft Ltd as G-18-8. First flight 9.10.59. Delivered to CPAL as CF-CPD 16.10.59. Returned to Bristol Aircraft Ltd 12.2.61. Re-registered as G-ARKA 15.2.61. Leased to Cunard-Eagle Airways 8.3.61. Lease transferred to British Eagle 9.8.63. Transferred to Bristol Aircraft Services Ltd 10.3.64 but lease to British Eagle continued. Sold to British Eagle 1.12.67. Sold to CCT (Aircraft) Leasing Ltd 21.3.69. Leased to Tellair 24.3.69–10.69. Withdrawn from use and stored Coventry 11.69. Sold to Airline Engineering for spares 6.71. Broken up at Coventry 10.71.

**c/n 13517** srs 324, Filton-built. First flight 4.11.59. Delivered to CPAL as CF-CPE 13.11.59. Returned to Bristol Aircraft Ltd 11.4.61. Re-registered as G-ARKB 13.4.61. Leased to Cunard-Eagle Airways 1.5.61. Lease transferred to British Eagle 9.8.63. Transferred to Bristol Aircraft Services Ltd 10.3.64 but British Eagle lease continued. Parked at Luton 11.68–3.69. Sold to CCT (Aircraft) Leasing Ltd. 11.4.69. Leased to Tellair 4.69–10.69. Withdrawn from use and stored Coventry 11.69. Sold to Airline Engineering for spares 6.71. Broken up at Coventry 10.71.

# Bibliography

During the preparation of this book the following sources of references were used, and are recommended to anyone with an interest in the Britannia or old airliners in general.

## Books

Air-Britain, *The Bristol Britannia* (Air-Britain)

Aviation Data Centre, *Airliners and Airlines – Bristol Britannia* (Aviation Data Centre, 1996)

Barnes, C.H., *Bristol Aircraft Since 1910* (Putnam, 1994)

Cuthbert, Geoffrey, *Flying To The Sun* (Hodder and Stoughton, 1987)

Merton Jones, A.C., *British Independent Airlines Since 1946 Vols 1–4* (Merseyside Aviation Society and LAAS International, 1976)

Russell, Sir Archibald, *A Span of Wings* (Airlife, 1992)

Stroud, John, *The Annals of British and Commonwealth Air Transport, 1919–60* (Putnam, 1962)

The Aviation Hobby Shop, *Turbo-Prop Airliner Production List* (TAHS, 1990)

## Periodicals

*The Aeroplane*, the Britannia Association's quarterly magazine
The Britannia Association Secretary
15 Haywood Drive
Carterton
Oxon OX18 3HX, UK

*Flight*

*Propliner*
'New Roots'
Sutton Green Road
Sutton Green
Guildford
Surrey GU4 7QD, UK

## Other Sources

Various Bristol Aeroplane Co. publications

*The Bristol Britannia Story* (video) (1st Take Video, 2000)

### Websites

www.Air-Britain.com
Air-Britain Information Exchange (available to members of Air-Britain only)

Contact details for membership/subscription enquiries:
Howard J. Nash
Air-Britain Membership Secretary
'The Haven'
Blacklands Lane
Sudbourne
Woodbridge
Suffolk IP12 2AX, UK

www.airliners.net

www.oldprops.f9.co.uk

www.aviation-safety.net

# Index